Marketing and Promotion

Pippa Riley

Viva Books

New Delhi | Mumbai | Chennai | Kolkata | Bengaluru | Hyderabad | Kochi | Guwahati

First Indian Edition 2011

VIVA BOOKS PRIVATE LIMITED

- 4737/23 Ansari Road, Daryaganj, New Delhi 110 002
  E-mail: vivadelhi@vivagroupindia.net, Tel. 42242200
- 76, Service Industries, Shirvane, Sector 1, Nerul, Navi Mumbai 400 706
  E-mail: vivamumbai@vivagroupindia.net, Tel. 27721273, 27721274
- Jamals Fazal Chambers, 26 Greams Road, Chennai 600 006
  E-mail: vivachennai@vivagroupindia.net, Tel. 28290304, 28294241
- B-103, Jindal Towers, 21/1A/3 Darga Road, Kolkata 700 017
  E-mail: vivakolkata@vivagroupindia.net, Tel. 22836381, 22816713
- 7, Sovereign Park Apartments, 56-58, K. R. Road, Basavanagudi, Bengaluru 560 004
  E-mail: vivabangalore@vivagroupindia.net, Tel. 26607409, 26607410
- 101-102 Mughal Marc Aptt., 3-4-637 to 641, Narayanguda, Hyderabad 500 029
  E-mail: vivahyderabad@vivagroupindia.net, Tel. 27564481, 27564482
- First Floor, Beevi Towers, SRM Road, Kaloor, Kochi 682 018, Kerala
  E-mail: vivakochi@vivagroupindia.net, Tel: 0484-2403055, 2403056
- 232, GNB Road, Beside UCO Bank, Silpukhuri, Guwahati 781 003
  E-mail: vivaguwahati@vivagroupindia.net, Tel: 0361-2666386

Published by arrangement with

BPP Learning Media Ltd.
BPP House, Aldine Place
London W12 8AA

ISBN : 978-81-309-1764-1

Published by Vinod Vasishtha for Viva Books Private Limited, 4737/23, Ansari Road, Daryaganj, New Delhi - 110 002.

Printed and bound by Raj Press, R-3, Inderpuri, New Delhi - 110 012.

Contents

Introduction

Viva-BPP Learning Media's Business Essentials range is the ideal learning solution for students studying for business-related qualifications and degrees. The range provides concise and comprehensive coverage of the key areas that are essential to the business student.

Qualifications in business are traditionally very demanding. Students therefore need learning resources which go straight to the core of the topics involved, and which build upon students' pre-existing knowledge and experience. The BPP Learning Media Business Essentials range has been designed to meet exactly that need.

Features include:

- In-depth coverage of essential topics within business-related subjects
- Plenty of activities, quizzes and topics for discussion to help retain the interest of students and ensure progress
- Up-to-date practical illustrations and case studies that really bring the material to life
- A full index, with key terms highlighted in bold

Each chapter contains:

- An introduction and a list of specific study objectives
- Summary diagrams and signposts to guide you through the chapter
- A chapter roundup, quick quiz with answers and answers to activities

Titles in the Series

- Accounts
- Business Decision Making
- Business Environment
- Business Maths
- Business Strategy
- Economics
- Finance: Management Accounting and Financial Reporting
- Human Resource Development and Employee Relations
- Human Resource Management
- Management: Communications and Achieving Results
- Management: Leading People and Professional Development
- Managing Finance
- Marketing and Promotion
- Marketing and Sales Strategy
- Marketing Principles
- Organisations and Behaviour
- Research Project

Study Guide

This Course Book includes features designed specifically to make learning effective and efficient.

- Each chapter begins with a summary diagram which maps out the areas covered by the chapter. There are detailed summary diagrams at the start of each main section of the chapter. You can use the diagrams during revision as a basis for your notes.
- After the main summary diagram there is an introduction, which sets the chapter in context. This is followed by learning objectives, which show you what you will learn as you work through the chapter.
- Throughout the Course Book, there are special aids to learning. These are indicated by symbols in the margin:

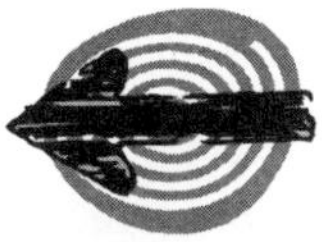

Signposts guide you through the book, showing how each section connects with the next.

Definitions give the meanings of key terms. The *glossary* at the end of the book summarises these.

Activities help you to test how much you have learned. An indication of the time you should take on each is given. Answers are given at the end of each chapter.

Topics for discussion are for use in seminars. They give you a chance to share your views with your fellow students. They allow you to highlight holes in your knowledge and to see how others understand concepts. If you have time, try 'teaching' someone the concepts you have learned in a session. This helps you to remember key points and answering their questions will consolidate your knowledge.

Examples relate what you have learned to the outside world. Try to think up your own examples as you work through the Course Book.

Chapter roundups present the key information from the chapter in a concise format. Useful for revision.

- At the end of each chapter, there is a **chapter roundup** and a **quick quiz** with answers. Use these to revise and consolidate your knowledge. The chapter roundup summarises the chapter. The quick quiz tests what you have learned (the answers often refer you back to the chapter so you can look over subjects again).
- At the end of the book, there is an index.

Part A

Marketing Intelligence

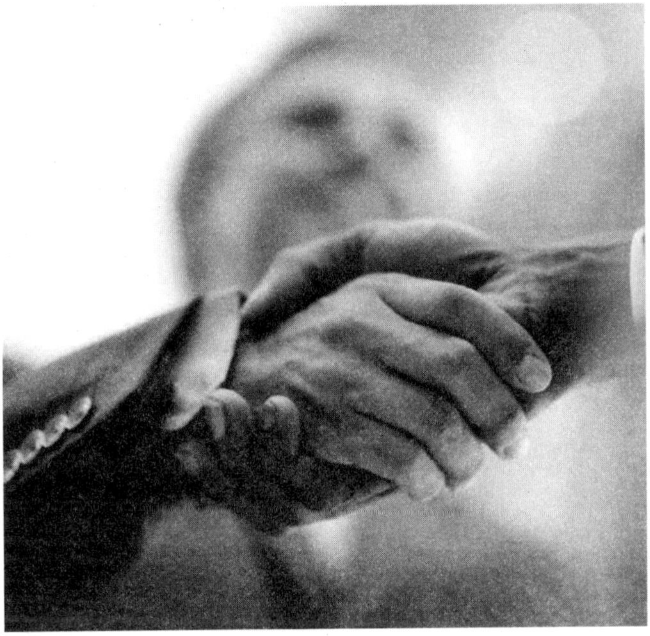

Chapter 1 :

BUYER BEHAVIOUR AND THE PURCHASE DECISION-MAKING PROCESS

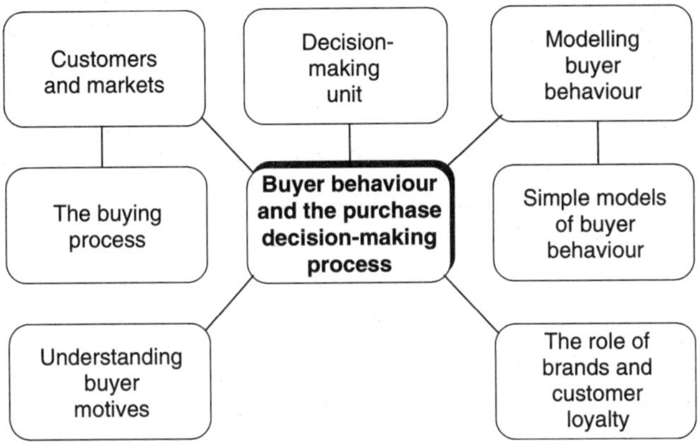

Introduction

The aim of this chapter is to introduce the basic principles of buyer behaviour. The first section offers a number of useful definitions and explains the purchase decision-making process. A simple decision process model is used to illustrate the buying process and this includes references to the *Engel, Blackwell and Miniard* model.

Section 2 goes on to discuss the modelling approach to buyer behaviour by looking at how models can be applied and evaluated. Simple models of buyer behaviour such as the black box and personal variable models are explained in Section 3.

The rate and extent of diffusion are then elaborated on, with emphasis on the variability of diffusion using the adopter categories to illustrate this.

In practice, many different people can be involved in decision-making both at a personal and organisational level. The different roles within the decision-making unit are discussed with reference to the personal influences of gender and children. The decision-making roles and processes within a personal and organisational context are compared.

The penultimate section is concerned with providing the reader with an understanding of the consumer's motivation mix. Psychological influences such as attitudes, loyalty and personality are assessed along with roles, reference groups, culture and sub-culture. This first chapter ends with a discussion regarding the role of brands and customer loyalty. Aspects which are covered include customer retention, relationship marketing and imagery.

Your objectives

In this chapter you will learn about the following.

(a) An overview of buyer behaviour

(b) The purchase decision-making process

(c) The function of modelling in buyer behaviour
(d) A range of simple models of buyer behaviour
(e) The importance of the decision-making unit
(f) The principles of buyer motives
(g) The role of brands and customer loyalty

1 CUSTOMERS AND MARKETS

1.1 Customers and users

Ted Johns (1999) makes the distinction between **customers** and **users**.

Definitions

- **Customers** are people who use goods and services and **pay** for them.
- **Users** are people who use the product or service, but **do not pay** for it.
- A **consumer** is the end user of a product or service who may or may not be the customer. For example, the consumer of a tin of cat food will be the family pet, while it was the pet owner who was the customer.
- The **payer** is the person who finances the purchase.
- The **buyer** participates in the procurement of the product from the market-place.

Not all organisations accepted this distinction between '**customer**' (the person who **pays**) and '**user**' (the person who **consumes**). In particular, **not-for-profit organisations** such as local authorities, libraries and schools often have a diversity of people and groups interested in the products and services they supply. These people and groups may be variously described as 'clients', 'users' or 'customers'.

The roles can be combined in many different ways.

User's role		**Example**	
Payer	Buyer	Business	Consumer/domestic
No	No	• Furniture, eg equipment used by employees but procured	• Cat food • Car purchased by parents for sole use of child • Health insurance policy paid by the company
Yes	No	Office manager may buy and pay for stationery for use by others	Stockbrokers are agents who buy shares on behalf of the user

No	Yes	Business-related examples: corporate sponsorship can mean that universities can select a building contractor and enjoy the subsequent benefits of the builder's work (in the form of, say, a dedi-cated business school or residential conference centre) without having to meet the costs.	Consumer-based examples: the driver who selects a car breakdown service with the costs reimbursed by an insurance company; the bride who specifies prospective wedding gifts from a 'list' maintained through a retail operation.
Yes	Yes	Small-business entrepreneurs often combine all three roles when they acquire office equipment, furniture, and the services of an accountant.	Most consumers purchase and pay for products intended for their personal use, such as clothing, watches, airline tickets, haircuts, and so forth.

1.2 Reasons for role specialisation

Users are unlikely to play other customer roles when the:

User lacks:

- Expertise/knowledge to make a choice
- Time to evaluate choice
- Buying power
- Access to the product

Product is:

- Unaffordable
- Subsidised (eg staff canteen)
- Free (eg public library)

Distinctions between user, payer and buyer are important because their clarification of the buying process helps potential product/service suppliers to **focus their marketing efforts** to optimal advantage. On the other hand, these same distinctions, even when clarified, do not necessarily show where (or how) power and influence are exercised, and by whom.

EXAMPLE

In a family, it is still mostly women who are the main food shoppers. Some food items however are clearly targeted at men or children. A pork pie manufacturer introduced a new range of mini pies. You may think these were developed as a party food item or for other snacking occasions. However, they were cleverly positioned to appeal to female food shoppers as well as the male consumers. The smaller size was specifically developed to meet the needs of women who were concerned about the high levels of fat their male partners were eating but didn't want to stop buying a favourite food.

FOR DISCUSSION

In the **children's toys** market, for example, it seems a straightforward argument to say that the child is **user** and the **parent is payer**. However:

(a) Who is the buyer, ie who is it who chooses which toy will be purchased?

(b) Does the fact that the parent is payer mean that **power** automatically resides with the parent?

Activity 1 **(10 minutes)**

Try to think of some more examples where the distinction between customer and user is significant.

1.3 The purchase decision-making process

A simple decision process model

A simple descriptive model of the decision process consists of these elements.

EXAMPLE

Imagine the scenario when purchasing a snack at an airport. The thoughts and behaviour of the consumer at each stage are likely to vary considerably but at a simple level can be considered in the following table.

Buying process stage	Buying a snack at an airport
Need recognition	Feeling hungry but flight due to be called
Information search	Look for a vending machine, cafe or shop
Evaluation of alternatives	Consider alternatives such as hot, cold – sweet or savoury, decide on sweet, view alternative sweets in nearest shop – chocolate bar close to the till chosen for speed and ease.
Purchase decision	Make fast decision based on known brands – Mars bar
Post purchase evaluation	Glad chose Mars bar rather than hot meal, as had to dash due to flight boarding

The table below now outlines in detail each of the purchase stages and some issues that marketers need to consider.

Element	Comment
Need/problem recognition	Leads to motivation. (In a more complex model, would be shown to be triggered by psychological, physiological and social factors.) Marketers can identify needs/problems for the consumer, through product positioning.
Pre-purchase/ information search	In a more complex model, would be affected by sources, attitudes, perceptions. Marketers can provide product information, tailored to need.
Evaluation of alternatives	Marketers can make products available for evaluation and provide comparative information about competing products: the important thing, though, is to get the product onto the short-list of options.
The purchase decision	(In a more complex model, would be affected by situational factors: intention is not everything.)
Post-purchase evaluation	Experience 'feeds back' to the beginning of the process, providing positive or negative reinforcement of the purchase decision. If the consumer is dissatisfied, he will be back at the problem recognition stage again. If the consumer is satisfied, the next decision process for the product may be cut short and skip straight to the decision, on the basis of loyalty (or, in a more complex model, expectations and learning constructs)

Such a model provides a useful descriptive framework for marketers, with indications of strategy requirements at each stage. It is still, however, too simple to be predictive, unless a large number of extra social, psychological and cultural variables are added or assumed. This means that the marketer will need to remember the strategies involved and provide the context for different purchase scenarios.

FOR DISCUSSION

Think about alternative buying scenarios such as when buying clothes. The way we behave when we buy an outfit to wear to a wedding, work clothes or beachwear differs considerably because there are different levels of importance and risk associated with the need to make a positive purchase. What might be some of the details associated with such a purchase which are not included in the simple DMP model?

1.4 *Engel, Blackwell and Miniard* model

This model was originally developed in 1968 by Engel, Kollat and Blackwell but has since undergone several revisions. The 1990 version is considered here.

The basis of the *Engel-Blackwell-Miniard* model takes the simple process of consumer behaviour described above as its basis but then adds more context and detail.

The **influencing variables** are divided into four main categories.

- Stimulus inputs
- Information processing
- Decision process
- Variables influencing the decision process

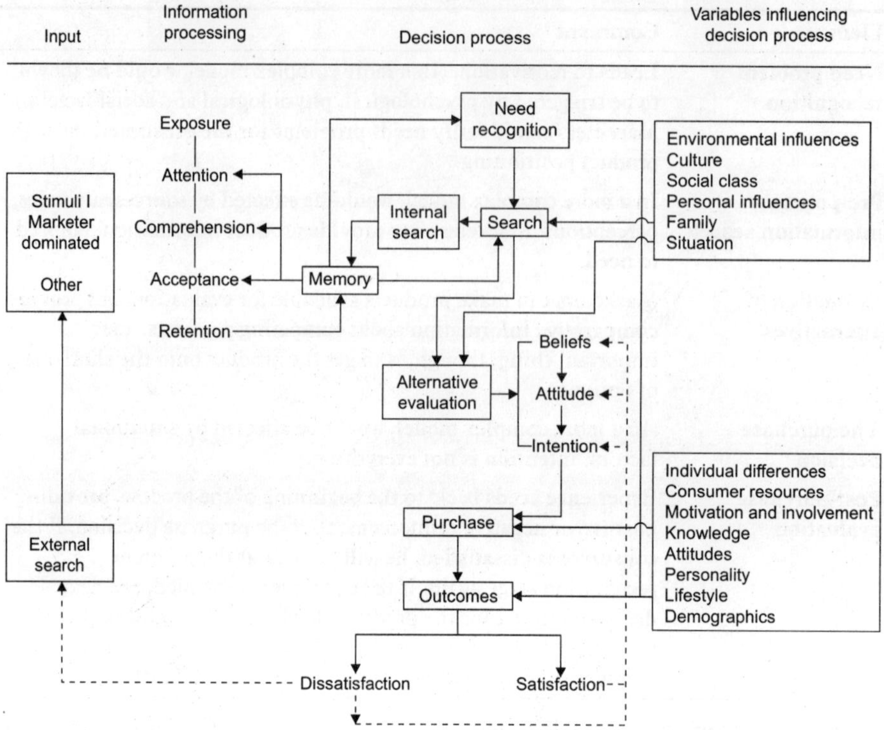

Figure 1.1: The Engel-Blackwell-Miniard model

Step 1

The starting point of the process is the customer's perception of a want or a problem which must be satisfied.

Step 2

This stimulates the start of the next stage, information search, which can be divided into two further stages. First, the customer searches his **internal memory** to ascertain what is known about potential solutions to the problem. If insufficient information is found through this course of action, the customer will begin the process of **external search**. The likelihood of external search is also affected by environmental factors, such as the urgency of the need, and also the individual characteristics of the customer. For example, individuals who are low risk-takers will tend to seek more information before making a decision.

Step 3

This search process identifies the various ways in which the problem can be solved. Those various ways are then evaluated. The **alternative evaluation** stage involves comparing the alternative brands against evaluative criteria, which are 'product judging standards that have been stored in the permanent memory'. This evaluation process may lead to changes in beliefs regarding the brands, which, in turn, leads to changes in attitudes and intentions to purchase.

Step 4

The process of **alternative evaluation** leads to an **intention** to make a purchase of the most favourably evaluated brand.

Step 5

This intention will be translated into action unless unforeseen circumstances intervene to postpone or prevent the purchase.

Step 6

Once purchased, the customer will use the product and will continue to evaluate the product by comparing performance against expectations. If the product chosen does not meet expectations, the result is dissatisfaction and this may lead to further search for information about the brand and/or changes in beliefs.

The overall process can, therefore, be seen as a continuous one, especially given the desirability of repeat purchase.

1.5 Types of buying decisions

Types of consumer buying decisions

On a continuum of effort ranging from very high to very low, three specific levels of consumer decision-making can be distinguished.

(a) **Extensive problem-solving**

When consumers have no established criteria for evaluating a product category or specific brands in that category or have not narrowed the number of brands they will consider to a small, manageable subset, their decision-making efforts can be classified as extensive problem-solving. At this level, the consumer needs a great deal of information to establish a set of criteria on which to judge specific brands and a correspondingly large amount of information concerning each of the brands to be considered, for example, when buying a new item for the first time.

(b) **Limited problem-solving**

At this level of problem-solving, consumers already have established the basic criteria for evaluating the product category and the various brands in the category. However, they have not fully established preferences concerning a select group of brands. Their search for additional information is more like 'fine tuning', they must gather additional brand information to discriminate among the various brands, or within brand families but between products with differing features, for example, when buying a new TV.

(c) **Routinised response behaviour**

At this level, consumers have experience with the product category and a well-established set of criteria into which to evaluate the brands they are considering. In some situations, they may search for a small amount of additional information, in other they simply review what they already know, for example when buying breakfast cereal.

Types of organisational buying decisions

The level of problem-solving in an organisational buying decision will also vary in its complexity.

(a) Some purchases will be a **straight rebuy** or the routine topping up of stocks without changing supplier or product specifications: for example, the re-ordering of stationery supplies. (This may be done on an automatic re-ordering system by the purchasing department or even the supplier, requiring only post-purchase review to ensure satisfaction.)

(b) Some purchases will be a **modified rebuy**: the organisation wants to change product specifications, prices, terms or suppliers (which should stimulate competitive offerings from existing and alternative suppliers). Any or all stages of the buying decision may be revisited.

(c) Some purchases will be a **new task** situation: the organisation is buying a product or service for the first time. In such circumstances, an extensive and systematic decision-making process may take place. This is an opportunity for the marketer to reach key members of the buying centre and to offer support and information in making the decision.

2 MODELLING BUYER BEHAVIOUR

2.1 Rationale and objectives

The 'modelling approach' is based on the idea that any phenomenon or process can be **simplified**, by leaving out of the 'picture' any aspects or variables that are not of interest to the modeller, while still portraying something **meaningful** about the real phenomenon or process. This is particularly true of **consumer behaviour models**.

Because a model is a simplification of reality based on the modeller's interests, different models may be developed to describe the same phenomenon or process, **showing different aspects of the same thing**.

2.2 Objectives

(a) **Help researchers to develop theories**. Models provide a simplified framework within which research can be directed to confirm or refute/modify hypotheses about the relationships between variables and about the nature of the 'invisible' intervening variables.

(b) **Describe and explain behaviour and aid prediction**. Models which have been substantially confirmed by research and practice offer a useful tool to the marketer who wishes to understand the consumer decision process, and to predict consumer reactions to a marketing strategy based on the manipulation of stimulus and intervening variables.

2.3 Applications

Micro versus macro	A micro-model deals with the **individual** or other small unit, while a macro-model deals with a **wider environment.**
Descriptive, diagnostic, predictive	Descriptive models **describe** historical or current phenomena, while diagnostic models set out to find **causes** – to explain – and predictive models try to show what **outcomes** will result from given inputs in given circumstances.
Low-level, medium-level, high-level	These terms denote the complexity of the model and the number of variables included.
Static or dynamic	A static model is a '**snapshot**' of a phenomenon at a **particular point in time,** while a dynamic model can take account of **variations over time.**
Qualitative and quantitative	Qualitative models do not make explicit variable **measurements,** while quantitative models do, weighting the variables according to importance and so offering a more accurate predictive model.
Data-based versus theory-based	A data-based model is based on logical analysis of **available data,** while a theory-based one is developed by means of logical **extension of existing theories,** often of marketing but sometimes of psychology or sociology.
Behavioural versus statistical	A behavioural model is based on **stimulus response theories,** that is on how people are expected to behave, while a statistical model uses numerical analysis without prior assumptions about motivation.
Generalised versus *ad hoc*	A generalised model is constructed to apply to a **wide range of markets,** while an *ad hoc* one applies just to one market or brand.

2.4 Evaluating models

(a) **Validity.** We **should be able to verify** the model, that is **test** its proposed relationships.

(b) **Factual accuracy.** Is the model consistent with known facts (even if it is an admittedly intuitive or theoretical model)?

(c) **Rationality.** Is the model logical and internally consistent (not contradicting itself or requiring irrational 'leaps')?

(d) **Completeness.** The model may by definition leave out aspects of the phenomenon/ process, but are all assumptions explicitly stated? Are the exogenous variables identified?

(e) **Simplicity.** Is the model accessible? Are the relationships portrayed as direct and easily-perceivable as possible?

(f) **Originality.** Does the model include new elements, or put elements together in a new way, which will further our insight or knowledge?

(g) **Effectiveness for its purpose,** whether that be:

(i) **Explanation** – does the model show causal relationships which explain how and why the phenomenon occurs?

(ii) **Prediction** – does the model enable the behavioural response/output to be predicted, given knowledge of the relevant input/stimulus and intervening variables?

(iii) **Heurism** – does the model identify gaps in our knowledge, and so suggest new or further areas of research?

3 SIMPLE MODELS OF BUYER BEHAVIOUR

As examples we shall discuss some of the lower-level forms of modelling.

(a) Black box models leave out the **internal** variables, the mental processes of decision making.

(b) Personal variable models leave out the **external** variables, concentrating only on the mental processes of decision making.

3.1 Black box models/stimulus-response

Black box models assume that **observable behaviour** is the only valid object of study. Concentrating as they do on environmental factors, such models in the context of consumer behaviour are **market models** which may be used in market research to identify, for example, the following.

(a) The **decision environment**. Factors external to the individual which influence his buying behaviour, are shown – but the individual is a black box.

(b) The **marketing distribution process**. The 'flow' of products, or information, or influence, is plotted – from producer to salesforce to retail outlet to consumer to other consumers. Competitors can be similarly plotted on the model.

(c) The **buying process** – taking into account only inputs and outputs.

Black box models

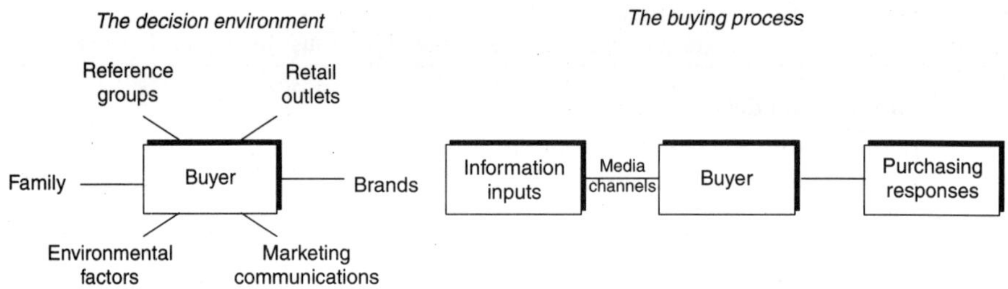

Figure 1.2: Source: Kotler et al.

Why are Black box models useful?

(a) They include **observable, quantifiable variables** which are easier to measure and to manipulate

(b) They concentrate on a **manageable number of relevant input variables**, on which a strategy can be based – without 'analysis paralysis' from speculating about all the possible intervening factors.

(c) **Stimulus variables** such as price, quality, availability, service, or advertising, can be identified by models, and the results of each – in terms of product/brand or supplier choice, quantity and frequency of purchase – set out in a simple, direct way. If a model indicates that decreased price results in increased purchase quantity, the marketer is able to respond accordingly: it does not matter, to an extent, why the phenomenon occurs.

(d) Black boxes are, however, limited to **simple, unambitious functions**. They do not attempt to predict behaviour in a wide range of circumstances, nor to explain behaviour.

Activity 2 **(5 minutes)**

Analyse a simple regular purchase that you make – a litre of milk, say, or a chocolate bar – in terms of the black box model depicted above.

3.2 Personal variable models

Personal variable models are simple models of **internal processes** – beliefs, intentions, motives, perceptions etc – without any of the **external, environmental influences**.

Examples of personal variable models

(a) **Compensatory or trade-off model**. When faced with a choice between products composed of certain attributes or benefits in different proportions, a consumer will **compromise** on his image of the 'ideal' product, and accept less of one attribute in return for more of another. This is a judgement about which combination of attributes offers the highest overall utility, or value.

(b) The **threshold model**. For each perceived attribute of a product, there is a perceived threshold of acceptability, below which the product will be rejected. Each attribute is assessed, until the product falls short on one (usually, price) and is discarded.

3.3 Diffusion of innovation model

New products represent a significant opportunity to both **consumers** (who may find a better means of satisfying their needs) and **marketers** (who may find a new source of profit or competitive advantage). The **first buyers** of a product are the **most important**, since there is no established frame of reference within which the product will be considered: no experience, association or reference group adoption to build on.

Definitions

An **innovation** is anything new (product, service, practice or idea) from the point of view of:

(a) The organisation ('We've never done this before').

(b) The product ('It hasn't been done quite like this before').

(c) The market ('You may not have seen this before').

(d) The consumer ('I don't think I've seen this before').

Everett Rogers' definition of innovation is: 'any idea or product perceived by the potential innovator to be new.' This is the essence of the customer-focused approach to innovation.

Diffusion of innovation is the 'macro' process by which the innovation is spread or disseminated from the source to the consuming public.

Adoption is the 'micro' process by which a consumer makes the decision to accept or reject an innovation.

Diffusion of innovation (*Rogers*, 1962)

You may have noticed that some new ideas 'catch on' suddenly (eg Crocs shoes and iPods), while others take a long time to gain acceptance (eg web only based banking), and others never get beyond the fringes (eg liquid furniture polish). The **rate and extent of diffusion** of an innovation depend on:

- The **characteristics** of the innovation/new product
- The **channels of communication** used
- The **social system** within which communication takes place
- The **stages of the adoption process** reached by members of the social system

Product characteristics that influence diffusion

(a) **Relative advantage**

Relative advantage is the degree to which potential consumers perceive the product innovation to be better than previous or competing products.

(b) **Compatibility**

Compatibility is the degree to which potential consumers perceive the product innovation to be comparable or consistent with their existing values, attitudes, needs and practices.

(c) **Complexity** is the degree to which potential consumers find the product innovation **difficult to understand or use**.

(d) **Trialability**

Trialability is the degree to which potential consumers can test or sample a product innovation before committing themselves to adopting it.

(e) **Observability**

Observability, or 'communicability' is the degree to which a product innovation's benefits or attributes are visible to the potential consumer – by his own observation, or imagination, or the descriptions of others.

Fashion items, for example, have high 'social visibility' and are more easily disseminated than products for private use, which are 'shared' less with other people.

Activity 3 **(10 minutes)**

Whenever you see a product or service which claims to be 'new' in some way, apply the tests of relative advantage, compatibility, complexity, trialability and observability to it.

EXAMPLE

Sony ("Make. Believe.") one of the best known names in consumer electronics, has a consistent record of outstanding and constant product innovations. Its success stories include the Walkman personal stereo, the 3.5" floppy disc, the Compact Disc, the Sony Play Station and the Mini Disc. It is now at the forefront of a new wave of innovation as the consumer electronics market continues to evolve rapidly with digitalisation. Audio-visual and information technology have effectively merged with the rise of digital technology to create opportunities for a further generation of products. Sony remains proactive in R&D to fuel innovation. Here are some of its latest products:

Full HD 1080

At Sony we have a passion for enriching life. And to help do that we create ground-breaking new technologies that constantly improve the quality of what the world views, hears, captures, records and experiences.

Motionflow 200Hz

Motionflow 200Hz is a world-first technology that delivers the smoothest picture ever experienced on an LCD TV.

RGB Dynamic LED backlight

RGB Dynamic LED uses coloured backlight technology to enrich colours, darken shadow and sharpen picture contrast on selected BRAVIA Full HD LCD TVs.

Blu-ray

Blu-ray is the industry standard High Definition disc format that delivers the extraordinary sound and picture quality of Full HD 1080 movies, music and games to your living room.

OLED (Organic Light Emitting Diode) TVs

A complete new era of TV design, breathtaking colour, extraordinary picture quality and increased viewing angles opens up with the introduction of the world's first OLED television.

See http://www.sony.com.au/section/leadingtech for more.

Rate of diffusion: 'adopter categories'

Diffusion research has indicated that diffusion of an innovation follows a normal distribution (a **bell-shaped curve**) over time, and that consumers can be classified according to the time they take to adopt an innovation, relative to other consumers.

Five adopter categories have been identified (by *Rogers* (1962) and others). (Note that although they are 'adopter' categories, we are still looking at 'diffusion', not 'adoption' as a process: we are still at the 'macro' level of society and the whole life of the product innovation.)

(a) **Innovators** (2.5% of the population that eventually adopts the product).

Innovators are the first people to adopt an innovation. Their main characteristic is said to be 'venturesomeness': they are not averse to risk, are eager to try new ideas, are varied and extensive in their social networking.

(b) **Early adopters** (13.5% of the population that eventually adopts the product).

Early adopters are next to adopt the innovation. Their main characteristic may be called 'respectability': they take fewer risks than innovators (watching to see how they get on before themselves adopting the innovation), and are integrated into their social system and culture. They have the highest number of opinion leaders and role models, and so are important in the communication process.

(c) **Early majority** (34% of the population that quickly adopts the product).

The early majority are the first of the general mass of the population to adopt a new idea: just before the 'average' adoption time. Their main characteristic is said to be 'deliberation'. They are slightly above average in education, age and income, but tend to be followers, seldom holding leadership positions, and relying heavily on information from others.

(d) **Late majority** (34% of the population that eventually adopts the product).

The late majority are the last of the general mass of the population to adopt a new idea: just after the 'average' adoption time. Their main characteristic is said to be 'scepticism': they are cautious about new ideas and tend to adopt only as a result of economic necessity, or social pressure.

(e) **Laggards** (16% of the population that eventually adopts the product).

Laggards are last to adopt. Their main characteristic is said to be 'traditionalism': they tend to be oriented to the past and custom, parochial in their social outlook and suspicious of anything new.

Remember that these are **not stages** people go through: they are '**types**' or categories of people. The stages refer to the **diffusion process over time**, and the points in it at which the different categories of people adopt the innovation.

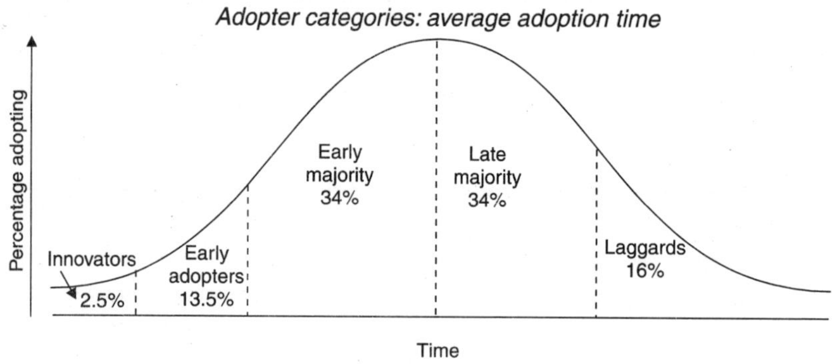

Figure 1.3: Adopter categories
Source: s 1962 (Roger)

The main problem with using this model is that the categories appear to add up to 100% of the social system – the target market. This is not a reflection of marketers' experience, since some potential consumers do not adopt/purchase at all.

EXAMPLE

A survey carried out by AXA has found that retired people are browsing the internet rather than the more traditional pastimes of gardening and DIY.

The AXA report, which looked at the online habits of retired people in 11 countries, calls these internet users '*silver surfers*'. In the US, Canada, Australia and the UK, silver surfers are using the internet more than six hours a week.

In the survey, 41% of pensioners listed browsing the internet as their preferred pastime, ahead of gardening and DIY.

Other findings were:

- Four in ten retired people are regular e-shoppers, with travel tickets the most popular item, with 45% regularly booking online.
- 84% use the internet for keeping in touch with friends and relatives via email. The next most popular online activity was 'looking for information', selected by 83%.
- 35% go online for banking activities.
- Pensioners in the US spend most time online, at an average of nine hours a week, closely followed by Canada and Australia at seven hours.
- The survey also found that pensioners in Italy, Spain were the least internet-savvy, spending an average of only 2 hours a week online.

However, according to Ofcom stats from July 2006, just 28% of people over the age of 65 have home internet access, lower then the average of 57% for the UK as a whole.

The adoption model

Definition

> **Adoption** is the process by which a consumer arrives at a decision to try (or not to try) and – having tried – to continue using (or discontinue using) a new product.

Based on the premise (not universally accepted) that consumers tend to engage in fairly extensive information search and problem-solving in order to reach a purchase decision, a five-stage model of product adoption has been proposed.

(a) **Awareness.** Consumers have been exposed to the product innovation, and are aware that it exists, but their attitudes to it are neutral at this stage.

(b) **Interest.** Consumers become curious about the innovation or aware of its potential to fulfil a need or want of theirs: they become interested in it to the extent of seeking out more information.

(c) **Evaluation.** Consumers use the information they have gathered in order:

  (i) To decide whether more information is necessary: delayed decision.

  (ii) To establish a positive or negative attitude (favourable or unfavourable evaluation) of the innovation.

(iii) To decide whether to purchase/try or reject the innovation.

The perceived product characteristics discussed earlier will influence this stage.

(d) **Trial.** Consumers try out the innovation, if possible on a limited, low-risk basis: their experience then provides them with the decisive information to adopt or reject.

(e) **Adoption** (or rejection). Based on evaluation ('mental trial') and physical trial of the innovation, consumers decide to continue to use it on a full committed basis – or to reject it.

Some researchers suggest that following trial, there are **two intermediate stages** (direct product experience and product evaluation: confirmation) before rejection or adoption.

Value of the adoption model

The adoption model offers a useful framework for marketers.

(a) To concentrate on **relevant aspects of the consumers' state of mind** at each stage. The most important goal, initially, will be to get attention, in competition with other stimuli. The next will be to arouse interest by suggesting motivations. The next will be giving information relevant to evaluation, then making the product available for trial etc;

(b) To study **which information media are most effective at each stage**. Awareness is best served by mass media, but in later stages, especially evaluation, mass media influence declines in favour of more personal sources: salespeople, opinion leaders and so on.

Definition

> **Opinion leader** – person who is knowledgeable about a product and is frequently able to influence others' attitudes or behaviours with regard to a product category.

However, the traditional adoption model has been **criticised** for:

(a) **Leaving out the problem/need recognition stage**, which may have to precede awareness if the message is going to be perceived

(b) **Suggesting that the stages are distinct and in sequence**. In practice, evaluation may take place throughout the decision-making process. Trial may occur before evaluation or interest – or not at all

(c) **Leaving out the possibility of post-adoption discontinuance**, because of further experience, post-purchase dissonance, forgetting and competing innovations

4 DECISION-MAKING UNIT (DMU)

In practice, many different people are involved in taking the buying decision. We hinted at the various different roles – the consumer is not necessarily the person who pays for the good.

Definition

Decision-making unit – all people influencing a buying decision – sometimes this may constitute just one person.

Role	Comment
Initiator	Suggests the idea of buying a particular product
Influencer	Provides information about a product/service to other members of the DMU.
Gatekeeper	Controls the flow of information about a product/service into the family (for example by 'giving the gist' of a consumer article, or selecting the advertising message that is relayed to the family).
Decider	Has the power to determine whether to purchase a specific product/service.
Buyer	Makes the purchase of the product/service.
Preparer	Makes the product into a form suitable for family consumption (by preparing food, say, or assembling DIY furniture).
User	Consumes or utilises a particular product/service.
Maintainer	Services or repairs a product so that it continues to satisfy.
Disposer	Initiates or performs the disposal or termination of the product/service.

This model can be used in a number of contexts. We now discuss two of these, the family and organisational DMUs.

4.1 The family DMU

Within a family group as a decision-making unit various members may occupy these roles. Let us consider the examples of the purchase of a child's toy and a family car.

Toy		*Car*	
Initiator	Child, parents	**Initiator**	Main earner, salesperson, family
Influencer	Parents Relatives Friends Salesperson	**Influencer**	Family Friends/colleagues Salesperson
Decider	Parents, child	**Decider**	Parents
Buyer	Parents	**Buyer**	Parents
User	Child (and possibly parents!)	**User**	Parents (and perhaps older children)

Marketers will be interested in reaching each of these roles: to make the product attractive to the initiator (if it is not a product automatically bought), **influencer** and

decider in particular. They would need to make the product readily **available** for the **purchaser**, and satisfying enough for the user to initiate future repurchase.

These roles – and the number and nature of the individuals who adopt them – will **vary from product to product, and from family to family**.

If the **buyer** of a product is a **different** person from the **decision-maker**, the marketer would need to **redirect promotional effort** from packaging and point of sale (attracting the buyer in-store) to advertising and promotional activity outside the store (where the decision-maker would be reached). If powerful influencers can be identified, they can be targeted as a way of getting to decision-makers.

Media which are designed for **sharing by the whole family** unit like television, Sunday newspapers, or cinema (when 'family' films are showing) offer marketers the opportunity of reaching influencers, decision-makers, buyers and users at the same time, facilitating discussion and influence within the decision-making unit.

4.2 The influence of gender

The pattern of decision-making roles has also **varied in society generally**, over time, particularly in relation to **gender roles**. The relative influence of male and female partners is of particular interest to consumer researchers, who commonly classify decisions as being male-dominated, female-dominated, joint, equal or 'syncratic', or unilateral or autocratic.

The relative influence of male and female partners, and the extent to which decisions are shared, may vary according to a variety of factors.

(a) The **family's attitudes to gender roles.**

(b) The **surrounding culture's attitudes to gender roles.**

(c) The **product or service.** Car purchase is a particularly interesting example: several decades ago, it was strongly male-dominated, while now, although still mainly male-dominated for the purchase of the main family car, the female car-buyer forms a rapidly expanding market segment (for second cars, cars for single and/or working women etc). The reverse trend is true for products like food and household items.

As the couple's education increases, more decisions are likely to be made together.

Activity 4 **(30 minutes)**

(a) Look out for car advertisements featuring women buyers and drivers, stressing independence and equality.

(b) Look out for advertisements in which the male partner (or even child) is 'sent out' shopping for food, washing powder and other such items: note how some choices they make change the female partner's mind and the family purchase pattern ('Well done. We'll be getting your brand from now on. Won't *you*?')

(c) Look out for advertisements which, on the other hand, reinforce traditional gender-related buying patterns: 'You're not a 'real'/'proper' mum if you don't buy/give them X.' 'Real men buy x.'

4.3 The influence of children

Children also have (or attempt to have) an influence on purchase decisions, not only those which are **relevant** to their particular wants ('I want toy X', 'I want chocolate bar Y') but also those which – **however irrelevant to them personally** – they relate to attractive messages they have seen and heard on television, or at friends' houses (a brand of dishwashing liquid marketed as having lots of soft bubbles, a car that a friend's dad has and so on).

Definition

> **Parental yielding** – when a parental DM is influenced by a child's request and makes a purchase.

There is still controversy over whether pre-school children are able to distinguish between television programmes and advertising: the impact of television in general, however, is undeniable, because of its **power of creating associations** which become part of child learning. Children are able to recall slogans and recognise symbolism in TV advertising even before they can read.

> **Activity 5** **(20 minutes)**
>
> For each of the following five product categories – groceries, cars, holidays, furniture and domestic appliances – describe the ways in which you believe a married couple's choices would be affected if they had children.

4.4 The DMU within organisations

All **organisational buying decisions** are **made by individuals or groups of individuals**, each of whom is subjected to the same types of influences as they are in making their own buying decisions. However, there are some real **differences** between personal and organisational buying decision processes.

(a) Organisations buy because the products/services are **needed to meet wider objectives**: for instance, also to help them to meet their customers' needs more closely. (However, as individuals also do not buy products and services for themselves but for the benefits they convey, it could be argued that both are forms of derived demand.)

(b) A **number of individuals are involved** in the typical organisational buying decision. Again, a personal buying decision may involve several family members, for example, and so may not be very different in some cases.

(c) The **decision process may take longer** for corporate decisions: the use of feasibility studies, for example, may prolong the decision process. Tendering processes in government buying also have this effect.

(d) Organisations are **more likely to buy a complex total offering** which can involve a high level of technical support, staff training, delivery scheduling, finance arrangements and so on.

(e) Organisations are **more likely to employ experts** in the process.

There are many examples of different types of organisational buying behaviour ranging from simple reordering (for example, of stationery supplies) to complex purchasing decisions (such as that of a consortium to build a motorway with bridges and tunnels, for example).

One system of categorisation for corporate buying decisions, devised by Howard and O'Shaughnessy, is based on the **complexity of organisational behaviour**. They identify three types:

Routinised buyer behaviour	This category is the habitual type, where the buyer knows what is offered and is buying items which are frequently purchased. It is likely that the buyer has well-developed supplier preferences and any deviation in habitual behaviour is likely to be influenced by price and availability considerations.
Limited problem-solving	This category is relevant to a new or unfamiliar product/service purchase where the suppliers are nevertheless known and the product is in a familiar class of products, for instance a new model of car in a company fleet.
Extensive problem-solving	This category relates to the purchase of unfamiliar products from unfamiliar suppliers. The process can take much time and effort and involve the need to develop criteria with which to judge the purchase. For example, the construction and refurbishment of new offices where previously buildings were looked after by managing agents.

4.5 The DMU in a business-to-business context

The **DMU is a particularly useful concept** in marketing industrial or government goods and services where the customer is a **business or other organisation**. The marketing manager then needs to know **who** in each organisation makes the effective buying decisions – this might be one person, or a group of people – and the DMU might act with formal authority or as an informal group reaching a joint decision. Many large organisations employ **purchasers** – but the autonomy of the buyers will vary from situation to situation.

Purchasing decisions may be influenced by several people in the consuming organisation.

(a) **Employees or managers** in operational departments might make recommendations about what type of supplies should be purchased.

(b) A **junior purchasing manager** might decide what he would like to buy, but **submit his recommendation** to a superior for approval.

(c) In large organisations, there will be **several purchasing managers**, who might work independently, but might also work closely together, either formally or informally.

(d) Technical specifications for component purchases might be provided by **engineers or other technical staff**.

(e) **Accountants** might set a limit on the price the organisation will pay.

(f) Large items of purchase might require approval from the **board of directors**.

The relationships between **members of the DMU** are also important.

The **user** may have influence on the technical characteristics of the equipment (and hence the cost) and on reliability and performance criteria, and so on.

Activity 6 **(15 minutes)**

Whenever you have the chance – when visiting businesses, or the newsagents browse through the trade magazines that you find (*Campaign, Farmer's Weekly, Banking World, The Grocer etc*).

What do you notice about the way products and services are marketed in such publications? Is more technical language used? Are the advertisements less 'glossy'? What do you learn about price and place?

5 UNDERSTANDING BUYER MOTIVES

5.1 The consumer's motivation mix

Customer behaviour is determined by **economic, psychological, sociological** and **cultural** considerations. The reasons for buying a product may vary from person to person, or product to product, or the reasons may be the same, but the weighting given to each reason in the mind of the customer may vary. These reasons make up the motivation mix of the customer.

The **motivation mix** leads a customer to choose:

- The type of goods or services they want to buy (food or a new haircut, say)
- The brand
- The quality
- The quantity
- In what place
- From whom
- At what price
- By what method of payment (cash, cheque, credit card)
- The timing of their purchase

The motivation mix of a customer for **consumer goods** will be different from that of a buyer of **industrial goods**.

(a) The **domestic buyer** might buy on impulse, attracted by the branding, packaging or display of an article, as well as to meet the family's needs within the shopping budget. The homemaker has a variety of demands to satisfy, within the limits of the family budget.

(b) An **industrial buyer** might be expected to give more emphasis to rational motives for purchasing – a clear need for the article, its price and quality, delivery dates and after-sales service.

Motives sit between **needs and action**. Motives are derived from needs in that a need motivates a person to take action. The difference between needs and motives are as follows.

(a) Motives **activate behaviour**. Being thirsty (need) causes (motivates) us to buy a drink (action). If the need is sufficiently intense, we are motivated to act.

(b) Motives are **directional**. Needs are general but motives specify behavioural action. A general need to belong may lead to a specific motivation to join a rugby club.

(c) Motives serve to **reduce tension**. If we are too cold, we are motivated to reduce the tension in our bodies that this causes by seeking a source of warmth.

Although we know that motives arise from needs and can lead to purchase actions, motives do not tell us **how** consumers choose from the options available to satisfy needs. Other influences are clearly at work.

5.2 Psychological influences on buyer behaviour

Attitudes and beliefs

Some writers have suggested that a buyer's attitude towards a product is an important element in the buying decision. However, there is no empirical evidence to link a favourable attitude directly with consumer purchases.

Loyalty

A consumer may demonstrate a loyalty towards a particular company's goods or to a brand, or even to a particular shop or retail chain. It is not clear, however, that marketing efforts can be successful in trying to increase customer loyalty. Although it is an important phenomenon, it may well be outside the sphere of management influence or control.

Personality

Inevitably, a consumer's buying behaviour will be influenced by their personality. For example, the latest computer might be purchased by a customer whose personality traits include self confidence, dominance and autonomy. Coffee producers, on the other hand, have discovered that heavy coffee drinkers tend to have sociability as a principal personality trait.

FOR DISCUSSION

Why is it that it is accepted practice to haggle about the price of some purchases (a house, or a second-hand car, say, in the UK) but not others?

5.3 Attitudes and behaviour

An **attitude** is a **relatively consistent, learned predisposition** to behave in a certain way in response to a given object.

(a) **Relative consistency**. Attitudes are not permanent: they can be changed. However, they tend to be reasonably well established, and so lead to behaviour with a reasonable degree of predictability. (If someone prefers coffee to tea, they are likely to choose coffee over tea fairly consistently.)

(b) **Learned**. Attitudes are 'learned' or conditioned, formulated with experience as a result of learning factors such as motivation, association and reinforcement.

(c) **Predisposition**. Attitudes are a predisposition to behaviour: they do not imply that a given behaviour will *necessarily* follow.

(d) **An object**. Attitudes relate to some aspect of the individual's environment: it may be a thing, person, event, concept or whatever.

Definition

> An **attitude** is an overall favourable or unfavourable evaluation of a product or service.
>
> *Jobber* (2007)

There is no automatic, direct relationship between attitude and behaviour. Insofar as attitudes and behaviour are inter-related, the process may be portrayed as a **tendency** for an individual to behave in a given way: not a **prediction** of how he will behave.

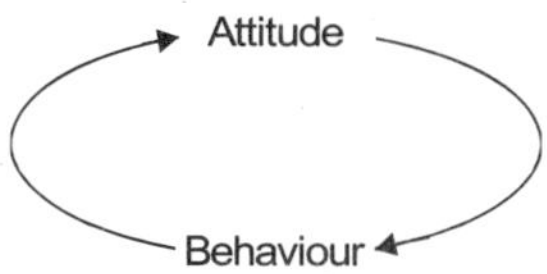

Situational factors affect our behaviour: attitudes are not the sole variable involved.

(a) An individual's **behaviour** may be influenced by the **situation**, to contradict his attitudes. For example, you may have a strong liking for organically-grown produce (you believe it is 'right' to buy such produce, and you intend to buy it) – but it is more expensive in the supermarket, so for economic reasons you do not buy it every week.

(b) An individual's **attitudes** may also be influenced by the **situation**. People who generally avoid chocolate for health and diet reasons may feel differently in situations where they are physically exhausted and need a boost in blood sugar, or where they are in a festive mood and sharing a bar/packet/cake with friends – especially if told that 'A Mars a day helps you work, rest and play!'

5.4 Attitude formation

Attitude theories are based on the premise that individuals seek **cognitive consistency**.

(a) Consistency between the attitudes they hold.

(b) Consistency between their attitudes/perceptions and their experience of reality.

(c) Consistency between their behaviour and their self-image.

When **discrepancies or inconsistencies** occur (and are perceived) the individual experiences **tension.** In order to alleviate that tension, the individual has to change one or more of the factors creating the inconsistency: to **change one of their conflicting attitudes** to 'fit' the other, to change their attitude to 'fit' their behaviour, or to change their behaviour to 'fit' their attitude.

Balance theory is simple, which is useful when it comes to application. However, it has been **criticised** as too simple to adequately portray the complexity of attitude systems and conflicts, particularly since it **uses only the dimensions 'positive' and 'negative'** without taking into account the **strength** of positive or negative feeling, which would allow us to predict which way people would choose to resolve an unbalanced situation (*Heider*, 1958).

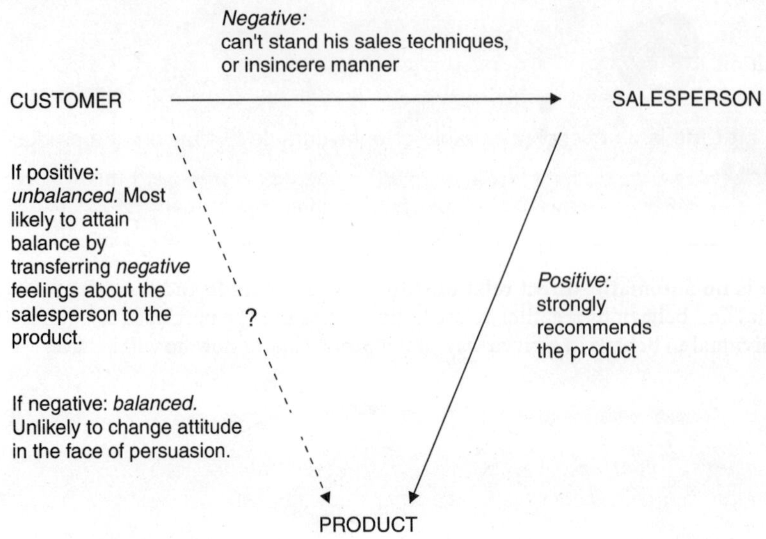

Figure 1.4: An application of balance theory

Definition

> **Balance theory** – considers relations among elements which a person might perceive as belonging together, and people's tendency to change relations among elements in order to make them balance.

5.5 Cognitive dissonance theory: *Festinger* (1957)

Cognitive dissonance is the discomfort experienced by an individual when they receive **new information which appears to contradict a belief or attitude they hold**. The theory is particularly concerned with **decision-making**.

(a) In making a decision – for example, to buy a product – individuals frequently have to **weigh up positive and negative factors** and compromise on that basis. Post-purchase dissonance occurs when somebody regrets or feels anxious about a choice they have made.

(b) They may also find themselves acting in a way that appears to contradict a belief or attitude they holds: they have chosen a foreign-made car because of a special financing deal or promotional campaign, when they had previously always believed in 'buying British'.

The individual may experience psychological discomfort as a result.

Marketers can use dissonance theory in several ways.

(a) To persuade people to **try or buy first** and develop a **positive attitude afterwards** (eg money back if not satisfied).

(b) **To reinforce purchase decisions.** The consumers will only be able to convince themselves they like the product if you *tell* them in your advertising they've done the right thing!

(c) **Be careful to avoid disappointing your customers.**

FOR DISCUSSION

Research investigating whether a quality mark would improve customer satisfaction with the financial services industry found that 45% of all respondents had, at one time or another, regretted taking out a financial product. The overwhelming reason was because the product was inappropriate for the person who bought it. 42% said this was because they were given wrong or incomplete information about the product, and a further 23% realised too late that they couldn't afford the payments. (*Phillips*, 2001)

5.6 Socio-psychological influences

Definition

> According to *Williams* (1981), **socialisation** is 'the process by which the individual learns the social expectations, goals, beliefs, values and attitudes that enable him to exist in society'. In other words, socialisation is the process by which an individual acquires sufficient knowledge of a society and its ways to be able to function and participate in it.

The **learning** of gender-related, consumer and occupational roles is part of the socialisation process: what it means to 'be' or 'behave like' a girl or boy, what money is for, what 'buying' is, what 'work' is and what sorts of work different 'sorts' of people do.

We can therefore identify a number of agencies who are instrumental in the socialisation of individuals.

(a) The **family** is probably the most enduring and extensive source of influence, because it is here that the dependent child learns from their parents and siblings. The family has a particularly strong influence on the child's perception of appropriate roles and on their self-esteem, which in turn affects aspirations.

(b) **School** is an important source of values, particularly as they relate to other people.

(c) **Peer groups** exert influence on social groups which can control a person's social and emotional satisfactions, say by appointing a person unelected leader or by 'sending him to Coventry'. As a person grows, peer groups become more of an influence, eventually superseding the family.

(d) The **mass media** is extremely pervasive and has a profound effect on all consumers.

'**Consumer socialisation**' is the process by which children acquire the skills, knowledge and attitudes that enable them to **function in society as consumers**.

(a) **Children** observe the consumption behaviour of their parents or older siblings (while pre-adolescents), or their peers (once adolescents and teenagers), and model their own behaviour accordingly.

(b) **Parents** use consumption-related events to socialise children generally: promises of gifts or shopping expeditions are used as incentives to behave in a desired way; withholding of money for self-directed purchases is threatened as a deterrent to undesirable behaviour.

(c) **Children** are socialised into attitudes, values and motivations which are indirectly related to consumption: products or particular brands are means of satisfying socialised needs and wants. Socialisation creates consumer motivations.

5.7 Reference groups

Definition

> A **reference group** is any person or group that serves as a point of comparison (or reference) for an individual in forming either general to specific values, attitudes, or a specific guide for behaviour. *Schiffman and Kanuk* (2004)

A reference group is an actual or imaginary individual or group perceived as having significant relevance upon an individual's evaluations, aspirations or behaviour.

Groups can serve as a benchmark for:

(a) General behavioural norms.
(b) Specific attitudes or behaviour – such as 'fashionable' product purchases.

An individual may be influenced by a non-contractual or secondary group, as well as a primary one with which they are intimately in contact. Note, too, that the individual **does not need to be a member of a group** in order to measure his behaviour by it.

(a) An **aspirational group** can impel an individual to act as it does, or to wear the same 'badges', in order to feel closer to attaining actual membership.

(b) A **dissociative group** can impel an individual to disown any behaviour or object associated with it.

Reference groups influence a buying decision by making the individual **aware** of a product or brand, allowing the individual to **compare** his attitude with that of the group, encouraging the individual to **adopt an attitude consistent** with the group, and then **reinforcing and legitimising** the individual's decision to conform.

EXAMPLE

Group membership has entered cyberspace as people around the world rapidly form virtual communities. Electronic anonymity opens up exciting new opportunities for many. New technologies allow people to chat about their mutual interests, to help one another with enquiries and suggestions, and to obtain suggestions for new products and services. Websites such as FaceBook and YouTube have become major social networking platforms and have grown to become a powerful media option for advertisers.

It has been suggested that we adopt **different reference groups** for **different areas** of our lives and consumer choices. Miles carried out a study of adolescent girls, and found that the **peer group** was most influential in, for example, the choice of clothes and books, while in matters such as the choice of boyfriends, their **parents**' opinions were more valued. **Youth**, however, is the stage at which we are most **personally insecure**, and at which the reference group has the most power: consider the market for training shoes or music, for example.

EXAMPLE

The Harley-Davidson brand is all about authority and prestige. It is not a bike for the sports motorcyclist: it seems to attract a significant number of men in their late 30s and early 40s, usually professionals seeking a bit of escapism. For many of them, ownership of a product that could not be afforded in their distant youth is a symbol of their achievement and success in life. Harley-Davidson dominates the cruiser/touring market, one of four market segments in the motorbike industry. The Harley-Davison owners' group claims to have over one million members with one dream: to make the Harley Davidson dream a way of life.

http://www.harley-davidson.com (accessed 6 December 2009)

5.8 Roles

Definition

> A '**role**' is the sum or 'system' of expectations which other people have of an individual in a particular situation or relationship. Role theory is concerned with the roles that individuals act out in their lives, and how the assumption of various roles affects their attitudes to other people.

An example may help to explain what is meant by 'roles'. An individual may consider himself to be a **father** and **husband**, a good **neighbour** and an active member of the **local community**, a **supporter** of his sports club, an amateur **golfer**, a conscientious **church-goer**, a man of certain **political** views, a **professional** and a **marketer**.

The other individuals who relate to him when he is in a particular role are called his **role set**. At work, he will have one role set made up of colleagues, superiors and subordinates, and any other contacts in the course of business: at home, he will have another role set consisting of family members.

Roles are **shaped** by:

(a) The **expectations** of other people as to how a person in a given role should or usually does behave.

(b) **Norms** – the customs and informal 'rules' of behaviour which society has formulated.

We learn, growing up in society and experiencing different role sets, **what is expected of us**, and what the '**rules**' are in given situations.

(a) We learn, for example, the '**appropriate**' **behaviour for our gender**

(b) When we start a **new job** – or first become a student – we are confronted with a whole new set of expectations and norms, and have to 'learn the ropes'

Individuals give expression to the role they are playing at any particular time by giving **role signs**. One example of role signs is **clothing or uniform**. A **white coat** indicates that an individual is performing his role as a hospital doctor, a certain shirt indicates that an individual is acting in the role of a **football team** supporter, and a **school** or **college scarf** is a sign that a person is in the role of student.

Note that **role signs** can be embodied as **particular products**. Many products are purchased because they reflect or reinforce social roles. Clothing and accessories are bought as symbols of role, for example; people buy gifts for each other which reinforce the nature of their role relationship (intimate and familial or formal and professional).

The nature of roles is not dependent on the particular people who fill them: people fit into roles. Roles are therefore valid units of analysis, in themselves. Knowledge of roles can:

(a) **Enable marketers to predict the kind** of role signs people will want to buy, for a wide range of roles.

(b) **Suggest role models** – ideal figures who embody the highest expectations of particular roles – who can be associated with a product (through licensing, advertising or promotions) in order to appeal to the aspirations of people in those roles.

(c) Offer the basis of **market segmentation** and product positioning: categories such as executives, or young mothers, carry with them a range of role expectations, norms and signs which can be appealed to or catered for.

Since roles depend on learning and perception, and since an individual occupies multiple roles, there are situations in which **problems** occur.

(a) **Role ambiguity** is a term which describes a situation when the individual is not sure what his role is, or when some members of his role set are not clear what his role is.

EXAMPLE

Role ambiguity is perhaps inherent in the way certain complex financial services, such as pension plans, have been sold. Is the person that sells the pension a 'financial advisor' or 'an insurance salesperson'?

The difference is important – a financial adviser is required to offer 'best advice' to the customer but, at the same time, may be required to meet sales targets.

Role ambiguity might sometimes emerge as 'conflict of interest'.

(b) **Role conflict** occurs when an individual, acting in several roles at the same time, finds that the roles are incompatible. A businessman who receives a telephone call from his wife, who wants him to leave work and go home, will experience conflict in his roles as businessman and family man. Similar conflict might be experienced by a working woman, who must reconcile her roles as a businesswoman and a mother. A trade union member may be reluctant to obey a strike call, because he disapproves of its reasons.

EXAMPLE

Ratners was a jewellery chain famous for its 'cheap and cheerful' products. Its managing director told an audience of investors that the products were 'crap', to explain its market position. This suggests role conflict between:

(a) The MD's role as being responsible to investors, explaining the business strategy.

(b) The MD's role as spokesman for the company as a whole to its other publics, including its customers.

Not long after this classic comment, the company ceased trading!

5.9 Secondary groups: the social environment

If we are to understand our customers we need to have some idea of how far the individual's cognitive processes and behaviour, including his/her decision whether to become our customer, depend on his/her perception of and interaction with **other people**. In this section we will cover two particular ways in which we see ourselves, and behave, **in relation to others**.

Some roles are perceived as **superior or inferior** in relation to others. The roles of employer and employee, or parent and child, have this connotation in traditional Western societies. One role may be superior to another because it is perceived that a person in that role has power or authority.

A combination of such factors – power, wealth, expertise, position – determines 'where' a person is in relation to other people, or in the framework of society as a whole. This relative position of superiority or inferiority is called status.

Definition

> In social class research, **status** is frequently thought of as the relative ranking of members of each social class in terms of specific status factors. For example, relative wealth (amount of economic assets), power (the degree of personal choice or influence over others) and prestige (the degree of recognition received from others) are three status factors frequently used when estimating social class. *Schiffman and Kanuk* (2004)

Status may be:

(a) **Ascribed,** or attributed to someone by society, on the basis of perceived factors such as their sex or age, intelligence or race. Improved status comes automatically with seniority in some cultures – such as the Japanese – while the male has traditionally had higher status than the female in Western cultures.

(b) Achieved by **deliberate effort** on the part of the individual. Professional and occupational status are *achieved*.

Status may be achieved by **acquiring appropriate roles and behaviours.**

FOR DISCUSSION

It is suggested that people play different roles and that their consumption behaviours may differ depending on the particular role they are playing. Do you agree or disagree with this perspective, and can you give examples to illustrate?

Some cultures are 'status-conscious', while others are not.

Marketing, as well as management, will need to take into account the extent of status-awareness. **Low-status** individuals, in a status-conscious society, may **aspire to achieve higher status**: products can be positioned accordingly. **High status** individuals may wish to be '**congratulated**', or to emphasise the exclusivity and power of their position in society: premium quality (and price) products frequently appeal to this sense. Status symbols are products that are purchased and displayed to signal membership of a desirable social class.

5.10 Social class: stratification of UK society

However, in practice, class strata or divisions are commonly derived from the specific **demographic factors** of:

- **Wealth/income** – economic resources
- **Educational** attainment
- **Occupational** status

From a marketer's point of view, it is also possible to infer **shared values, attitudes and behaviour within a social class,** as distinct from those of a higher or lower class: some research has been able to relate consumption behaviour to class standing. This makes social class an attractive proposition for market segmentation.

5.11 Class distinction and mobility

Social class tends to perpetuate itself, **where people are highly class-conscious: they do not tend to move between classes,** or indeed to interact socially with members of other classes. Sociologists note that some societies have a very rigid class system, while others do not.

Social mobility has several **implications for marketers.**

People aspire to upward mobility, given a reasonable expectation of success, and will exhibit purchase and consumption patterns suitable to the class to which they aspire.

The **'lower' classes will become a less significant proportion of the population** (and therefore target market), as people move up out of them – assuming that the country's economy can support a widespread increase in per capita income.

People are **afraid,** in a society of increasing inequality, of **downward mobility.**

FOR DISCUSSION

What consumption differences might you expect to observe between a family characterised as under-privileged versus one whose income is average for its social class?

5.12 Education and achievement

(a) *Social Trends (2009)* reports that the workforce is becoming **increasingly well qualified, although there are still inequalities. For example,** married or cohabiting parents in the UK in the second quarter of 2008 were more likely to be educated to degree level or higher than lone parents (23 per cent compared with 11 per cent)

(b) The number of people leaving school without qualifications is lower than the past. Women are doing increasingly well. In fact, fewer girls leave school without educational qualifications than boys. Overall in the UK, **girls outperform boys.**

The changes in educational attainment could be attributed to:

(a) The expansion of higher education after World War II
(b) Government policy, which has been to extend the scope of education
(c) Removal of maintenance grant entitlements.

5.13 Buying patterns

Demography and the class structure are relevant in that they can be both **behavioural determinants** and **inhibitors** of household buying behaviour.

(a) **Behavioural determinants** encourage people to buy a product or service. The individual's personality, culture, social class, and the importance of the purchase decision (eg a necessity such as food or water, or a luxury) can predispose a person to purchase something.

(b) **Inhibitors** are factors, such as the individual's income, which will make the person less likely to purchase something.

Socio-economic status can be related to buying patterns in a number of ways, both in the amount people have to spend and what they spend it on. It affects both the quantity of goods and services supplied, and the proportion of their income that households spend on goods and services.

FOR DISCUSSION

When the government provided funding to allow national museums and galleries in the UK to abolish admission charges and become more accessible to a wider range of people, an extra 7% of the population paid a visit. But visitors continued to come predominantly from the AB social groups. The DEs, who make up 30% of the population, still only accounted for 20% of museum visits and 11% of gallery visits. *(Museums Journal,* 2002)

5.14 Secondary groups: cultural issues

Culture is a concept crucial to the understanding of buyer behaviour and can be thought of as the collective memory of a society.

Culture embraces the following aspects of social life.

(a) **Beliefs** are perceived states of knowing: we feel that we know about 'things', on the basis of objective and subjective information.

(b) **Values** are the comparatively few key beliefs which are:

   (i) Relatively enduring

   (ii) Relatively general – not tied to specific objects

   (iii) Fairly widely accepted as a guide to culturally appropriate behaviour – and therefore as a 'standard' of desirable and undesirable beliefs, attitudes and behaviour

(c) **Customs** are modes of behaviour which represent culturally approved ways of responding to given situations: usual and acceptable ways of behaving.

(d) A **ritual** is a type of activity which takes on symbolic meaning, consisting of a fixed sequence of behaviour repeated over time. Ritualised behaviour tends to be public, elaborate, formal and ceremonial – such as marriage ceremonies.

(e) The different **languages** of different cultures is an obvious means of distinguishing large groups of people.

(f) **Symbols** are an important aspect of language and culture: the symbolic nature of human language sets it apart from animal communication. Each symbol may carry a number of different meanings and associations for different people, and some of these meanings are learned as part of a society's culture. The advertiser using slang words or pictorial images must take care that they are valid for the people he wants to reach – and up-to-date.

(g) Culture embraces all the physical **'tools' or artefacts** used by people for their physical and psychological well-being. In our modern society, the **technology** we use has a very great impact on the way we live our lives, and new technologies accelerate the rate of social change.

(i) Appearance and dress
(ii) Food and eating habits
(iii) Gender roles
(iv) Mental processing and learning styles
(v) Time and time consciousness

FOR DISCUSSION

Summarise an episode of a weekly television series that you have watched recently. Describe how the programme transmitted cultural beliefs and values.

5.15 Characteristics of culture

Having examined the areas included in the definition of culture, we can draw together some of the underlying characteristics of culture itself.

(a) **Social**. Culture exists to satisfy the needs of people. 'It offers order, direction and guidance in all phases of human problem solving, by providing 'tried and true' methods of satisfying physiological, personal and social needs'.

(b) **Learned**. Cultural norms and values are taught or 'transferred' to each new member of society, formally or informally, by socialisation. This occurs in institutions (the family, school and church) and through on-going social interaction and mass media exposure in adulthood.

(c) **Shared**. A belief or practice must be common to a significant proportion of a society or group before it can be defined as a cultural characteristic.

(d) **Cumulative**. Culture is 'handed down' to each new generation, and while new situations teach new responses, there is a strong traditional/historical element to many aspects of culture.

(e) **Adaptive**. Culture must be adaptive, or evolutionary, in order to fulfil its need-satisfying function. Many factors may produce cultural change – slow or fast – in society: eg technological breakthrough, population shifts, exposure to other cultures, gradual changes in values. (Think about male-female roles in the West, or European influences on British lifestyles.)

Activity 7 **(30 minutes)**

Schiffman & Kanuk (2004) give the following summary of American core values and their relevance to consumer behaviour. Consider how far they are applicable to your social culture.

Value	*General features*	*Relevance to consumer behaviour*
Achievement and success	Hard work is good; success flows from hard work	Acts as a justification for acquisition of goods ('You deserve it')
Activity	Keeping busy is healthy and natural	Stimulates interest in products that are timesavers and enhance leisure time
Efficiency and practicality	Admiration of things that solve problems (eg save time and effort)	Stimulates purchase of products that function well and save time
Progress	People can improve themselves; tomorrow should be better than today	Stimulates desire for new products that fulfil unsatisfied needs; ready acceptance of products that claim to be 'new' or 'improved'
Material comfort	'The good life'	Fosters acceptance of convenience and luxury products that make life more comfortable and enjoyable
Individualism	Being oneself (eg self-reliance, self-interest, self-esteem)	Stimulates acceptance of customised or unique products that enable a person to 'express his or her own personality'.
Freedom	Freedom of choice	Fosters interest in wide product lines and differentiated products
External conformity	Uniformity of observable behaviour; desire for acceptance	Stimulates interest in products that are used or owned by others in the same social group
Humanitarianism	Caring for others, particularly the underdog	Stimulates patronage of firms that compete with market leaders
Youthfulness	A state of mind that stresses being young at heart and a youthful appearance	Stimulates acceptance of products that provide the illusion of maintaining or fostering youthfulness
Fitness and health	Caring about one's body, including the desire to be physically fit and healthy	Stimulates acceptance of food products, activities, and equipment perceived to maintain or increase physical fitness

FOR DISCUSSION

The practice of coffee drinking has deep cultural roots. While Parisians may associate it with smoky cafés, metallic espresso machines, miniature china cups, spoons and sugar cubes, Americans are more likely to envisage it as something to be consumed at a book shop or a comfortable coffee bar with sofas and newspaper, from a large disposable cup. In Bangkok coffee is routinely sold by street vendors, poured into plastic bags of ice and mixed with evaporated milk.

The UK has developed its own coffee bar culture, modelled closely on the coffee bars of the US rather than those of continental Europe.

5.16 Micro-culture

Culture is a rather broad concept, embracing whole societies. It is possible to subdivide (and for marketers, further segment) a macro-culture into **micro-cultures** (or **sub-cultures**) which also **share certain norms of attitude and behaviour.**

Definition

> The members of a specific **subculture** possess beliefs, values and customs that set them apart from other members of the same society. In addition, they adhere to most of the dominant cultural beliefs, values and behavioural patterns of the large society.
>
> So subculture can be defined as a distinct cultural group that exists as an identifiable segment within a larger, more complex society.
>
> *Schiffman and Kanuk* (2004)

The main **micro-cultures relevant to the UK** are defined by the following demographic factors.

(a) **Class** (discussed in detail earlier).

(b) **Nationality**. Nationality refers to the birthplace of one's ancestors. The UK is home to many nationalities. The key issue for marketers is whether these offer segmentation opportunities.

(c) **Ethnicity**. Ethnicity refers to broader divisions. There are identifiable differences in lifestyles and consumer spending patterns among these groups, but it is only relatively recently that attention has been given to reaching and serving ethnic minority market segments, as distinct from mass marketing which would 'also reach' the racial minorities.

(d) **Geography or region**. Even in such a small country as the United Kingdom, there are distinct regional differences (eg lifestyle), brought about by the past effects of physical geography (poor communication between communities separated by rivers or mountains, say) and indeed its present effects (socio-economic differences created by suitability of the area for coal-mining, say, or leisure, or urbanisation). There is talk of a 'North/South' divide.

EXAMPLE

Just as marketers have discovered that it is a mistake to group together all members of racial minorities, the same principle can be applied to Caucasian consumers. In the US, there are significant differences in income levels among subcultures of various European extractions. These differences often reflect the length of time members of a subculture have been settled in the US. This is because groups who have been there longer have had more time to develop business networks and amass wealth. French-Americans are the most likely to be affluent – almost 42% have a household income greater than £50,000, while Polish-Americans have the lowest income among these segments.

(e) **Religion**. Adherents to religious groups tend to be strongly oriented to the norms, beliefs, values, traditions and rituals of their faith. Food customs are strict in religions such as Judaism, Hinduism and Islam. Values and lifestyle are also likely to vary according to the teachings and customs of the religion.

(f) **Age**. Age micro-cultures vary according to the period in which individuals were socialised, to an extent, because of the great shifts in social values and customs in this century. (You may have seen specially branded products for 'Baby-boomers': those born between 1946 and 1964 in the post-war birthrate explosion.)

(g) **Gender**. We have already discussed gender roles in family buying behaviour, and their gradual erosion – despite which, marketers make frequent appeals to gender-linked stereotypes. The Working Woman and the New Man are perhaps the most important current micro-cultural markets segmented on this basis.

Marketers also need to **avoid exaggerating the exclusivity of micro-cultures**. Promotional strategies need not target a single micro-cultural membership, since each consumer is **simultaneously a member of many micro-cultural segments**. (You do not need to sell cornflakes specifically to a ethnic minority, when its members are also Protestants, women, young people, living in the West Midlands – and part of the mainstream UK culture, as far as cornflake consumption is concerned.)

Activity 8 **(30 minutes)**

(a) Find at least one example of marketing communication targeted at a segment of each of the above micro-cultures. You do not have to confine yourself to commercial enterprises or to TV advertising. The Metropolitan Police ran a recruitment drive using a poster that featured a white man chasing a black man – or so one concluded until one read the copy. Actually both men were policemen chasing an unseen criminal.

(b) Visit shops or look through magazines that are not targeted at the micro-cultures into which you happen to fit. Make a note of the differences that you perceive.

5.17 Economic influences

Economic man

Economists have believed that the consumers make **rational decisions**, that is:

(a) They are aware of all product alternatives,

(b) They are capable of correctly ranking the alternatives having assessed their merits and disadvantages, and

(c) They are able to identify the best alternative.

This probably sounds pretty far-fetched to you and indeed the theory has been roundly criticised on a number of grounds.

(a) People do not have perfect information.

(b) People tend to act in accordance with their existing values and goals, and are limited by existing habits, skills and reflexes.

Passive man

(a) The objections to the economic man model give rise to a second model, the **passive man**. Such a person is irrational and impulsive, and is therefore entirely prey to the aims and strategies of marketers. The model suggests that the consumer can be manipulated at will.

(b) It is a simplistic model and ignores the fact that consumers can and usually do seek some information about product alternatives (even if the information is not perfect) and then make a choice which gives *them* satisfaction, not the marketer (even if the choice is not perfectly satisfying).

Cognitive man

Cognitive man is a thinking *problem solver* who seeks information on which to base consumption decisions from a range of choices. He is aware of the risks involved in making a choice, and will use various strategies to handle them.

Risks	Strategies for handling risks
'the uncertainty that consumers feel when they cannot foresee the consequences of their purchase decisions'	
Functional risk: will the product do what 'they' say it will, and what I want it to do?	Seek information Brand loyalty ('I was happy before')
Economic risk: will it be worth the cost? Am I getting a good deal? Ought I to be spending this money?	Brand image (expert opinions reduce perceived risk)
Physical risk: is it difficult or dangerous to use? Is it environmentally friendly?	Store image ('it's John Lewis, it must be good') Pay more for premium quality
Social risk: will the Jones's be jealous or contemptuous?	Seek reassurance (warranties etc)
Psychological risk: will I feel good about it?	
Time risk: is this all going to be a waste of time as the product doesn't work?	

Emotional man

This model confirms what many of us instinctively know – that our feelings and emotions play a large part in our purchase decisions. Many people buy impulsively, without any information search, because it makes them feel good at the time. In fact, buying something because it affords emotional satisfaction is a rational thing to do because it satisfies a need, the need to feel good. This is in many instances a more important need than the need for food or for a particular brand of fragrance.

5.18 Scarcity

It is a fact of life that there are limits to available resources. For the individual (often called the *consumer* or deemed to be collected together in *households* by economists), the scarcity of goods and services might seem obvious enough. Most people would like to have more: perhaps another car, or more clothes, or a bigger house of their own. Being physical commodities, these are called *goods*. Most people would also like to have more *services*, which can be defined as things which can be consumed only at the time of production. Examples of services include live theatre performances, public passenger transport and child-minding.

Since resources are scarce and there are not enough goods and services to satisfy the total potential demand, choices must be made. Choice is only necessary because resources are scarce.

5.19 Opportunity cost: the cost of one use for resources rather than another

Choice involves sacrifice. If there is a choice between having books and having butter, and a person chooses to have books, he will be giving up butter to have the books. The cost of having books can therefore be regarded as a sacrifice: not being able to have butter.

The cost of an item measured in terms of the alternatives forgone is called its *opportunity cost*. Thus the opportunity cost of buying six eggs can be measured as the two litres of milk or the one bus ride that could have been bought instead. Similarly, at a national level the opportunity cost of a country having a nuclear could be measured in capability terms of the number of hospitals that could have been built and staffed with the same amount of resources.

5.20 Income levels

Disposable income

Whether a customer will buy, and what he buys – his demand – depends to a very large extent on whether he has the disposable income available to make the purchase. His disposable income will be considerably less than this total income since a large part of that will be committed elsewhere (to his mortgage, basic food bills, electricity bills etc). In economic terms, demand is affected by disposable income levels.

Change in household income

More income will give households more to spend as their disposable income rises (the necessities form a smaller percentage of the total), and they will want to buy more goods at existing prices. However, a rise in household income will not increase market demand for all goods and services. The effect of a rise in income on demand for an individual good will depend on the nature of the good.

Demand and the level of income may be related in different ways.

(a) A rise in household income may increase demand for a good. This is what we might normally expect to happen, and goods for which demand rises as household income increases are called *normal goods*.

(b) Demand increases up to a certain point and then remains unchanged as household income continues to rise. Examples are basic foodstuffs such as sugar or bread for which demand can reach a maximum level because there is a limit to what consumers need or want to consume.

(c) Demand may rise with income up to a certain point but then fall as income rises beyond that point. Goods whose demand eventually falls as income rises are called **inferior goods**: examples might include offal and cheap alcohol.

5.21 Change in price

Two things happen when the price of a good falls.

(a) First, the fall in price raises the real income of the consumer, thus increasing the demand for normal goods, but decreasing the demand for inferior goods. This is called the *income effect*.

(b) Second, now that the good is cheaper, it will tend to be substituted for other goods by the *substitution effect*, leading to a rise in demand for the good. For normal goods, the price fall thus results in greater demand for the good because the two effects work in the same direction.

5.22 Change in fashion and expectations

A change in fashion will alter the demand for a product.

EXAMPLE

Bottled water was once rarely purchased in the UK, but came into fashion in the early 1980s, as a result of clever marketing and public concern – unjustified according to the water industry – about tap water. Since then, the explosion in the market for bottled water has led some to question if it is really worth paying the extra money (not to mention the environmental impact of producing all of those plastic bottles).

If consumers believe that prices will rise, or that shortages will occur, they may attempt to stock up on the product, thereby creating excess demand in the short term which will increase prices. This can then lead to panic buying.

5.23 Elasticity of demand

Where demand is **inelastic**, the quantity demanded falls by a smaller percentage than price, and where demand is elastic, demand falls by a larger percentage than the percentage rise in price.

EXAMPLE

Salt has a very low price elasticity of demand. We spend such a tiny fraction of our income on salt that we would find little difficulty in paying a relatively large increase in price. In contrast, a major item of expenditure has a much greater price elasticity of demand. If mortgage interest rates rise (the 'price' of loans for home purchase) people may have to cut down substantially on their demand for housing, being forced to buy somewhere much smaller and cheaper or live in rented accommodation.

Activity 9 **(5 minutes)**

Do cigarettes have elastic or inelastic demand? What about durable products such as white goods?

For most commodities an increase in income will increase demand. The exact effect on demand will depend on the type of product. For example the demand for some products like bread will not increase much as income rises. Therefore, bread has a low **income**

elasticity of demand. In contrast, the demand for luxuries increases rapidly as income rises and luxury goods therefore have a high income elasticity of demand.

5.24 Elasticity of supply

The elasticity of supply indicates the responsiveness of supply to a change in price. Where the price of goods is fixed, for example in the case of antiques, vintage wines and land, whatever price is offered, the elasticity of supply is zero.

5.25 Psychographic and life cycle factors

Psychographic, or lifestyle, analysis is based on people's subjective feelings and attitudes towards life in general. Psychographic and lifestyle influences on behaviour include the following.

(a) **Age.** Individuals consume different products and services, and respond to different marketing messages, according to their age. This is particularly relevant to lifestyle products such as clothes, furniture and recreational pursuits. It also impacts on the kinds of media which will be effective in reaching the target audience.

(b) **Stage in the family life cycle**, through which families pass as they mature over time. The traditional stages are shown in the table below.

Young singles	Few financial burdens; recreation/fashion led.
Young married couples	Strong financial position; focus on home
'Full nest' stages:	
Young couple, child under 6	Peak financial burdens; reliance on credit; child focus
Young couple, child over 6	Better financial position (wife return to work); child focus
Older couple, dependent child	Better financial position (more wives work); school focus
'Empty nest' stages:	
Children left, head of family working	Strong financial position; focus on travel, leisure
Children left, head of family retired	Cut in income; focus on health
Solitary survivor	Reduced spending; focus on health, hobbies, care, companionship

However, new markets are emerging with non-traditional households: single parents, childless couples and so on.

(c) **Occupation**; influencing income, status, interests and attitudes. Marketers may target occupational groups with particular interest in their products or services.

(d) **Economic circumstances**; level and stability of disposable income, savings and assets, borrowing power – and attitudes towards spending and saving.

(e) **Lifestyle.** an individual's mode of living as identified on key AIO dimensions: *Activities* (work, shopping, hobbies, sports, events attended),

Interests (family, recreation, fashion, computers, food and drink, travel) and *Opinions* (about products, issues, events, people). Marketers will seek to identify how their products/services 'fit' different lifestyle groups or profiles (of which there are many researched classifications).

6 THE ROLE OF BRANDS AND CUSTOMER LOYALTY

6.1 Is customer loyalty the same as customer retention?

There are differences between loyalty and retention.

Definition

> Properly understood, **customer loyalty** can be defined as **voluntary, profitable repurchasing and referral**.

It is voluntary in the sense that it is not a result of so-called 'incentives' like loyalty cards. In other words, customers are genuinely loyal when they return to a product/service supplier of their own accord and not merely (or principally) because if they do so they will collect 'points'.

It is **profitable** because it generates financial advantage for the product/service supplier (plus, presumably, a sense of 'value' for the customer).

It involves **repurchasing** and not merely window-shopping.

It includes **referrals** and recommendations to others – again without any financial or material 'consideration' being expected or offered.

Customer retention, on the other hand, may occur for a variety of reasons which have little to do with loyalty.

(a) Some customers may be '**tied in**' to the purchase of 'software' which is essential for the effective operation of previously-acquired 'hardware'. Thus, for example, users of a proprietary type of shaver may find it essential to buy razor blades which are only manufactured by a single source. Their frequent re-purchasing can scarcely be defined as genuine customer loyalty, as it arises from the realisation that **switching costs** are prohibitive.

(b) Customers may continue to use a particular product/service supplier through **inertia**: perhaps the supplier's performance, while not impressive, is not yet bad enough to justify a switch.

(c) **Switching costs** may also be prohibitive, literally so, in cases where customers have benefited from temporarily lower prices whilst accepting a long-term contractual commitment. This applies particularly with house mortgages: 'special [lower-interest] rates' are almost always linked to the existence of penalty redemption charges where mortgages are redeemed within a defined time period.

'**Customer satisfaction produces customer loyalty**'. Many organisations still claim that one of their strategic goals is the achievement of exceptional levels of customer 'satisfaction'. However, customers can be 'satisfied' and still defect to alternative suppliers, if apparently better deals suggest themselves.

Most customers now **expect** to be satisfied: they are not surprised when they buy something and it works.

6.2 Relationship marketing

Relationship marketing helps them to do this. Technology is the key factor. Software developments have made **databases** flexible and powerful enough to hold large amounts of **customer specific data**. While the corner shop of old recognised customers visually, companies today can recognise them electronically.

Definition

> Relationship marketing is the process of creating, maintaining and enhancing strong relationships with customers and other stakeholders. (*Jobber,* 2007)

The justification for relationship marketing comes from the **need to retain customers**.

In a **relationship approach**, 'smart marketers try to build up long-term, trusting, win-win relations with valued customers, distributors, dealers and suppliers ... it is accomplished by building strong economic, technical and social ties with the other parties.'

Relationship marketing may be contrasted with **transactional marketing**.

Differences between transactional and relationship marketing

Transactional	Relationship
Importance of single sale	Importance of customer relation
Importance of product features	Importance of customer benefits
Short time scale	Longer time scale
Less emphasis on service	High customer service
Quality is concern of production	Quality is concern of all
Competitive commitment	High customer commitment
Persuasive communication	Regular communication

The **rewards from effective relationship marketing** are potentially impressive (and are linked to the whole exercise of **customer retention**).

(a) One credit card company calculated that a 5% increase in customer retention would create a 125% increase in profits.

(b) American Express believes that by extending customer lifecycles by five years, it could treble its profits per customer.

(c) According to Coca-Cola, a 10% increase in retailer retention should translate to a 20% increase in sales.

Kotler says 'marketing can **make promises** but only the whole organisation can **deliver satisfaction**'. *Adcock* expands on this by remarking that relationship marketing can only exist when the marketing function fosters a customer-oriented **service culture** which supports the network of activities that deliver value to the customer.

Relationship marketing is thus as much about **attitudes** and **assumptions** as it is about techniques. The marketing function's task is to inculcate habits of behaviour at all levels and in all departments that will enhance and strengthen the alliance. It must be remembered, however, that the effort involved in long-term relationship building is **more appropriate in some markets than in others**. Where customers are purchasing intermittently and switching costs are low, there is always a chance of business. This tends to be the pattern in commodity markets. Here, it is reasonable to take a **transactions approach** to marketing and treat each sale as unique. A **relationship marketing approach** is more appropriate where switching costs are high and a lost customer is thus probably lost for a long time. Switching costs are raised by such factors as the need for training on systems; the need for a large common installed base and high capital cost and the incorporation of purchased items into the customer's own designs.

It is possible to discern five different levels of customer relationship.

Level	Comment
Basic	The salesperson sells the product without any further contact with the customer. This is, essentially, the transactional marketing described above.
Reactive	The customer is encouraged to call the salesperson if there are any problems.
Accountable	The salesperson phones the customer to see if there are any problems and to elicit ideas for product improvements.
Proactive	The salesperson contacts the customer on a regular basis.
Partnership	The salesperson and customer work together to effect customer savings. The commercial buyer works closely with the supplier to ensure that the deal suits both parties. This should encourage repeat business.

Broadly speaking, the greater the number of customers and the smaller the profit per unit sold, the greater the likelihood that marketing will tend to be at the **basic** end of the spectrum. At the other extreme, where a firm has few customers, but where profits are high, the **partnership** approach is most likely.

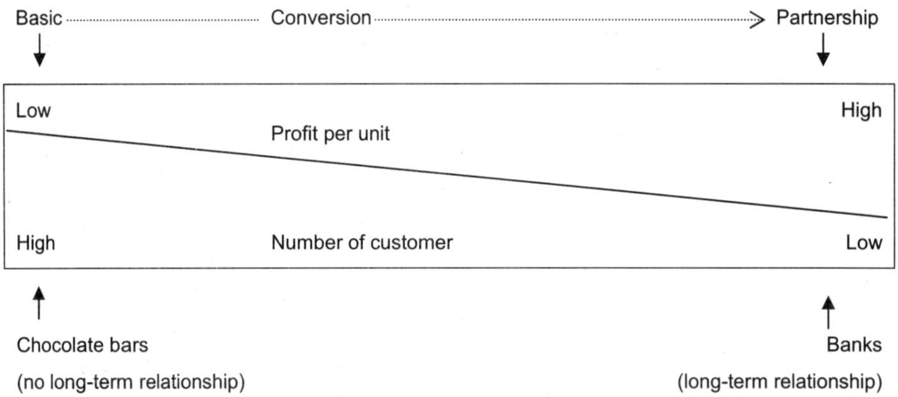

Figure 1.5 Levels of customer relationship

Implementing relationship marketing

The conceptual or philosophic nature of relationship marketing leads to a simple principle, that of enhancing satisfaction by precision in meeting the needs of individual customers. This depends on extensive two-way communication to establish and record the customer's characteristics and preferences and build a long-term relationship. *Adcock* mentions three important practical methods which contribute to this end.

- Building a customer database
- Developing customer-oriented service systems
- Extra direct contacts with customers

Modern computer database systems enable the rapid acquisition and retrieval of the individual customer's details, needs and preferences. Using this technology, relationship marketing enables the sales person to greet the customer by name, know what he purchased last time, avoid taking his full delivery address, know what his credit status is and what he is likely to want. It enables new products to be developed that are precisely tailored to the customer's needs and new procedures to be established that enhance his satisfaction. It is the successor to mass marketing, which attempted to be customer-led but which could only supply a one-size-fits-all product. The end result of a relationship marketing approach is a mutually satisfactory relationship that continues indefinitely.

Lifetime value

In determining which customers are worth the cost of long-term relationships, it is useful to consider their lifetime value. This depends on three things.

- Current profitability computed at the customer level
- The propensity of those customers to stay loyal
- Expected revenues and costs of servicing such customers over the lifetime of the relationship

Building relationships makes most sense for customers whose **lifetime value** to the company is the highest. Thus, building relationships should focus on customers who are currently the most profitable, likely to be the most profitable in the future, or likely to remain with the company for the foreseeable future and have acceptable levels of profitability.

Relationship marketing is grounded in the idea of establishing a **learning relationship** with customers. At the lower end, building a relationship can create cross-selling opportunities that may make the overall relationship profitable. For example, some retail banks have tried selling credit cards to less profitable customers. With valuable customers, customer relationship management may make them more loyal and willing to invest additional funds. In banking, these high-end relationships are often managed through private bankers, whose goals are not only to increase customer satisfaction and retention, but also to cross-sell and bring in investment.

Software

The goal of relationship management is to increase customer satisfaction and to minimise any problems. By engaging in 'smarter' relationships, a company can learn customers' preferences and develop trust. Every contact point with the customer can be seen as a chance to record information and learn preferences. Complaints and errors must be recorded, not just fixed and forgotten. Contact with customers in every medium, whether over the Internet, through a call centre, or through personal contact, is recorded and centralised.

Many companies are beginning to achieve this goal by using customer relationship management (CRM) software. Data, once collected and centralised, can be used to customise service. In addition, the database can be analysed to detect patterns that can suggest better ways to serve customers in general. A key aspect of this dialogue is to learn and record preferences.

6.3 Consumer imagery

An 'image' is an established and enduring perception of something or someone. We all have or hold images of people and things that we have experienced or imagined. For marketers, the images most relevant to consumer behaviour are:

(a) The self-image of the consumer; and

(b) The image consumers have of products and brands, retail and manufacturing organisations.

Self-image

Each individual has a self-image of being a certain type of person, with certain qualities and circumstances: this is his self-image. It is partly developed by reflection from other people, through the interpersonal contacts made in life: the way others respond.

In fact, the self-image is not a single 'snap shot' of what the individual is like, but consists of:

(a) **Actual self-concept**: how the individual perceives himself – what he is

(b) **Ideal self-concept**: how the individual would like to perceive himself – what he wishes to be, and

(c) **Expected self-concept**: how the individual expects to perceive himself in future – what he aspires to be.

Self-image affects **product and brand choice.**

(a) Products have a symbolic value for consumers: they 'say' something which may or may not be consistent with an individual's actual or aspirational self-image

(b) Consumers need to support or enhance their self images, and can do this by buying products that 'fit' the desired image, and avoiding those that do not

(c) Consumers may also identify with the image of a marketing campaign or retail outlet

(d) Consumers want to achieve their expected self-concept. Apart from a thriving 'personal image consultancy' industry (advice on wardrobe, presentation etc), there is a general vogue for aspirational products, such as mobile phones, Porsches, or membership of a health club.

Activity 10 **(10 minutes)**

(a) Are you a 'boutique' person or a Marks & Spencer person? Does this image hold true across all product ranges (does M&S food have a different image to M&S clothes, say)?

(b) What kind of shop-window displays do you identify with (or not)?

(c) What kind of car do you drive? What kind of car would you like to drive? What is the most desirable kind of car you can really see yourself driving?

6.4 Product image

The creation of an image of a product or brand in the market's perception is known as **product positioning.** It is a very important marketing technique. Whatever the actual physical attributes of a product, it is important that consumers perceive that product to possess the attributes that will fulfil their particular needs better than any competing product.

The image presented by a product or brand may:

(a) make the product/brand distinctive in the consumer's mind (differentiate it from its competitors)

(b) make the product/brand fit a distinctive market niche or segment.

> 'Positioning strategy ... conveys the concept, or meaning, of the product (how it fulfils a consumer need) rather than the product idea (the physical properties of the product itself). Different consumer meanings can be assigned to the same product. Thus, it can be 'positioned' differently to different audiences, or it can be 'repositioned' to the same audience, without being physically changed.'
>
> (*Schiffman and Kanuk, Consumer Behaviour*, 2004)

One technique used by marketers to determine how their products are perceived by consumers, in relation to competing products, is *perceptual mapping*. A grid or cruciform chart is drawn up, indicating key features or benefits. Consumer respondents' perceptions of the products, with reference to those features, are then plotted.

The perceptual map can then be used to identify:

(a) Areas where consumers do not feel their needs are being met

(b) Competing brands are perceived to be similar to your brand – which may therefore need to be differentiated more clearly; and

(c) The strengths and weaknesses of your product in relation to others

The following example of a perceptual map uses toilet tissue as an example. The dotted line indicates where the product would like to be.

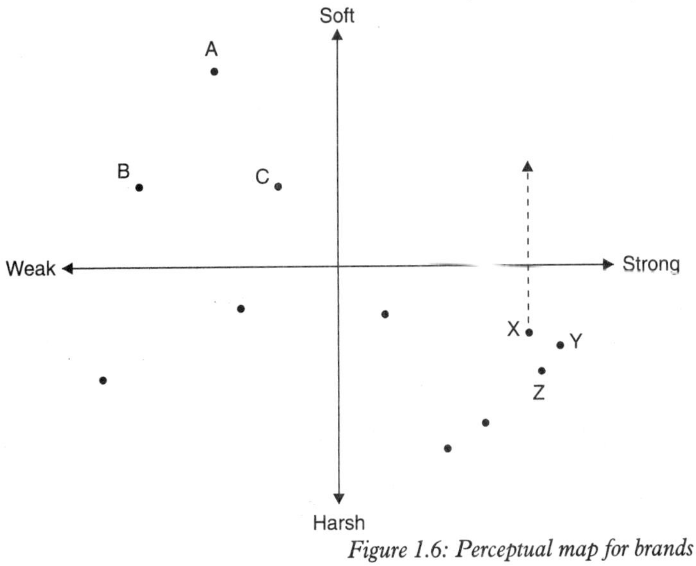

Figure 1.6: Perceptual map for brands of toilet tissue

6.5 Company image

Organisations also have images in people's minds.

(a) Retailers have their own image, reinforced by own-brand products and labels, in-store design and marketing 'style'. A consumer's perception of a product may be enhanced by the knowledge of its origin.

(b) Manufacturers and service providers have their own image, distinct from the brand names they produce. Large corporations with a variety of subsidiary companies and brands are increasingly at pains to establish a unifying ('The name behind all these great brands') corporate image: McVitie's and Scott are two recent examples. **Corporate image** may be based on community and environmental responsibility, sponsorship of sporting or artistic events, or sound managerial/financial performance.

EXAMPLE

In the UK, the corporate image of the Virgin group is very much tied to the image of Richard Branson. The group covers a host of different services from trains to IT and cosmetics.

Organisations have an image as employers, both internally and in the external labour market.

Activity 11 **(30 minutes)**

Select a product and brand that you use frequently and list what you consider to be the brand's determinant attributes. Without disclosing your list, ask a friend of the opposite sex to make a similar list for the same product (the brand may be different). Compare and contrast the identified attributes and report your findings.

Chapter roundup

- Individuals are important in all buying decisions, either for themselves or on behalf of an organisation. Marketers need to understand their motives, psychology and influences, and how these combine to form a motivation mix.
- Different types of consumer decision-making can be distinguished by the level of time and effort expended.
- Different types of organisational decision-making depend on the nature of the buying decision.
- Models are used to illustrate buyer behaviour as a means of simplifying a complex process.
- Essentially there are two formats for simple buyer behaviour models, black box models which exclude internal variables and personal variable models which exclude external variables.
- The key elements of the buying process are problem recognition, information search, evaluation of alternatives, the purchase decision and post-purchase evaluation.
- Diffusion of innovation is the term used to describe the process by which an innovation is spread or disseminated from the source to the consuming public.
- The family is of critical importance to individuals, as a network of relationships, reference group and social unit. The decision-making unit operates most often in a family context, with different family members adopting different consumption and hence DMU roles.
- Organisational decision-making is based on the same DMU model but is generally more rational yet inert. The interaction of DMU members is influenced by a great many variables. The AMA model can be used to describe this.
- The DMU is a particularly useful concept in marketing industrial or government goods and services where the customer is a business or other organisation.
- The marketing department of a supplier aiming at corporate clients therefore needs to be aware of:
  - How buying decisions are made by the DMU
  - How the DMU is constructed
  - The identities of the most influential figures in the DMU
- Buyer behaviour is determined by economic, psychological, sociological and cultural considerations.
- The term 'culture' encompasses the sum total of learned beliefs, values, customs, rituals, languages, symbols, artefacts and technology of a society or group.

Chapter roundup (cont'd)

- Different societies vary greatly in most aspects of culture, but all culture is social, learned, shared, cumulative and adaptive.
- Products can be invested with cultural meaning by marketing efforts; that meaning is transferred to a buyer who uses the product in a cultural context and hence imbues it with further cultural meaning. This is called transfer of cultural meaning.
- Micro-cultures within a culture are usually structured on the lines of class, nationality, ethnicity, geography, religion, age and gender.
- Marketing cross-culturally has many advantages for marketers but brings with it a number of new challenges. Two approaches can be used: localised markets (marketing a product so that it fits into the existing culture) or global marketing (capitalising on the fact that culture changes and develops, so a 'foreign' product can gain acceptance into different cultures in the same form worldwide).
- Customer loyalty and retention can be aided by relationship marketing techniques, whereby companies attempt to convert customers from basic transactional partners into lifelong 'advocates' for their product or service.

Quick quiz

1. What is a consumer?
2. What are the four influencing variables in the *Engel, Blackwell and Miniard* model?
3. What are the three types of consumer buying decisions?
4. Why are models used to describe buyer behaviour?
5. Name three criteria that should be applied when evaluating models.
6. What is the basic underlying assumption of black box models?
7. Why are black box models useful?
8. What do personal variable models focus on?
9. List four product characteristics that influence diffusion.
10. What are the five adopter categories?
11. Name four roles in any DMU.
12. Decisions which are reached by both spouses are known as?
13. List four differences between personal and organisational buying decision processes.
14. What are the three key psychological influences on buyer behaviour?
15. What is meant by the term 'cognitive dissonance'?
16. Which agencies could be said to be instrumental in the socialisation of individuals?
17. What are status symbols?
18. What are the underlying characteristics of culture?
19. What is a micro-culture?
20. What are the stages of the family life cycle?
21. What is relationship marketing?
22. What are the five different levels of customer relationship?
23. What does self-image consist of?

Answers to quick quiz

1. A consumer is the end user of a product or service who may or may not be the customer.
2. Stimulus inputs, information processing, decision process and variables influencing the decision process.
3. Extensive problem-solving, limited problem-solving and routinised response.
4. Models can help researchers to develop theories and they can describe and explain behaviour and so aid prediction.
5. Three from: validity, factual accuracy, rationality, completeness, originality and effectiveness
6. That observable behaviour is the only valid object of study.

7 They include observable, quantifiable variables; they concentrate on a manageable number of relevant input variables, and they help identify stimulus variables.

8 They focus on internal processes such as beliefs, intentions, motives and perceptions.

9 Relative advantage, compatibility, complexity and trialability.

10 Innovator, early adopter, early majority, late majority and laggard.

11 Initiator, gatekeeper, decider, buyer.

12 Syncratic.

13 Organisations need to meet wider objectives, they usually have a greater number of people involved, the decision process may take longer and they are more likely to buy a complex total offering.

14 Attitudes, loyalty and personality.

15 Cognitive dissonance is the discomfort experienced by an individual when they receive new information which appears to contradict a held belief or attitude.

16 Family, school, peer groups and the mass media.

17 Status symbols are products that are purchased and displayed to signal membership of a desirable social class.

18 Social, learned, shared, cumulative and adaptive.

19 A micro-culture is a distinct and identifiable cultural group within society as a whole: it will have certain beliefs, values, customs and rituals that set it apart – while still sharing the dominant beliefs, values, customs and rituals of the whole society.

20 Young single, young married couple, full nest, empty nest, solitary survivor.

21 Relationship marketing is the process by which information about the customer is consistently applied by the company when developing and delivering products and services.

22 Basic, reactive, accountable, proactive and partnership.

23 Actual self-concept, ideal self-concept and expected self-concept.

Answers to activities

1 Your own examples were required. Our examples are medical supplies, office stationery, and restaurant and catering supplies.

2 The result of, or answer to, this activity will depend on the item you have chosen.

3 The result of, or answer to, this activity will depend on the item you have chosen.

4 There is no specific answer to this activity.

5 Groceries: May need to spend less money
Will need to buy baby food
May be the subject of pressure from older children
Likely to buy less exotic, overseas and sophisticated foods.

Cars: More influenced by issues of safety
Likely to buy a bigger car
Less likely to buy a sports car
Influenced by amount of space for luggage, equipment etc

Holidays: Will want childcare facilities (cots, early supper etc)
Will want children's entertainment
Will want a safe environment (beach, swimming pool)
May have to travel in the peak holiday periods
Less likely to buy long haul or luxury holidays

Furniture: Likely to spend less
Will want durable furniture, unlikely to suffer damage
Will need children's furniture (bunk beds etc)
Furniture purchases will be lower on the list of priorities once initial baby/child furniture has been bought

Domestic appliances: Will want durability
Will expect reliability
May expect guarantees of prompt repair

6 The result of, or answer to, this activity will depend on the publications you have chosen.

7 The answer to this activity will depend on your own social culture.

8 The result of, or answer to, this activity will depend on the samples you have chosen.

9 Cigarettes have a fairly inelastic demand. Purchases of cigarettes do not form a significant part of most people's budget; people who smoke will tend to pay for an increase rather than face the prospect of giving up smoking.

10 The result of, or answer to, this activity will depend on your own self-image.

11 The result of, or answer to, this activity will depend on the item you have chosen.

Grandma	[illegible] to spend [illegible] Will need to buy baby food [illegible] [illegible]
[illegible]	More [illegible] [illegible] Less likely to buy a sports car [illegible]
	Will [illegible] [illegible] [illegible] May have to [illegible] [illegible]
[illegible]	[illegible] Will [illegible] durable furniture [illegible] Will need [illegible] [illegible] [illegible]
	[illegible]

[illegible]

The [illegible] will [illegible]
have [illegible]

[illegible]

Chapter 2 :
MARKETING RESEARCH

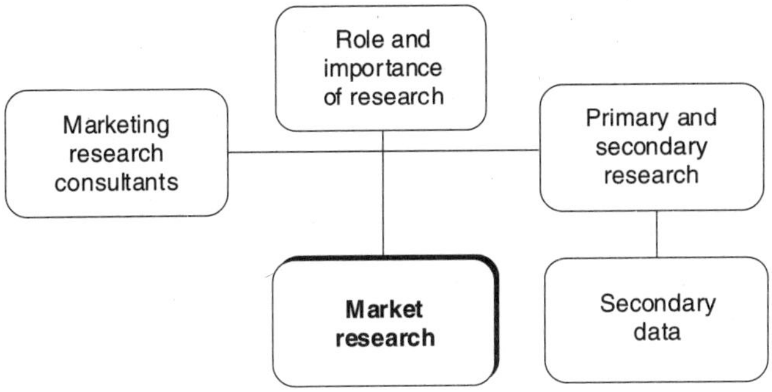

Introduction

Having covered some of the key issues underlying buyer behaviour, we now move on to focus on the techniques firms use to understand how customers behave. The chapter begins by discussing the components of an effective marketing information system. It goes on to discuss what marketing information an organisation might need and suggests how that information might be obtained.

The second section compares and contrasts primary and secondary research and offers some advantages and disadvantages of each type of data. The third section suggests sources of secondary data and offers a set of criteria which can be used when evaluating secondary findings.

The chapter concludes with an overview of marketing research consultants. This includes how they are selected and the relative advantages and disadvantages of outsourcing research.

Your objectives

In this chapter you will learn about the following.

(a) An overview of the marketing information system

(b) The scope of different types of research

(c) The range of different types of data

(d) The importance of secondary data

(e) The role of marketing research consultants

(f) Ethical considerations

1 ROLE AND IMPORTANCE OF MARKETING RESEARCH

Market research and marketing research are often confused. 'Market' research is simply research into a specific market. It is a very narrow concept. 'Marketing' research is much broader. It not only includes 'market' research, but also areas such as research into new products, or modes of distribution such as via the Internet. Here are some definitions:

(a) "Marketing research is about researching the whole of a company's marketing process." Palmer (2000).

(b) 'The objective gathering, recording and analysing of all facts about problems relating to the transfer and sales of goods and services from producer to consumer or user.' (*Chartered Institute of Marketing*)

(c) The function that links the consumer, customer and public to the marketer through information – information used to identify and define marketing opportunities and problems; generate, refine and evaluate marketing actions; monitor marketing performance; and improve understanding of marketing as a process. Marketing research specifies the information required to address those issues; designs the method for collecting information; manages and implements the data collection process; analyses the results; and communicates the findings and their implications. (*AMA definition*)

(d) The gathering of data and information on the market (*Jobber*, 2007)

The role of marketing research in consumer markets has become well established on a global scale. It is particularly important for manufacturers because of the way in which retailers and other intermediaries act as a buffer between manufacturers and their end consumers. If the manufacturer is not to become isolated from market trends and changing preferences, it is important that an accurate, reliable flow of information reaches the marketing decision-maker.

Another factor facing the consumer goods marketer is the size of the customer base. With such a potentially large number of users and potential users, the onus is on the organisation to make sure that it generates a backward flow of communication from those customers.

1.1 The marketing information system

Definition

The collection, organisation and analysis of marketing information is the responsibility of a **marketing information system** (MkIS) which in itself is part of the hierarchy of information systems that exist within organisations. The information collected, organised and analysed by an MkIS will typically include the following.

- Details on consumers and markets
- Sales – past, current and forecast
- Production and marketing costs
- Data on the operating environment: competitors, suppliers, distributors and so on

Typically, an MkIS will have four interlinked components.

(a) **The internal database.** This includes information on costs, production schedules, orders, sales and some types of financial information relating to customers (such as credit ratings). Financial analysis and tools would provide much of this information.

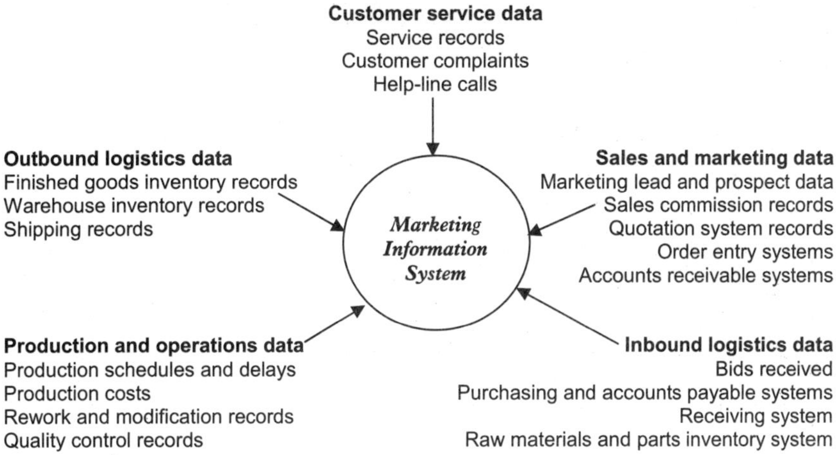

Figure 2.1: Marketing information systems

(b) **The external database**. This includes all types of information collected from external sources, commonly described as **marketing intelligence**. This database may take the form of press cuttings and so forth, but can also incorporate subscriptions to external sources of competitive data.

(c) **The marketing research system**. Generally such a system involves the process of information search undertaken on an ad hoc basis to provide answers to specific questions.

(d) **The decision support system**. A DSS is a set of analytical techniques that enable marketing managers to make full use of the information provided by the other three sources. This analysis may range from simple financial ratios and projections of sales patterns to more complex statistical models, spreadsheets and other exercises in extrapolation.

The marketing information needs of the organisation can be assessed by examining the information needed to answer each of the **four key strategic questions**.

(a) Where are we **now**?
(b) Where do we **want** to be?
(c) How might we **get there**?
(d) How can we **ensure** we get there?

The following table covers these four questions, shows what marketing information is needed to answer each question, and suggests how the information may be obtained.

Stage	*Information needed*	*Sources of information: forms of marketing research*
1 **Where are we now?** Strategic, financial and marketing analysis	Current sales by product/ market	Internal accounting
	Market share by product/market	Market analysis/surveys
	Competitor shares by product/market	Competitor intelligence
	Corporate image versus competitors'	Customer surveys
	Company strengths and weaknesses	Internal/external analyses
	Financial position versus competitors'	Company accounts
2 **Where do we want to be?** Strategic direction and strategy formulation	Market forecasts by segment	Industry forecasts/surveys
	Environmental changes	PEST analysis
	Growth capabilities	PIMS
	Opportunities and threats	Competitor research
	Competitor response	Product/marketing research
	New product/market potentials	
3 **How might we get there and which way is best?** Strategic choice and evaluation	Marketing mix evaluation	Internal/external audits
	Buying behaviour	Customer research
	New product development	Concept testing/test marketing
	Risk evaluation	Feasibility studies/CVP analysis
	Alternative strategic options	NPV analyses/competitor response modelling/focus groups/marketing mix research
4 **How can we ensure arrival?** Strategic implementation and control	Performance evaluation	Internal accounting/external auditing

This information-seeking process can be best expressed as a flow diagram.

Step 1 → Internal →

- The organisation's marketing information system (MkIS)
- Official company records
- Employees

↓

Step 2 →External (published)→

- Government statistics
- Trade association information
- Trade magazines
- Other magazines and newspapers
- Published reports
- Conference papers
- Research registers
- Books

↓

Step 3 →External (surveys) ⟶

- Shared cost or syndicated surveys
- Consumer panel tracking data
- Omnibus surveys
- Interfirm comparison
- Industry surveys

↓

Step 4 → Own survey ⟶

- Use Marketing research Agency
- Conduct own survey

Figure 2.2: Information seeking process flowchart

Generally, organisations do not use all of the sources outlined above continuously but may well use a range over the course of a planning year and choose according to specific project needs. For example, a chocolate manufacturer may purchase sales data from an organisation such as AC Nielsen, who buy till data from the major grocery retailers and prepare syndicated reports. This information is used for a range of purposes mostly related to performance tracking on their existing brands or markets they are interested in possibly entering. This type of continuous research would contribute significantly to the marketing information system. The same manufacturer is also likely however to use other research sources on an *ad hoc* basis when specific projects emerge. During the new product development project for example they may employ a marketing research agency to conduct taste tests on alternative product concepts with the potential target market.

1.2 Sources of research data

Primary research involves the marketing researcher in collecting data for a specific problem which has to be solved or decision which has to be made. Primary data may come from surveys, questionnaires, experiments etc.

Secondary research is based on data which for the most part has been collected for some other purpose. Examples include environmental scanning, published statistics and bought-in reports.

1.3 Marketing research organisation categories

The above categories of marketing research are those used generally in textbooks. In the marketing research industry different categories of research techniques are used.

1.4 Qualitative and quantitative research

(a) **Qualitative research** is geared towards gathering qualitative information about, for instance, attitudes and motivation, often in the form of pictures and words and using techniques such as discussion groups.

Definition

> **Qualitative research** – research data not subject to quantification or quantitative analysis.

(b) **Quantitative research** is involved with data as numbers, often using questionnaires and surveys.

Definition

Quantitative research – studies that use mathematical analysis.

1.5 *Ad hoc* and continuous research

Ad hoc research, as the name suggests, is a 'one-off' which comes into being with an initial brief and ends with a report. It is not designed, for instance, to monitor change but rather to find answers to specific problems, often using qualitative research methods. This should be contrasted with *continuous* research which has no identifiable beginning or end but keeps the data constantly 'topped up', so that changes in the environment can be identified. Continuous research often requires a sophisticated management or marketing information system, and frequently involves panels.

1.6 Customised and syndicated research

Customised research is also to some degree 'one off' research, since it comes into being thanks to a commission by a single organisation. *Syndicated* or 'off the peg' research is material which has been put together by one organisation (often a specialist marketing research organisation) and then sold to a number of clients to whom it is more or less equally relevant. Continuous research is often syndicated, mainly so as to spread the considerable cost of initiating and constantly updating the information.

1.7 Contract and consultancy research

Often marketing organisations will ask a research organisation simply to do one part of the marketing research process – such as collecting data which the commissioning organisation then analyses. This is known as *contract* research. This can be contrasted with the increasingly popular *consultancy* research, where the marketing research organisation may be involved in every stage of the process.

1.8 Consumer and business research

Research can be distinguished on the basis of who the end-user of the product concerned will be. Hence *consumer* research concentrates on individuals and households, while *business* research looks at customers who are organisations.

FOR DISCUSSION

The role of marketing is to create exchanges. What role might marketing research play in the facilitation of the exchange process?

1.9 Ethics

Brassington and Pettitt (2003) note that the ethical concerns surrounding marketing research have been the subject of an ongoing debate in the industry for a long time. As much consumer research involves specific groups of consumers, including children and other groups that might be considered vulnerable, it is essential that the researchers' credibility is maintained and that the highest standards of professional practice are demonstrated. This is vital if researchers are to maintain the confidence of their clients, as well as that of the general public and the government, and so the industry has established a set of professional ethical guidelines.

Members are expected to comply with these guidelines, although there is still some debate about their interpretation. The marketing research guidelines include such matters as protecting the confidentiality of respondents and clients, not distorting or misrepresenting research findings, using tricks to gain information from respondents, conducting an experiment and not telling those being studied and using research as a guise for selling.

FOR DISCUSSION

To what extent do you think it would be ethical for a condom manufacturer to undertake a survey of fourteen to sixteen year olds?

---

2 PRIMARY AND SECONDARY RESEARCH

Here, in brief, are the types of data.

2.1 Sources of research data

	Secondary data	**Primary data**
What it is	Data neither collected directly by the user nor specifically for the user, often under conditions unknown to the user – in other words, data collected not by YOU but by someone else for their own purposes or for general use	Data that is collected specifically by or for the user, at source.
Quantitative, 'factual' or 'objective' example	**Government reports** – in the UK a good example is Social Trends, which contains government statistics about British society, employment in different industries, attitudes and so on.	A survey you conduct with a questionnaire you have designed, with regard to a sample. You aim to get a statistically significant result. An experiment.
	A company's **published financial statements** summarise and interpret company transactions data for the benefit of **shareholders,** not the needs of the Research and Analysis project.	

Qualitative example	An article or a book about theories of motivation.	A focus group you have conducted to talk about motivation.
Advantages	• Cheap • Widely available • Suggests further primary research	• Clear target • Controlled • Up-to-date
Disadvantages	• Lack of focus	• Expensive • Time consuming

3 SECONDARY DATA, INCLUDING THE INTERNET

3.1 Internal sources of secondary data

Most employers probably have large amounts of information, not designed for your research, but useful to you. Monthly management accounts are only part of what is available for your research. And remember, the accounts department is rarely the **driver** of a business.

Accounts department

- Procedures manual
- Management accounts – balance sheets
- Financial data
- Accounting policies
- Tax details
- Working capital

Sales and marketing department

- Sales reports by region
- Sales by customer
- Sales by product
- Competitor intelligence
- Market prospects and reports
- Customer complaints
- Marketing research reports
- Brand strategy and values
- Distribution chains

Production and operations department

- Operations data
- Efficiency and capacity detail
- Process flow charts
- Detailed product costings
- Input prices
- Supply chain

Human resources department

- Number of employees
- Recruitment procedures
- Training programmes
- Staff turnover details
- Details of pay

In many instances internal data is gathered in a relatively unorganised manner and people in the organisation may have little knowledge of what data is actually available. The growth of marketing information systems alongside the trend towards the computerisation of all records in a business can do much to simplify the organisation and accessibility of internal data.

3.2 External secondary data

It is hard to give detailed rules about where you should look, except that you should search for **relevant** data, and make use of the Internet.

Books

Books tend to date quickly but can provide a useful tool.

Journals and articles

Academic journals, such as the *Harvard Business Review*. Again, rather than list them here, you may be able to find a list from your own college library of what is published – perhaps an article may be obtained or copied for you.

Other business or current affairs journals and newspapers, such as *The Economist, Euromonitor, Asian Wall Street Journal* etc, may have surveys relevant to different business areas.

Trade journals are also useful – most countries have journals produced by relevant trade bodies, detailing developments in the industry. You can use the Internet to access the websites of **trade associations**. Increasingly, businesses in an industry are setting up electronic markets

The **Internet** is an excellent source of secondary data, if used with care.

(a) You can use a **search engine** to bring up websites of interest. Some websites will allow you to download articles. Some of these websites – the **Economist Intelligence Unit** is one – offer articles for download. Another is www.ft.com. Many of these will be in PDF (portable document file) format.

(b) Your Internet service provider may also refer you to magazines and online newspapers.

Government ministries and agencies

Government agencies are good sources of economic and other statistical information. Most countries have an agency that provides national statistics. This varies significantly from country to country in terms of what is produced and the format, but you should be able to find:

(a) Economic data (eg UK Annual Abstract of Statistics)
(b) Social data (eg on population size and structure – social trends)
(c) Market data (eg export promotion)

Regulatory bodies and industry associations

There are many quasi-government and other public sector bodies which can provide data on particular industry sectors.

EXAMPLE

The BCCCA (The Biscuit, Cake, Chocolate and Confectionery Association) represents major manufacturers such as Cadbury, Nestlé, United Biscuits and Ryvita together with over 70 smaller and specialist manufacturers in this food sector. While representing the interests of the industry through its PR work, part of the Association's role is to provide industry-specific information for its funding members and to encourage the sharing of best practice through forums such as its annual conference. The Association, also however, is a useful source of information for a wide range of interested parties as they publish papers in a range of subjects such as obesity management and eating behaviours through its annual publication *Snack Facts*. In 2006, for example, *Snack Facts* included research on pupils' attitudes to school meals. In light of the publicity celebrity chef Jamie Oliver raised concerning the nutritional value of food in schools, there are likely to be a number of non-snack food organisations (government bodies, schools and catering providers) who are not members of the trade association but who would benefit from using this information.

Trade associations are often overlooked as a source of information but marketers who take time to search for related organisations are often richly rewarded with free information.

3.3 Using secondary data

Secondary data is used in many business situations, not just in academic research.

Backdrop to primary research

Secondary data may also be used to set the **parameters** for primary research. In an **unfamiliar field**, it is natural that the researcher will carry out some **basic research** in the area, using journals, existing reports, the press and any contacts with relevant knowledge.

Substitute for primary research

The (often substantial) **cost** of primary research **might be avoided** should existing secondary data be sufficient. Given the low response rate available for questionnaires, secondary research might do the job just as well. There are some situations however, in which secondary data is bound to be **insufficient**.

Some types of information can **only be acquired through secondary data**, in particular **trends** over time. The **historical data** published on, say, trends in the behaviour of an industry over time, cannot realistically be replaced by a one-off study.

3.4 Syndicated services

If the expense of conducting their own surveys is too great, companies and organisations can obtain general surveys that they can buy into on a shared basis, for example the Nielsen Retail Audit. A particular form of shared cost research is the omnibus survey, a variety of which are advertised in the Marketing research Society Newsletters and range from general weekly surveys done by telephone (such as phonebus) to special sector surveys (for example, Omnicar – motoring, Carrick James – children and youth, small businesses and so on).

The advantage is that for a few hundred as opposed to a few thousand pounds, a company can ask a few questions of a reasonably representative sample and have a report sent within two or three weeks.

Examples are: Nielsen, AGB, and Taylor Nelson Sofres (TNS).

Secondary data, while not necessarily fulfilling your information needs, can be of great use by:

(a) **Setting the parameters**, defining a hypothesis, highlighting variables, in other words, helping to focus on the central problem

(b) **Providing guidance**, by showing past methods of research and so on, for primary data collection

(c) **Helping to assimilate the primary research** with past research, highlighting trends and the like

3.5 Issues to bear in mind in using secondary data

Topic	Comment
Relevance	The data may not be relevant to the research objectives in terms of the data content itself, classifications used or units of measurement.
Cost	Although secondary data is usually cheaper than primary data, some specialist reports can cost large amounts of money.
Availability	Secondary data may not exist in the specific product or market area.
Bias	The secondary data may be biased, depending on who originally carried it out and for what purpose. Attempts should be made to obtain the most original source of the data, to assess it for such bias.
Statistical accuracy	Was the sample representative? Was the questionnaire or other measurement instrument(s) properly constructed? Were possible biases in response or in non-response dealt with and accounted for? Was the data properly analysed using appropriate statistical techniques? Was a sufficiently large sample used? Does the report include the raw data? In addition, was any raw data omitted from the final report, and why?
Sufficiency	Even after fulfilling all the above criteria, the secondary data may be insufficient and primary research would therefore be necessary.

Activity 1 **(20 minutes)**

Look for secondary research based on the telecommunications industry over the past twelve months. Use the above criteria to evaluate your findings.

EXAMPLE: FINDING OUT WHAT CHILDREN ARE UP TO

When marketing researchers have to investigate children's behaviour and motivation as consumers, they have to proceed with extreme caution. It is very easy to step over both the legal line and industry codes designed to protect children and young people from predatory practices. Nevertheless, marketers cannot afford to ignore the needs of a segment estimated to be worth £300 billion. Marketing research is especially important among these five to sixteen-year olds because they can change their minds and preferences frequently and not always with reason, and there is a real risk that today's best selling product is tomorrow's uncool fad from the past. Thus implementing carefully designed research that generates reliable insights and data ethically and with due respect to both children and their parents is well worth the effort.

The Marketing research Society (MRS) has issued strict guidelines for researchers. Measures such as obtaining parental consent for interviews with under 16s in the home and preventing interviewer and child being alone together help to protect the rights of children and ensure that they are not exploited. The MRS Code of Conduct also seeks to reassure parents and protect the researchers from unfortunate claims

Researchers also have a responsibility to prepare valid reports for their clients. Children are not easy to engage in research unless considerable care is taken in selecting research methods, location, group and interviewer dynamics, and response mechanisms. Children are often eager to please, may be intimidated by adult interviewers and may not understand the concepts and language used in research. Creative ways of engaging children often have to be employed, using pictures, toys, play and multimedia stimuli.

The resulting profiles are no doubt read avidly by marketers keen to keep up with events and to tap into the potential. It does, however, raise perhaps another more serious social question: to what extent to we want today's youth to be exposed to better informed and targeted marketing effort? Who should decide what is acceptable? Is it right to target sports and music-related merchandise at this age group? Is the marketing of violent television programmes and video games or overt appeals to materialism in the child's best interests? High degrees of professionalism and ethical standards are adopted by most marketing research companies and brand suppliers when children are involved, but that does not take away the need to question the societal impact of excessive exposure to naked commercialism. Does the profile above simply lead branded goods thinking, or is it a product of previous marketing exposure?

FOR DISCUSSION

Marketing research has traditionally been associated with manufacturers of consumer goods. Today, we are experiencing an increasing number of organisations both profit making and non-profit, using marketing research. Why?

---

4 MARKETING RESEARCH CONSULTANTS

Marketing research has been a growing source of organisational expenditure in recent years. Very few organisations can shoulder the cost of a large full-time staff of marketing research workers, especially a 'field force' of researchers spread around the country. In addition to marketing research agencies, there are marketing research departments in many of the large UK advertising agencies.

Definition

> **Field service firms** – companies that only collect survey data for corporate clients or research firms.

4.1 Choosing and using consultants

Choosing the right agency or consultant to work with is a key element in a successful working relationship. The external expert must become a trusted part of the team.

It is equally important that the marketing researcher has the specialist knowledge and research service capabilities needed by the organisation. In the UK you would expect a research organisation to be affiliated to the professional body, the Marketing Research Society, and for those working on the account to have relevant qualifications.

It helps if the agency has some knowledge of the market or business in which the company operates. Therefore, it is worthwhile developing a **long-standing relationship** with the research organisation. As the understanding of the company's business and the marketplace develops over time, there is a real dividend from the two operations working together.

4.2 Steps in choosing a research firm

Step 1 Check sources for finding names of research companies.

Step 2 Compile a list of firms and decide on two or three that appear to be the most promising.

Step 3 Contact the research firm in writing, giving as full a description as possible of the problem.

Step 4 Arrange an interview with the research firm, preferably in its office.

Step 5 Find out more about the research supplier and its previous clients.

Step 6 Explore how the research firm prefers to work with clients.

Step 7 Ask for a written proposal.

Step 8 Come to a clear understanding that further discussions may change the proposal in some ways.

Step 9 Agree about who will be the prime contacts between client and researcher.

Step 10 Make it clear to a firm submitting a proposal that proposals from other firms are also being considered when this is the case.

In selecting an outside agency, account should be taken of the degree to which an in-depth knowledge of the employing company and its field is required and the agency's skill in the type of study to be undertaken. An outside agency often needs some weeks of training or instruction about the company and its marketing problems before it can understand what the client requires.

4.3 Types of consultants

Outside agencies offering research may be categorised according to their type and location.

(a) **Local firms offering specialist types of assistance**

These firms may specialise in interviewing, mall intercepts, telephone research etc. They may take on special local assignments for large, nationwide research companies.

(b) **National research firms**

Agencies of this kind may be able to do almost all forms of marketing research. The companies often offer consulting in marketing and even general management. They also may offer computer-based information for use in databases, marketing strategy decisions and the like.

(c) **Consultants in various specialities**

These firms may consult and advise about packaging, advertising and personnel problems. They also may offer to do some research relating to their specialities. These firms may have a major field of interest such as engineering. The research offered by consultants can include necessary external studies, both marketing and technical.

4.4 External agencies versus in-house programmes

There are a number of advantages and disadvantages to each alternative.

(a) **Using an external agency**

(i) *Advantages*

(1) External agencies **specialising** in research will have the necessary expertise in marketing research techniques. This should allow them to develop a cost-effective research programme to a **tighter timescale**.

(2) Skills in **monitoring and interpreting data** will allow the programme to be reviewed and modified as required.

(3) There will be **minimal disruption** to the normal working of the marketing department which might result from releasing internal staff from existing duties.

(4) An external agency can provide an **objective input** without the bias which often results from a dependence on internal resources.

(5) **Costs** can be determined from the outset, thereby allowing better **budgetary control**.

(6) Such an approach might be advantageous when conducting **confidential research** into sensitive areas, there being less risk of information being 'leaked' to competitors.

(ii) *Disadvantage*

Agency knowledge of the industry will be limited. This would be a serious drawback if the agency requires a disproportionate amount of time to familiarise itself with the sector.

(b) **In-house programme**

(i) *Advantages*

(1) **Costs can be absorbed** into existing departmental overheads.

(2) It offers an opportunity to **broaden the experience** and skill levels of existing staff.

(3) It might be useful in promoting a **team spirit** and encouraging a 'results-oriented' approach.

(ii) *Disadvantages*

(1) There is a danger of **overstretching current resources** and adversely affecting other projects.

(2) There is a risk of developing an **inappropriate programme,** yielding insufficient or poor quality data with inadequate analysis and control.

(3) If additional **training or recruitment** is required this could prove expensive and time consuming.

(4) **Bias** could result from using staff with pre-conceived views.

(5) **Company politics** may influence the results.

(6) Considerable **computing resources** with appropriate software packages would be required to analyse the data.

(7) There may be a lack of **appropriate facilities**. For example, focus group research would normally be conducted off premises during an evening or weekend.

In view of the shortcomings of a purely in-house or external agency approach, a **combination** of the two might be more appropriate. For example, it might be deemed preferable to design the programme in-house but contract out certain aspects.

FOR DISCUSSION

Why is marketing research important to marketing executives? Try to think of several reasons.

Chapter roundup

- Marketing research can take some of the risk out of marketing decision-making by providing information that can contribute to sound marketing decision-making.
- This may be achieved in all elements of the marketing mix and, through involvement in problem formulation and solution-finding, marketing research becomes an integral part of the process of formulating marketing strategy.
- The collection, organisation and analysis of marketing information is the responsibility of a marketing information system.
- Ethical issues in marketing research are very important and researchers have to comply with codes of practice to protect vulnerable groups in society from exploitation.
- Marketing research can perform a variety of studies and makes use of both primary and secondary data sources.
- The growth of marketing information systems alongside the trend towards the computerisation of all records in a business can do much to simplify the organisation and accessibility of internal data.
- Research can be conducted either in-house or by marketing research companies which specialise in this form of consultancy. The latter offer a wide range of services from off-the-peg studies to tailor-made studies to meet the needs of individual clients.
- In selecting an outside agency account should be taken of the degree to which an in-depth knowledge of the employing company and its field is required and the agency's skill in the type of study to be undertaken.

Quick quiz

1. What categories of data would you expect to find on an effective internal database?
2. In a marketing research context, what does DSS stand for?
3. What are the four key strategic questions which organisations have to ask themselves?
4. What is primary research?
5. What is secondary research?
6. Define qualitative research.
7. How does quantitative research differ from qualitative research?
8. What is ad hoc research?
9. What is syndicated research?
10. List six issues to consider when using secondary data.
11. What do field service firms do?
12. Name two potential advantages of using an external agency.
13. Discuss two possible disadvantages to undertaking research in-house.

Answers to quick quiz

1. Customer service data, sales and marketing data, inbound and outbound logistics data and production and operations data.
2. A decision support system.
3. Where are we now, where do we want to be, how can we get there, how can we ensure arrival?
4. Primary research involves the marketing researcher collecting data for a specific problem which has to be solved.
5. Secondary research is based on data which for the most part has been collected for some other purpose.
6. Qualitative research is not subject to quantification or quantitative analysis.
7. Quantitative research involves studies that use mathematical analysis.
8. *Ad hoc* research is a one-off which comes into being with an initial brief and ends with a report.
9. Syndicated research is assembled by one organisation and then sold to a number of clients.
10. Relevance, cost, availability, bias, statistical accuracy and sufficiency.
11. Field service firms only collect survey data for corporate clients or research firms.
12. External agencies may have the expertise which is not available in-house and they can provide an objective input without the bias which can result internally.
13. There is a danger of overstretching current resources and thus adversely affecting other projects and there may be lack of appropriate facilities.

Answer to activity

1. The result of, or answer to, this activity will depend on your findings.

Chapter 3 :
THE PROCESSES AND FORMS OF MARKETING RESEARCH

Introduction

This chapter is concerned with the process and main types of marketing research. It begins by defining the concept of marketing research and establishing the way in which the results of effective marketing research can be used as an input to decision making.

The actual stages in the marketing research process are then described and this is followed by a discussion of the role of the research brief. Primary data collection is defined and the range of primary techniques available to marketers is evaluated. The importance of effective sampling is then explained along with an in-depth discussion of sampling theory which includes the sampling frame, types of sampling and the calculation of sample sizes.

Non-response bias results from the fact that individuals chosen for the sample who actually respond are systematically different in their attitudes or behaviour from those who are chosen and do not respond. The impacts of this upon the accuracy of the research findings are considerable. Methods to reduce this phenomenon are discussed. The challenges of the effective presentation of research findings are noted and the chapter concludes with a discussion of product, price and finally distribution research.

Your objectives

In this chapter you will learn about the following.

(a) An overview of the marketing research process

(b) The principles of primary data collection

(c) The importance of sampling and non-response bias

(d) The presentation of research findings

(e) The factors involved in product, price and distribution research

1 INTRODUCTION

Marketing research, however well organised, is no substitute for decision-making. It can help to reduce the risks in business decision-making, but it will not make the decision. Professional marketing depends partially on sound judgement and reliable information, but it also needs flair and creativity, and the ability to see the wood from the trees. Indeed, some of the world's most successful products would never have been launched had research results been solely used to make the decision. When conducted carefully however, it plays an important role in providing additional knowledge to assist decision-making.

2 THE MARKETING RESEARCH PROCESS

2.1 The process

The following ten-step marketing research process is the standard model.

Set the objectives of the research
↓
Define the research problem
↓
Assess the value of the research
↓
Construct the research proposal
↓
Specify data collection method(s)
↓
Specify technique(s) of measurement
↓
Select the sample
↓
Data collection
↓
Analysis of results
↓
Presentation of final report

Figure 3.1. Marketing research process. Source: Webb

Step 1 **Set the objectives of the research**

Webb, who developed this model, suggests that 'marketing research should reduce the need for a company to have to react, by making the organisation proactive, ie by sensitising management to oncoming threats and opportunities in a timely way, such that steps can be taken to avoid those threats or to take maximum advantage of the opportunities'.

Activity 1 **(15 minutes)**

Your company manufactures cruelty-free beauty products (bubble bath, talcum powder and so on) for a number of supermarket chains. You have been given responsibility for finding out about the market for a new line of cruelty-free cosmetics (lipsticks, eyeshadow and so on).

List the likely research objectives.

Step 2 Define the research problem

This vital step in the process establishes the area of research and the type(s) of data required. An accurate assessment of the environment in which the problem/opportunity exists must be made. This may necessitate building a model of the situation so as to allow researchers to put forward possible ways in which the research question may be answered.

Webb suggests the following summary of Step 2.

Overall research objective

↓ ← Exploratory research

Definition of the research problem

External expert advice → ↓ ← Exploratory research

Development of the hypothesis

↓

Research proposal

Step 3 Assess the value of the research

This step involves carrying out a **cost/benefit exercise** on the desired information. The cost of a research project should always be less than the value of the information provided.

Step 4 Construct the research proposal

If the results of marketing research are to prove useful they must provide 'a true, life-like representation of the situation and not a distorted cartoon-like image' (*Webb*). Both client and researcher must agree on the exact constituents of the research proposal.

The category of research (exploratory, descriptive or causal) must be decided upon.

(a) **Exploratory research** is the least formal and most flexible, looking at the variables which impact on a situation.

(b) **Descriptive research** describes the variables.

(c) **Causal research** (the most formal and inflexible) looks at the relationships between the variables, essentially cause and effect.

Step 5 Specify data collection methods

Data can be collected from either primary or secondary data sources. Secondary data, which we looked at in detail in Chapter 2, is 'data neither collected directly by the user nor specifically for the user, often under conditions that are not well known to the user' (American Marketing Association). Primary data is information collected specifically for the study under consideration and can use qualitative or quantitative methods.

Step 6 **Specify the techniques of measurement**

Measurement is the process of turning the factors under investigation into quantitative data. The scale will depend on both the data collection methods being used and the type of data required.

Step 7 **Select the sample**

Time and money will preclude the researcher from conducting a census of each member of the population in which he/she has an interest unless the population is very small. The researcher must therefore examine a sample.

Step 8 **Data collection**

This is when the researcher actually goes out and gets the data using the techniques as outlined in Step 5.

Step 9 **Analysis of results**

The data collected in Step 8 will not answer the research problem defined in Step 2. The data will have to be processed into information (as planned in Step 6). Note that certain types or levels of analysis are only possible if the data has been collected in a certain way and has been measured using certain instruments and scales of measurement. The researcher, prior to Steps 6, 7 and 8 should therefore have decided upon the way in which the data should be analysed. Often this is not done. The result is that the research simply shows that the information sought could not be collected.

Step 10 **Presentation of final report**

We will be looking at this aspect of the marketing research process in Section 6.

2.2 The research brief

The key to good research information, whether collected by an in house section or an external agency lies in the quality of the research brief. You need to be familiar with the content of a brief as you may be called upon to produce one in the examination.

The structure of a research brief will normally cover the following.

(a) **Background**. This covers relevant information about the company product, market place and the factors which have led to the current need for market information.

(b) **The problem**. This may be undertaken in conjunction with the researcher, but defining the problem carefully and agreeing objectives for the research is an essential first step in the research process and is central to the brief.

Sometimes this section is called 'information to be obtained'.

Too broad a definition leaves the researcher looking for 'everything and anything' while too narrow a view can blinker the researcher and limit the potential value of any research.

For example, the **objectives** of a research study into students' choices of text books might be as follows.

(a) Identify the main factors post-graduate students consider when selecting a text book.

(b) Assess the importance of the tutor as influencer in the decision-making process.

(c) Assess the importance of availability in the final selection of a text.

The brief should also contain any **constraining factors** relevant to the process. These can involve time scale, budget or the degree of secrecy necessary.

3 PRIMARY DATA COLLECTION

Definition

> **Primary data** is data collected by or specifically for the user (as opposed to secondary data).

3.1 Off the peg research

Off the peg research may consist of syndicated research or omnibus research.

(a) **Syndicated research** is collected by a research organisation on behalf of a number of organisations requiring the research. Syndicated research is usually too expensive for any individual organisation to collect. The research data is sold on to all the firms who have a use for it and hence the cost of data generation and collection is shared. This type of research generally uses large sample sizes or difficult-to-contact respondents.

(b) **Omnibus research** is where regular surveys of defined populations are undertaken. The research agency doing the work may make the service available as an 'omnibus' for other organisations to climb aboard. Each organisation climbing aboard the omnibus may be allowed to ask a few specific questions. For example, a company who advertises a new product on television may wish to identify how many of their target audience had actually seen the ad and would be able to recall it.

3.2 Made to measure research

'**Made to measure**' **research** is the most **expensive** type of research to undertake. The organisation requiring information decides what it is that it exactly wants to know. The organisation then has two choices.

(a) To carry out the research itself (in-house)
(b) To buy in the services of a research agency

Although it is the most expensive type of research to undertake, it is also the most useful type of research since it is '**customised**'.

This type of research is also classified according to whether it is to be conducted on an *ad hoc* (one-off) basis or is part of a longitudinal (long-term) study.

3.3 Field research methods

Definitions

Research in the field is concerned with the generation and collection of original research data.

Field research is the collection of primary data. Such collection methods can be divided into three types.

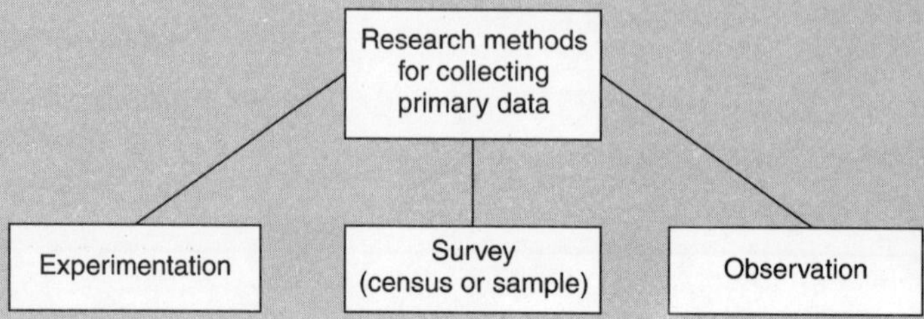

The most well-known of these is probably the **market survey**, with the stereotyped image of a woman with a clipboard. Each of the techniques has its particular strengths and the choice of approach is determined by the nature of the problem and the business.

3.4 Experimentation

In a **controlled experiment**, a controlled research environment is established and selected stimuli are then introduced. To the extent that 'outside' factors can be eliminated from the environment the observed effects can be measured and related to each stimulus. Controlled experiments have been used to find the best advertising campaign, the best price level, the best incentive scheme, the best sales training method and so on.

When experiments are conducted in more realistic market settings, results are less reliable because of the researcher's inability to control outside factors. Nevertheless, the local market reaction to a new product, for example, is often a prerequisite to a national launch. This is known as a **test market**.

FOR DISCUSSION

Dairy Crest decided to trial its two pint recyclable milk pouch system before a full-scale launch. Three UK counties were selected: Hampshire, Oxfordshire and Somerset. The bag was on offer at selected supermarkets and for doorstop delivery. The pouches can be frozen and are sold with a plastic container into which to pour the milk once it has been opened. Sainsburys started selling them in June 2008.

Such an innovation is good news for the environment as millions of plastic milk bottles are thrown away each year without being recycled. The pouch will mean fewer plastic bottles. Although relatively new to the UK, the concept has already been well accepted in Canada and Switzerland.

3.5 Survey (census or sample)

The **survey** approach involves asking questions of the target market or population. In marketing research for consumer goods, it will be impossible to obtain data from every consumer in the market. To obtain data, it is therefore usually necessary to obtain a **sample** to provide an estimate of the characteristics of the entire 'population'. The accuracy of the sample will depend on the following.

(a) **How** the sample is taken
(b) The amount of **variability** in the population
(c) The **size** of the sample

The larger the sample, the greater the likelihood that the sample will provide an accurate reflection of the population as a whole. Questions can be limited and highly structured, in the form of questionnaires delivered by post, telephone or in person.

On the other hand, questions can be asked in great depth of a relatively small sample. This is **qualitative or motivational research** and provides information on behaviour and attitudes.

3.6 Observation

Observation involves the personal or mechanical (eg video) monitoring of selected activities. It records actions as they occur and thus there is no lack of accuracy caused by a respondent's faulty recollection of their past actions or inadequate estimate of future ones.

Three conditions must usually exist if the observation method is to be effectively carried out:

1 The event must be observable: attitudes, motives and other mental activities are difficult to record

2 The event must occur frequently or be predictable

3 The event must be completed over a short period of time

Observation is often used in shopping studies, especially in retail outlets, when the customer is looking at the shelves and deciding what to buy. Observations of the in-store environment can include distribution, shelf price, shelf facings, shelf location, display activity, presence of point-of-purchase material.

Observation within both households and stores typically requires the setting up of a panel, making it subject to sampling difficulties and maintaining participation. Another problem is the quality of the data obtained.

FOR DISCUSSION

Love it or hate it, the Pop Idol 2002 competition won by Will Young, who beat 9,999 other contestants to win a recording contract was a great success for Thames Television. It was also an excellent piece of marketing research, as elimination of finalists one by one over ten weeks according to votes cast in a viewers' telephone pool identified which singers were most likely to capture the public imagination and thus could be the greatest success for the show's financial backers from the music industry. Effectively, the record company not only persuaded the public to participate willingly in the marketing research on a huge scale (over 8.5 million votes were cast in the final show) but also to pay for the privilege, with each call costing 10p. It was weekly test marketing and the voting arrangements gave virtually constant feedback (*Woods*, 2002)

So effective was this approach that over seven years later a plethora of similar format programmes and research gathering initiatives have swamped global television.

---

4 SAMPLING

Conducting a survey by sampling is one of the most important subjects in marketing research. In most practical situations a population will be too large to carry out a complete survey and only a sample will be examined. The results from the sample are used to estimate the perceptions of the whole population.

Definition

> **Sampling** techniques provide a range of methods that enable you to reduce the amount of data you need to collect by considering only data from a sub-group rather than all possible cases. *Saunders, Lewis and Thornhill (2003)*

Occasionally a population is small enough that all of it can be (or even needs to be) examined: for example, the examination results of one class of students. When all of the population is examined, the survey is called a **census**. This type of survey is quite rare, however.

Trade-offs clearly exist. To be 100% sure that the views of the sample really are representative of the views of the entire population you would need include an enormous sample (and even then statistically you could never be 100% certain). There is therefore a relationship between the size of your sample and the level of accuracy which can be expected in the results.

4.1 Why use sampling?

You may think that using a sample is very much a compromise, but you should consider the following points.

(a) In practice, a 100% survey (a census) rarely achieves the completeness required.

(b) It can be shown mathematically that once a certain sample size has been reached, very little extra accuracy is gained by examining more items.

(c) It is possible to ask more questions with a sample.

(d) The higher cost of a census may exceed the value of results.

Activity 2 **(5 minutes)**

What do you see as the advantages of sampling over complete coverage?

4.2 Selecting a representative sample

You need to be sure of the following.

(a) Your sample is not **unrepresentative or biased**. If the characteristics of the sample are different from those of the population, then the inferences drawn will be unreliable.

For example, a local leisure centre wishes to ascertain the opinions of working parents towards the possibility of a school holiday sports club designed as a form of childcare. For ease the centre may choose to question all existing leisure centre members. This sample would only be appropriate however, if a large proportion of members were working parents with children in the appropriate age bracket. The views of childless men and women who may be centre members are unlikely to be in favour of the most active proposed service. Including them in the sample for this specific research project would be wasteful and potentially misleading.

(b) The **cost and time** involved in selecting the sample produces the required benefits of **usefulness and accuracy**.

4.3 Biased samples, or sources of sampling error

Bias, or **sampling error**, can occur for the following reasons.

(a) Poorly defined or communicated **research objectives** leading to the wrong information being obtained

(b) **Measurement** errors, because the question posed by the researcher to elicit certain information produces different information entirely

(c) **Badly-defined population** (For instance, the population for a survey concerning purchase of football strips should not be 'young males 10 to 18 but should include young females, plus parents and grandparents, who actually pay)

(d) Inaccurate **sampling frame** (See below)

(e) **Unrepresentative random sample**, usually because the sample size is too small (This is also discussed below)

(f) **Selection error** where non-random sampling is used. (If a researcher has a quota of, say, 40 people to interview, and she positions herself outside a sports club at 5pm, she is likely to get 40 people of similar age and interest who are not representative of the population as a whole)

(g) Errors caused by **non-response** (See Section 5 below)

(h) **Mistaken responses**, particularly in answer to badly-worded questions or because the respondent is embarrassed

(i) **Data processing** or input errors

(j) **Collection errors** caused by the interviewers' preconceptions and prejudices when recording qualitative data

(k) **Data analysis** errors, were errors are introduced when data is subjected to further statistical analysis

4.4 Sampling frames

Definition

A **sampling frame** is the list, index, map or any other population record from which the sample can be selected.

Every factor of the survey design is influenced by the sampling frame – the population coverage, the stratifications that are used, the method of sample selection and so on.

(a) Does it adequately cover the population to be surveyed?

(b) Is it complete? Are all members of the population on it? Is it accurate and as up-to-date as possible?

(c) No items should appear more than once.

(d) Is it arranged in a convenient way for sampling? is it readily accessible?

No frame is likely to completely satisfy all the above criteria.

EXAMPLE

A typical sampling frame could be as simple as a database of contact details which is either constructed in-house or bought in, pages from a phone book or even a physical enclosure of a shopping centre. The sampling frame does not therefore have to always be a tangible written list but if your sample criteria is that you need to speak with shoppers within a town shopping centre, the sampling frame would be the centre itself, anyone who happened to be walking about in the centre belongs within the sampling frame and as a result should have a chance of being selected as a participant.

Types of sampling frame

These can be broadly classified as follows.

(a) **Lists of individuals**. Such lists, either of the whole population or of the groups within it can be used. Examples include the electoral register, the lists of members of professional bodies and lists of company employees.

(b) **Complete census returns**. Unfortunately the manner in which the data is collected and processed tends to prevent its use as a frame.

(c) **Returns from an earlier survey**. How useful previous surveys are depends on the questions asked in the original survey and if the data is up-to-date.

(d) **Lists of dwellings**. Council tax lists are useful as a frame for obtaining samples of dwellings.

(e) **Large scale maps**. Ordnance Survey maps have a grid system which enables areas to be broken down into suitably sized blocks. Sometimes a problem is the availability of up-to-date large scale maps, there having been much town and city re-development in recent years.

The two frames most generally available are council tax or valuation lists and electoral registers. These can be stratified along ACORN geodemographic lines to assist accurate stratified random sampling. An obvious sampling frame is the self-accumulated list: a list already in the hands of the marketing firm. It may include names and addresses of those who have made purchases, had deliveries made, used credit cards or registered at trade shows.

FOR DISCUSSION

What are the problems associated with using a telephone directory for a certain area as a sampling frame of the people who live in that area?

Activity 3 **(15 minutes)**

Locate any recent newspaper or magazine in which survey results are reported. Try to ascertain whether this survey was based on a census, a random sample or a non-random sample.

4.5 Sampling theory

Instead of looking at distributions occurring as a result of considering a whole 'population' of items, we can now construct probability distributions, known as **sampling distributions**, for samples rather than whole populations. And when we start taking fairly large random samples from a population and measuring the mean of those samples, we find an uncanny relationship with the normal distribution.

A sampling distribution of the mean has the following important properties.

(a) It is very close to being **normally distributed**. The larger the sample the more closely will the sampling distribution approximate to a normal distribution.

(b) The mean of the sampling distribution is the same as the population mean, μ.

(c) The sampling distribution has a standard deviation which is called the standard error (s) of the mean.

From our knowledge of the properties of a normal distribution, together with the rule that sample means are normally distributed around the true population mean, with a standard deviation equal to the standard error, we can predict the following.

(a) 68% of all sample means will be within 1 standard error of the population mean.

(b) 95% of all sample means will be within 1.96 standard errors of the population mean.

4.6 Deciding on a sample size

What this means is that if you take a reasonably large sample of representative items and find out something about them you can be confident up to a certain level that something that is true of the sample is true of the *whole* population of items.

Suppose, for example, you measured the height of 100 mature Labrador dogs and found that the average was, say, 30cm with a standard deviation of 2cm. You could then be 95% certain that the average height of all mature labradors in your market was in the range of $30 \pm (1.96 \times 2) = 26.08$cm to 33.92cm.

In practice you will probably be keen to leave the figurework to marketing research specialists or company statisticians. The important thing is that you understand enough of the jargon to appreciate the scientific basis of such an analysis rather than being blinded by it.

4.7 Practical points regarding sample sizes

Although it is possible to calculate an ideal sample size from a statistical point of view, administrative and practical factors have to be taken into account. These factors are summarised below.

(a) The amount of **money and time** available
(b) The **aims** of the survey

(c) The **degree of precision** required
(d) The number of **sub-samples** required

A sample therefore only need be **large enough to be reasonably representative** of the population.

The aim of sampling is to get accurate and usable data at a reasonable cost within a reasonable timescale. The two main sampling methods are random probability sampling and non-probability sampling.

4.8 Random sampling (quasi-random)

Definition

> A **simple random sample** is a sample selected in such a way that every item of the population has an equal and known chance of being selected.

Random samples are not perfect because they may be highly unrepresentative. It is important to appreciate that random selection does not guarantee that the sample will be free from bias – only that the method of selection is free from bias.

Random selection methods are, however, an essential part of the protection against selection error. 'Random' is not equivalent to 'haphazard'; random sampling is a careful, systematic procedure which generates data which is statistically valid and suitable for further statistical analysis.

There are various different approaches to taking a random sample. Some of these techniques are also often described as quasi-random because technically there are practical reasons why not every member of the population has an even and known chance of being selected.

4.9 Probability (random)

This method of selecting a sample is considered to be the only truly random approach. It is typical of the approach taken if you are using a random name generator for example within a database.

4.10 Systematic (quasi-random)

Systematic random sampling is one of the most frequently used sampling methods because it is easy to use. This method involves selecting the nth item within the sampling frame. In practice this means that a researcher may be wishing to randomly sample shoppers within a shopping centre. The directions they could have been given would be to approach every fifth person that passes by. The reason it is quasi-random is because if you were the second, person to approach the respondent you would not stand a chance of selection.

4.11 Stratified random sampling (quasi-random)

In theory, **stratification** uses knowledge of the population to increase the representativeness and precision of the sample. For example, a random sample of Europeans could result in the sample all being Germans. We would therefore select from each country in proportion to its population. Populations can be stratified in many ways such as by sex, age groups, regions and so on.

4.12 Multi-stage random sampling (quasi-random)

To reduce the distance a researcher would have to travel which would probably result from simple random sampling, **multi-stage sampling** can be used. The procedure is simple. The country is divided into areas, say counties, and three or four of these are selected at random. These large areas are divided and sub-divided until a sample of small areas is obtained and number of householders can be selected at random in each small area.

Area sampling is basically a form of random sampling in which maps are used in place of lists. This is common in the USA where cities are often laid out in regular patterns and roads dividing blocks make convenient area boundaries. An alternative is to place a grid over a map, number the squares and take a random sample of them.

4.13 Non-random sampling

A number of non-probability sampling methods exist. The main similarity between them is that the sample is not selected by chance but for the convenience, speed and ease.

Opinion on the validity of non-probability sampling is divided. Statisticians tend to criticise the method for its theoretical weakness, but market and opinion researchers defend it for its cheapness and administrative convenience.

Definition

Quota sampling is used to avoid the time and expense necessary to search for individuals chosen by a random sample. This method of sampling differs fundamentally from random methods in that once the general breakdown is decided (such as how many men and women, how many people in each age group and social class are to be included) the interviewers are left to select the persons to fit this framework.

The quotas given to the interviewers need to be arranged in such a way that for the whole country and maybe even for each region, the sexes, age groups, and social classes are represented in the correct proportions on the basis of available data. **Age** and **sex** present few problems but **social class** has always been one of the most dubious areas of marketing research investigation. 'Class' is a highly personal and subjective phenomenon, to the extent that some people are 'class conscious' or class aware and have a sense of belonging to a particular group. JICNAR's social grade definitions (A–E) has been the system most frequently used to classify people into social classes for marketing purposes.

FOR DISCUSSION

The major problem with the quota method of sampling is that interviewers are allowed discretion in choosing the individual respondents within the quota categories.

% of Population (2006)	JICNAR Social Grade	Social Status	Characteristics of occupation (of head of household)
4	A	Upper middle class	Higher managerial/professional eg lawyers, directors
22	B	Middle class	Intermediate managerial/administrative/ professional eg teachers, managers, computer operators, sales managers
29	C_1	Lower middle class	Supervisory, clerical, junior managerial/ administrative/professional eg foremen, shop assistants
21	C_2	Skilled working class	Skilled manual labour eg electricians, mechanics
16	D	Working class	Semi-skilled manual labour eg machine operators
			Unskilled manual labour eg cleaning, waiting tables, assembly
8	E	Lowest level of subsistence	State pensioners, widows (no other earner), casual workers

A researcher is conducting taste tests for a new low fat breakfast cereal and wishes to know the preferences amongst the potential target market. The target market is mostly female within the BC_1 social classification groups. The quota could be set as follows.

% of sample

Total	*Males 300*	*Females 700*
B	100	250
C1	200	450

4.14 Convenience sample (non-random)

This method selects respondents at the convenience of the researcher. So often they are the nearest of most contactable who are selected. An example could be where a student researching chocolate preferences amongst adults as part of a college project asks their friends to complete their survey. There are obvious limitations with this approach, but it is one which is used surprisingly frequently.

FOR DISCUSSION

What are the main problems associated with convenience samples?

4.15 Judgmental sample

The opinion and experience of the researcher is used to select appropriate respondents.

4.16 Snowball sample

Snowball sampling is used mostly within qualitative research where it is not necessary to use a large sample size. The method is used where respondents are especially difficult to find. The process works by finding one or a few respondents and using them to help identify other people. Imagine a retailer who is trying to conduct research amongst shop-lifters to try to identify the motivations behind their behaviour. It would be virtually impossible to find a list (that you could legally obtain) to use as a sampling frame. It might be possible however to identify one respondent and provided the research was conducted sensitively they may be willing to provide a route into a network of shop-lifters who would be willing to participate in the research.

FOR DISCUSSION

How each of the different sampling methods work is often difficult to visualise. If you are having problems seeing the differences between how the samples are selected then try working through the following activity.

You will need a tray and a bag of assorted sweets, coloured counters or different sorts of hard pasta. Throw the sweets onto the tray. Next, read through the descriptions of the sampling methods described in this chapter to direct you in sampling the sweets. A systematic sample for example would involve you counting the sweets from those nearest to you and picking out the eighth (or any other n^{th} you decide before hand) sweet you come across, then repeat until you have covered the whole tray extracting every eighth sweet. When you have finished, throw them back onto the tray and try to use another sampling method.

Often the act of using tangible items can help to clarify how the sampling method actually works.

4.17 Sample sizes and validity

The size of a sample is critical to whether or not the results of that sample can be taken to be valid for the population as a whole. It is common sense that a sample of, say, three people is not going to be representative of a total population of 100,000 people. To understand how a valid sample size can be decided on, researchers use **statistical techniques** involved in sampling theory, such as the normal distribution.

4.18 The normal distribution

In your earlier studies you will have seen frequency and probability distributions and the most common example, the **normal distribution**, which is often applied to continuous variables.

(a) A frequency distribution shows how many times each particular value occurs in a set of items.

(b) A probability distribution simply replaces actual numbers (frequencies) with proportions of the total.

For example the marks out of ten awarded to a sample of 50 students might be as follows.

Marks out of 10	*Number of students (frequency distribution)*	*Proportion or probability (probability distribution)*
0	0	0/50 = 0.00
1	0	0/50 = 0.00
2	1	1/50 = 0.02
3	2	2/50 = 0.04
4	4	4/50 = 0.08
5	10	10/50 = 0.20
6	15	15/50 = 0.30
7	10	10/50 = 0.20
8	6	6/50 = 0.12
9	2	2/50 = 0.04
10	0	0/50 = 0.00
	50	1.00

Examples of **continuous variables** include the following.

(a) The heights of people. The height of a person need not be an exact number of centimetres, but can be anything within a range of possible figures.

(b) The temperature of a room. It need not be an exact number or degrees, but can fall anywhere within a range of possible values.

The normal distribution can also apply to discrete variables which can take many possible values. For example, the volume of sales, in units, of a product might be any whole number in the range 100 – 5,000 units. There are so many possibilities within this range that the variable is, for all practical purposes, continuous.

Whether for continuous or discrete variables, the normal distribution can be drawn as a bell-shaped curve. Compare the curve below with the probability distribution column in paragraph 4.19 above.

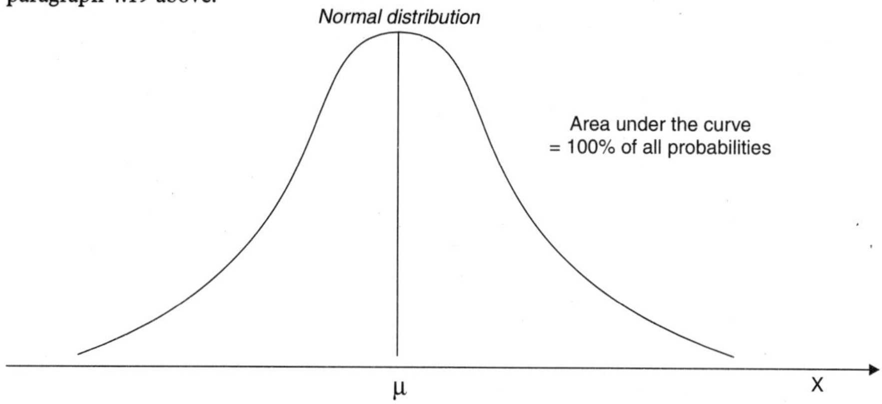

Figure 3.2: Normal distribution curve

The normal curve is symmetrical. The left-hand side of the area under the curve to the left of μ is the mirror image of the right-hand side.

- μ (the lower case Greek letter, mu) is the average of the distribution of the population as a whole
- $\bar{x}$ is the mean or average of the distribution of a sample

Because it is a probability distribution, the area under the curve totals exactly 100%.

4.19 The standard deviation

For any normal distribution, the dispersion around the mean of the frequency of occurrences can be measured exactly in terms of the **standard deviation**. This is the most important measure of spread in statistics, measuring the spread about the mean. It is denoted by σ or s.

(a) σ (the lower case Greek letter, sigma) is used for the standard deviation of a **population** of values (all cola-consuming households, say).

(b) The symbol s is used for the standard deviation of a **sample** of values (cola-consuming households in Swindon, say).

As the entire frequency curve represents all the possible outcomes and their frequencies of occurrence and the normal curve is symmetrical, 50% of occurrences must have a value greater than the mean value, and 50% of occurrences must have a value less than the mean value.

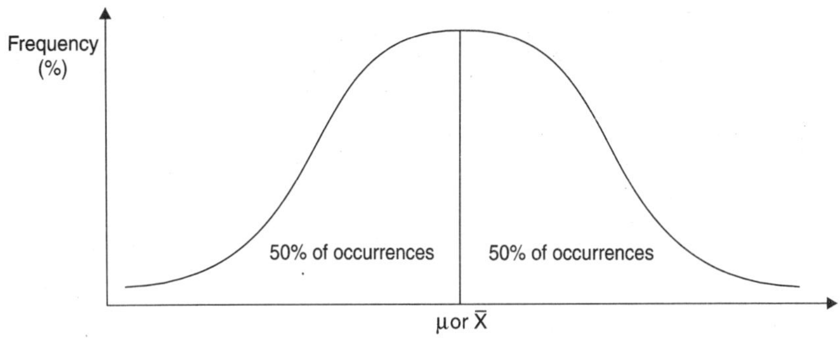

Figure 3.3: Frequency curve

It is known that 68% of frequencies have a value within one standard deviation either side of the mean.

Thus if a normal distribution has a mean of 80 and a standard deviation of 3, 68% of the total frequencies would occur within the range ± one standard deviation from the mean, that is, within the range 77 – 83.

Since the curve is symmetrical, 34% of the values must fall in the range 77 – 80 and 34% in the range 80 – 83.

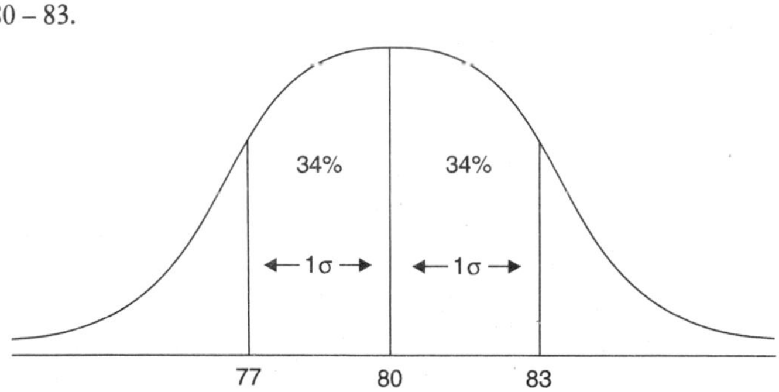

Figure 3.4: Standard deviation

It is known that 95% of the frequencies in a normal distribution occur in the range ± 1.96 standard deviations from the mean.

In our example, when $\mu = 80$, and $\sigma = 3$, 95% of the frequencies in the distribution would occur in the range

$$80 \pm 1.96 \times 3$$
$$= 80 \pm 5.88 \text{ (the range 74.12 to 85.88)}$$

Validity is concerned with whether the findings are really about what they appear to be about.

5 NON-RESPONSE

Non-response (of a sample member) cannot be avoided. It can, however, (apart from in mail surveys) be kept at a reasonable level. Experience has shown that the non-response part of a survey often differs considerably from the rest. The types of non-response are as follows.

(a) **Units outside the population.** Where the field investigation shows that units no longer exist (eg demolished houses), these units should be considered as outside the population and should be subtracted from the sample size before calculating the non-response rate.

(b) **Unsuitable for interview.** This is where people who should be interviewed are incapable of supplying responses perhaps through such factors as language barriers or physical infirmity.

(c) **Movers.** People who have changed address since the list was drawn up cannot be interviewed.

(d) **Refusals.** Some people refuse to co-operate.

(e) **Away from home.** People might be away from home for longer than the field work period and call-back might not be possible.

(f) **Out at time of call.**

There seems little doubt that social changes have influenced the level of non-response. Rising crime means that householders may be afraid to answer the door to strangers and, with women increasingly in full time employment, it is becoming more and more difficult to find the standard type of person who used to be the backbone of fieldwork.

Another problem is 'data fatigue', as the public becomes tired of filling in questionnaires and more cynical about the real motives of 'marketing researchers' because of 'sugging' (selling under the guise of research) and 'frugging' (fundraising under the guise of research).

5.1 How to deal with non-response

The interviewer can try to increase response rate.

(a) To minimise 'refusals', keep questionnaires as brief as possible, use financial or other tangible incentives such as free gifts, and use highly skilled interviewers.

(b) People 'away from home' may be contacted later, if this is possible or a minimum of three call backs used.

(c) People 'out at time of call' is a common problem. The researcher should plan calling time sensibly (for example, as most full time workers are out at work in the day-time so call in the evening).

(d) Make it easier to participate by doing simple things like including pens in self-completion surveys, on-site self-completions being collected in person etc.

The main things to remember and questions to address within your sampling plan therefore are:

- Who exactly do you need to talk to?
- How important is the level of accuracy to your research?
- Do you need a census or could you sample?
- Are their any sub-groups you need to break-out within your overall research?
- How easy will it be to reach your respondents?
- Do you have an already defined sampling frame?
- How much time and money do you have?

Exactly which sampling method you adopt will depend on your answers to these questions.

6 THE PRESENTATION OF RESEARCH FINDINGS

Once the research process has been completed, the researcher will usually present the findings in a face-to-face session, giving managers the opportunity to ask questions about the results. It takes time and skill to convert the findings into a well-structured oral presentation.

It is very likely that the research must be organised in report form as well. It is always a mistake simply to prepare the oral presentation from the already written report, since the conventions of report writing are quite different from the criteria that govern effective presentations.

The basic requirement is for a report and presentation that can be believed and trusted by everyone who will be affected by the research. The solution to a particular research problem should produce greater efficiency, lower costs and more benefits for the organisation. The presenter of the research results has to convince the audience that the research findings can be acted on for their own benefit. A written report needs to be put together so that interest and belief develop throughout its reading, and the recommended action appears as a natural outcome.

It may be beneficial to delete less important questions in order to emphasise the basic problem. Constant attention to the basic problem and its recommendations will make the study and its presentation more useable and interesting in the minds of the listeners and/or the readers of the final presentation. Presenters have the best chance of success if they have planned their research well and meet the expectations of their listeners.

Very often researchers will provide a copy of the raw data files if requested beforehand so that additional analysis could be conducted if required.

EXAMPLE

Many growers and retailers had been misled by surveys suggesting that 70 per cent of consumers would purchase organic vegetables and fruit. In the event a much smaller percentage are doing so, the remainder have demonstrated by their actions that *behaviour* and *attitudes* are not necessarily synonymous. Perhaps they had not seriously considered the possibility that organic produce would cost more or that it would look less attractive; quite possibly they gave 'ethically correct' responses when completing a questionnaire, but had no real intention of acting differently. The economic downturn experienced in 2008/2009 has also led to a decline in organic food sales:

Less UK consumers are buying organic products amid the recession hitting the country's economy, food and grocery analysts IGD has claimed. The percentage of UK shoppers buying organic food has fallen from 24% to 19%.

IGD surveyed over 1,000 UK shoppers in December and claimed that the country's consumers are still supporting ethical products despite the downturn. According to the survey, 25% of consumers bought Fairtrade products in the previous month, up from 9% in 2006.

The proportion of shoppers buying food made according to higher animal welfare standards has risen from 14% in 2008 to 18%, IGD said. IGD chief executive Joanne Denney-Finch said consumers had become more "price sensitive" but were still looking to buy ethical products.

Denney-Finch added: "Only organic seems to have suffered a small decline. We believe this is partly due to a swing towards other ethical options, and it is mainly among more casual organic shoppers. A strong core of dedicated organic shoppers remains."

http://www.just-food.com/article.aspx?id=105267

7 PRODUCT RESEARCH

Definition

Product research is concerned with the product itself, whether new, improved or already on the market, and customer reactions to it.

This aspect of marketing research attempts to make product **research and development** customer-oriented.

New product ideas may come from anywhere – from research and development personnel, marketing and sales personnel, competitors, customers, outside scientific or technological discoveries, individual employees or executives and so on. Research and development is carried out by company scientists, engineers or designers; much wasted effort can be saved for them, however, if new ideas are first tested in the market, in other words if product research is carried out.

7.1 The process of product research

New ideas are first screened by a range of specialists (marketing researchers, designers, research and development staff and so on) and are rejected if they have any of the following characteristics.

(a) They have a low profit potential or insufficient market potential.
(b) They have a high cost and involve high risk.
(c) They do not conform to company objectives.
(d) They cannot be produced and distributed with the available resources.

Ideas which survive the screening process should be product tested and possibly test marketed. Product research also includes the need to keep the product range of a company's goods under review for the following reasons.

(a) **Variety reduction** may be desirable to reduce production costs, or when there are insufficient sales of certain items in the product range to justify continued production. In practice, there is often strong resistance, both from within a company and from customers, to the elimination of products from the market.

(b) **Product diversification** increases a product range by introducing new items, and a wide range of products can often improve a company's market image.

(c) **Segmentation** is a policy which aims at securing a new class of customers for an existing range of products, perhaps by making some adjustments to the products to appeal to the new segments.

Product research also involves finding **new uses for existing products**, and this could be considered a means of extending a product range. The uses for plastics and nylon, for example, have been extended rapidly in the past as a result of effective research.

7.2 The product life cycle

The profitability and sales of a product can be expected to change over time. The **product life cycle** (PLC) is an attempt to recognise distinct stages in a product's sales history.

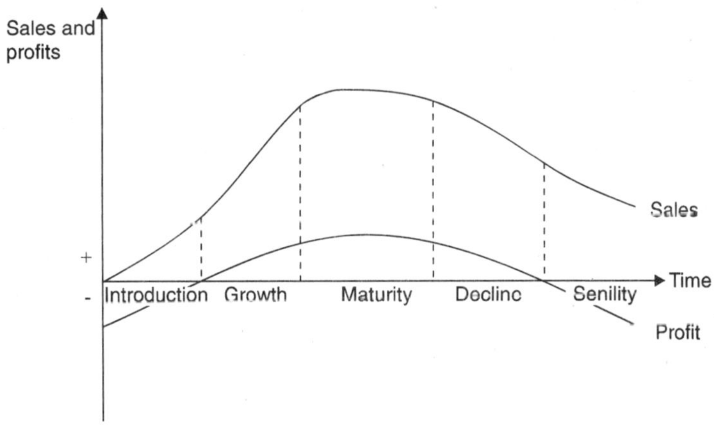

Figure 3.5: Product life cycles

Information about the stage a product has reached in its life cycle may be an important indication of how long its market will continue and how soon new product developments must be introduced to replace it.

(a) There ought to be a **regular review** of existing products, as a part of marketing management responsibilities.

(b) Information should be obtained about the likely future of each product and sources of such information might be as follows.

(i) An analysis of past sales and profit trends
(ii) The history of other products
(iii) Marketing research
(iv) If possible, an analysis of competitors

The future of each product should be estimated in terms of both sales revenue and profits.

Once the assessments have been made, decisions must be taken about what to do with each product.

Activity 4 **(20 minutes)**

Locate a marketing/design publication that describes how any new product was developed. Summarise and evaluate the product research conducted prior to the launch of this product.

8 PRICE RESEARCH

Price sensitivity will vary amongst purchasers. Those who can pass on the cost of purchases will be least sensitive and will respond more to other elements of the marketing mix.

(a) Provided that it fits the corporate budget, the business traveller will be more concerned about the level of service and quality of food when looking for an hotel than price. In contrast, a family on holiday are likely to be very price sensitive when choosing an overnight stay.

(b) In industrial marketing the purchasing manager is likely to be more price sensitive than the engineer who might be the actual user of new equipment that is being sourced. The engineer and purchasing manager are using different criteria in making the choice. The engineer places product characteristics as first priority, the purchasing manager is more price oriented.

8.1 Finding out about price sensitivity

Research on price sensitivity of customers has demonstrated the following.

(a) Customers have a concept of a '**just price**' – a feel for what is about the right price to pay for a commodity.

(b) Unless a regular purchase is involved, customers search for price information before buying, becoming price aware when wanting to buy but forgetting soon afterwards.

(c) Customers will buy at what they consider to be a bargain price without full regard for need and actual price.

EXAMPLE

Bell Telephones in the US were concerned about the lack of sales of extension telephones. When, as part of a marketing research survey, customers were asked to name the actual price of an extension telephone, most overestimated it. By keeping the existing price but running an advertising campaign featuring it, Bell were able to increase sales as customers became aware of the lower than anticipated price.

8.2 Factors affecting pricing decisions

(a) **Intermediaries' objectives**

If an organisation distributes products or services to the market through independent intermediaries, the objectives of these intermediaries have an effect on the pricing decision. Thus conflict over price can arise between suppliers and intermediaries which may be difficult to resolve.

(b) **Competitors' actions and reactions**

An organisation, in setting prices, sends out signals to **rivals**. These rivals are likely to react in some way. In some industries (such as petrol retailing) pricing moves in unison; in others (such as the supermarket sector), price changes by one supplier may initiate a price war, with each supplier undercutting the others.

(c) **Suppliers**

If an organisation's **suppliers** notice that the prices for an organisation's products are rising, they may seek a rise in the price for their supplies to the organisation.

(d) **Inflation**

In periods of inflation the organisation's prices may need to change in order to reflect increases in the prices of supplies, labour, rent and so on. Such changes may be needed to keep relative (real) prices unchanged (this is the process of prices being adjusted for the rate of inflation).

(e) **Quality connotations**

In the absence of other information, customers tend to judge quality by price. Thus a price change may send signals to customers concerning the quality of the product. A rise may be taken to indicate improvements, a reduction may signal reduced quality.

(f) **New product pricing**

Most pricing decisions for existing products relate to price changes. Such changes have a reference point from which to move (the existing price). But when a new product is introduced for the first time there may be no such reference points; pricing decisions are most difficult to make in such circumstances. It may be possible to seek alternative reference points, such as the price in another market where the new product has already been launched, or the price set by a competitor.

(g) **Income effects**

In times of rising incomes, price may become a less important marketing variable than, for instance, product quality or convenience of access. When income levels are falling and/or unemployment levels rising, price will become a much more important marketing variable.

EXAMPLE

In the recessions of the early 1990s and 2008/2009, the major grocery multiples such as Tesco, Sainsbury, and Waitrose, who steadily moved up-market in the 1980s with great success leaving the 'pile it high, sell it cheap' philosophy behind, suddenly found bargain stores such as Aldi, Kwik Save and Netto a more serious threat. They responded by cutting prices on 'staples' (such as baked beans) to draw consumers into their stores.

---

9 DISTRIBUTION RESEARCH

Place as an element in the marketing mix is largely concerned with the selection of distribution channels and with the physical distribution of goods.

In selecting an **appropriate marketing channel** for a product, a firm has the following options.

(a) **Selling direct to the customer.** Consumer goods can be sold directly through mail order catalogues, telephone selling, door-to-door selling or 'off the page' (magazine advertisements). Industrial goods are commonly sold directly by sales representatives, visiting industrial buyers.

(b) **Selling through agents or recognised distributors,** who specialise in the firm's products. For example, a chain of garden centres might act as specialist stockists and distributors for the products of just one garden shed manufacturer.

(c) **Selling through wholesalers** or to retailers who stock and sell the goods and brands of several rival manufacturers.

Some organisations might use unprofitable channels of distribution for their goods which should either be abandoned in favour of more profitable channels, or made profitable by cutting costs or increasing minimum order sizes.

As well as **cost and profitability analyses,** distribution research can embrace the following.

(a) To what extent is the distribution channel **actually working**? In other words, how effective is the distributor at delivering products to customers?

(b) To what extent is the distributor favouring its own brand or competitors' products over your own, in terms of shelf space and positioning and in-store promotions.

This latter point is important as own-brand products are highly competitive with branded goods. Supermarket chains promote their own brand extensively.

Normal **marketing research techniques** can be used to assess the effectiveness of distribution channels. Marketing research questionnaires can ask how easy it is for customers to obtain products and information, and where they are obtained. An example might be a newspaper readership questionnaire, which will ask where the customer acquires the newspaper (eg delivered at home, or bought on way to work).

Chapter roundup

- Marketing research can be defined as the objective gathering, recording and analysing of all facts about problems relating to the transfer and sales of goods and services from producer to consumer or user.
- Marketing research plays an important role in helping to solve problems and improve decision-making by producing information that helps to allay uncertainty.
- Like all project work, marketing research can be quite complex and requires considerable planning, scheduling and control.
- Primary data is data collected by or specifically for the user.
- It has been consistently demonstrated that a relatively small but carefully selected sample can quite accurately reflect the characteristics of the population from which it is drawn.
- Factors such as time, money, objectives and degree of precision required all affect sample sizes.
- A good knowledge and understanding of the audience are essential for good reporting. The presenter of a report should know in advance who will receive copies of the written report or who will attend an oral presentation.
- Product, price and distribution research are all aspects of marketing research.

Quick quiz

1. What are the first four stages of the marketing research process?
2. What two issues does a research brief usually cover?
3. What is an omnibus survey?
4. What is meant by the term field research?
5. Define sampling.
6. Suggest two reasons as to why a sampling error can arise.
7. What is a sampling frame?
8. What is a simple random sample?
9. Name three types of non-response.
10. What new product characteristics might cause it to be rejected at the screening stage?
11. What are the five stages in the product life cycle?
12. Name three factors that affect pricing decisions.
13. What are the three key distribution options?

Answers to quick quiz

1. Set objectives, define the research problem, assess the value of the research and construct the research proposal.
2. Background and the problem.
3. Omnibus research occurs where regular surveys of defined populations are undertaken.
4. Research in the field is concerned with the generation and collection of original research data.
5. Sampling involves taking a limited number of a large population so that by studying the part something may be learnt about the whole.
6. Poorly defined research objectives can lead to the wrong information being obtained and an unrepresentative random sample may be selected.
7. A sampling frame is the list, index, map or any other population record from which the sample can be selected.
8. A simple random sample is a sample selected in such a way that every item of the population has an equal and known chance of being selected.
9. Those who are unsuitable for interview, those who have changed addresses and those who refuse to co-operate.
10. Low profit potential, insufficient market potential, high cost and so high risk, do not conform to company objectives, cannot be produced and distributed with the available resources.
11. Introduction, growth, maturity, decline, senility.
12. Intermediaries' objectives, competitors' actions and reactions, and suppliers.
13. Direct selling to the customer, eg direct mail; selling through agents or distributors; selling through wholesalers or retailers.

Answers to activities

1. Research objectives need to be SMART.

Research objectives	Discover re Activity:
Specific	Size of market for *cruelty-free* cosmetics not cosmetics in general
Measurable	Respective market share in percentage terms of leading players
Actionable	Price range within which consumers will buy
Reasonable	A defined number of preferred colours
Timescaled	Information within three months so product can be marketed for Christmas

2. It saves time
It can focus on key items
It is cheaper
It can be regarded as mathematically accurate if done properly

3 The result of, or answer to, this activity will depend on the survey you have chosen.

4 The result of, or answer to, this activity will depend on the item you have chosen.

Chapter 4 :
MARKETING RESEARCH TECHNIQUES

Introduction

This chapter concentrates on the tools that can be used to capture marketing research information. Each tool has its own advantages and disadvantages and as such there is no perfect research tool, but the same tool may be used in widely different settings and for different purposes.

Research tools fit broadly into qualitative and quantitative classifications. Qualitative methods generate information which is highly detailed and contextually rich. This type of exploratory research is perfect when you need a depth of understanding or have a complex problem to investigate. Importantly qualitative research should not be analysed statistically due to its depth in nature which means that very small sample sizes are used. Quantitative methods on the other hand should be subjected to statistical analysis and use large sample sizes in order to quantify an understanding. The main objective of using quantitative methods is to be able to measure the research findings against the extent to which they are consistent with views or behaviour of the whole population of interest. Qualitative methods are considered first before the chapter moves to quantitative methods.

The first qualitative tool to be evaluated is interviewing, and this includes fully structured, semi-structured, unstructured and finally depth interviews. This is followed by group discussions and focus groups where the emphasis is on group dynamics and the skill of the moderator. Project techniques are then discussed with a range of tools such as word-association, sentence and story completion, cartoon tests and third person techniques being illustrated.

In covering quantitative methods the challenges of effective attitude measurement and the measurement scales that can assist in this task are evaluated.

Questionnaire design, along with postal and interview surveys are next. A discussion of the application of technology in managing data capture is noted in the section on scanning with reference to panel methodology. The advantages and disadvantages of panel research are then illustrated and observation techniques are discussed.

The chapter concludes with a section on data value and validity.

Your objectives

In this chapter you will learn about the following.

(a) The role of interviews and group discussions

(b) The importance of attitude measurement techniques such as self-reporting scales and projective techniques

(c) The principles of effective questionnaire design

(d) An overview of postal research questionnaires and interview surveys

(e) The scope of panel methodology, telephone research and observation

(f) The challenges of establishing data value and validity

(g) The use of research data

1 INTRODUCTION

Having looked at some of the underlying methodological issues concerned with the design and execution of a marketing research project, we are now going to explore the range of data capture techniques or research tools which may be used.

Often the same instrument may be used in widely different settings and for different purposes.

Research projects are also conducted in phases or 'waves' with both qualitative and quantitative methods being employed at different stages.

Questionnaires, for instance, are used not only in survey research, but also in some forms of qualitative research, continuous research and in a wide range of experimental scenarios. A quantitative survey on the other hand may also include an open-ended qualitative question.

As we shall see, the relationship between researcher and respondent may be direct (as in face-to-face interviews or telephone contacts) or indirect and even remote (as in postal questionnaires or in-home scanning).

Each method of data capture has its own characteristics and advantages or disadvantages. By the time you have read and absorbed this chapter you should be in a much better position to make informed judgements about matching data-gathering techniques to research objectives.

One of the most important things to remember when selecting and designing your data collection methods is that the original research objectives need to be met. This may sound obvious but when questionnaires or focus group guides are written often questions or topics raised do not seem to relate back to the overall research purpose. One way to avoid this is to use a table as used in the following example, in order to avoid redundancy in your data collection. The key things to remember are:

- Each research objective is likely to lead to a number of individual questions the research should address, these are known as research questions
- Individual research questions may (but not necessarily) need investigating in a number of different research phases
- Research questions are not those that you ask respondents. Fieldwork questions should address the individual research questions in full or part but in a more user friendly or appropriate format. You may need to ask more that one fieldwork question in order to fully address the research question.

Simplified example research project purpose for a dog food manufacturer investigating dog owners perceptions towards 'fresh' dog food.

Research objective:
To identify whether 'fresh' dog food is perceived as a premium offering

Research questions	Data collection method	Fieldwork question
Do consumers think fresh food is better quality than dried or tinned dog food?	Online survey	Please order the following types of dog food with the type you think is the highest quality at the top and the one you believe to be the lowest quality at the bottom (You should click and drag the items to put them in their correct positions) Dry Tinned Fresh Home made Frozen
Would consumers pay more for fresh dog food?	Online survey	Please state from the drop down list how much you would be prepared to pay per week for the following types of dog food Dry Tinned Fresh Home made Frozen
Is fresh dog food perceived as a healthier choice for dogs?	Focus group	Discussion topic – healthy dog food options

2 QUALITATIVE DATA COLLECTION METHODS

Qualitative research methods include: in-depth interviews; focus groups; group interviews and projective techniques.

2.1 Interviews

The main advantage personal contact methods have over other methods is that they normally achieve a **high response rate** and that the likely level of error being introduced into the research results is low.

Definition

> An **interview** has been defined as a conversation directed to a definite purpose other than satisfaction in the conversation itself.

This type of research is most useful in providing the researcher with **quantitative data** such as 'so many people said this, or think that or do this'. Fully structured questions should be easy to ask and easy for respondents to answer. The major limitation of fully structured questionnaires is in their **structure**. For example, if the researcher wanted to know which factors appeared to be most important in making choices about holiday destinations, a fully structured questionnaire may provide the respondent with five choices which the researcher feels are important. However, if the respondent identified other factors felt to be important, they would be overlooked.

2.2 Depth interviews

Motivational research often uses the method of **depth interviews**. Motives and explanations of behaviour often lie well below the surface. It is a time-consuming and expensive method of data collection. Taped interviews and analysis of transcripts is often the way in which the depth interview and subsequent data analysis are conducted.

The strengths of depth interviews include the following.

(a) **Longitudinal information** (such as information on decision-making processes) can be gathered from one respondent at a time, thereby aiding clarity of interpretation and analysis.

(b) **Personal** material can be more easily accessed and discussed.

There are, however, disadvantages to depth interviews.

(a) They are **time-consuming** to conduct and to analyse. If each interview lasts between one and two hours, a maximum of three or four per day is often all that is possible.

(b) They are more **costly** than group discussions.

2.3 Unstructured interviews

Interviewers may have a checklist of topics to cover in questioning, but they are free to word such questions as they wish. Unstructured interviews are a very useful way of capturing data which is **qualitative** in nature. Over the course of a number of interviews, questions are likely to become increasingly focused as the researcher becomes more knowledgeable about the topic under investigation.

2.4 Semi-structured interviews

Semi-structured interviews consist of both **closed questions** and **'open ended' questions** which offer respondents a free choice. For example, 'Which factors do you consider most important when making a choice of holiday destination?' provides the respondent with an open question to which they may respond freely.

The interviewer may decide to use **probing questions** such as: 'What other factors are there?' Probing questions may trigger further responses and the interviewer may be more confident about the data provided.

3 GROUP DISCUSSIONS/FOCUS GROUPS

Definition

> A **focus group** is a small group of people, considered to be representative of the target segment, invited to openly discuss products or issues at their leisure in a relaxed environment. *Brassington and Pettitt* (2003)

Group discussions are useful in providing the researcher with qualitative data. Qualitative data can often provide greater insight than quantitative data.

Group discussions usually consist of eight to ten respondents and an interviewer taking the role of **group moderator**. The group moderator introduces topics for discussion and intervenes as necessary to encourage respondents or to direct discussions if they threaten to wander too far off the point. The main emphasis, however, is that the moderator simply guides rather than taking full control of the group by asking lots of structured questions. General topic ideas are suggested rather than detailed questions.

Group discussions may be recorded for later analysis and interpretation. Group discussion is very dependent on the skill of the group moderator. It is inexpensive to conduct, it can be done quickly and it can provide useful, timely, qualitative data. It is often used at the early stage of research to get a feel for the subject matter under discussion and to create possibilities for more structured research.

According to Kent (1993) the key advantages of group discussions include the following.

(a) The **group environment** with 'everybody in the same boat' can be less intimidating than other techniques of research which rely on one-to-one contact (such as depth interviews).

(b) What respondents say in a group often **sparks off** experiences or ideas on the part of others.

(c) **Differences** between consumers are highlighted, making it possible to understand a range of attitudes in a short space of time.

(d) It is **easier to observe** groups and there is more to observe.

(e) **Social and cultural** influences are highlighted.

(f) Groups are **cheaper and faster** than depth interviews.

The principal disadvantages of groups are as follows.

(a) Group processes may **inhibit** some people from making a full contribution and may encourage others to become exhibitionistic.

(b) Group processes may **stall** to the point where they cannot be retrieved by the moderator.

(c) Some groups may take on a **life of their own**, so that what is said has validity only in the short-lived context of the group.

Quite often groups are conducted in specially designed research premises which are designed to be comfortable to put respondents at ease. A common feature of these facilities is a viewing window so additional researchers can observe without distracting the group.

FOR DISCUSSION

Conduct a focus group in your class on entertainment facilities in your area. What are the key problems with conducting such a focus group?

---

4 PROJECTIVE TECHNIQUES

The objective of any projective test is to delve below the surface responses in order to obtain true feelings, meanings or motivations. The rationale behind projective tests comes from the knowledge that people are often reluctant to, or cannot, reveal their deepest feelings. In other instances they are unaware of those feelings because of psychological defence mechanisms.

The most commonly applied projective tests used in marketing research are word-association tests, sentence and story completion, cartoon tests and third person techniques.

4.1 Word-association

A respondent is given a series of single words and then asked to match each with one of their own. The goal is to elicit quick, unrestrained answers: it can be used to select brand names, advertising campaign themes and slogans. For example, a cosmetic manufacturer might ask consumers to respond to the following potential names for a new perfume: infinity, encounter, flame, precious.

4.2 Sentence and story completion

Sentence completion follows the same kind of pattern, eg

The people who shop at Asda are ....

Asda should really ....

Story completion is a longer version of sentence completion in which participants are presented with incomplete scenarios and are asked to complete the story. For example,

Mrs X has just moved into the area. Her new neighbour Mrs Y goes to her home to welcome her. Mrs X does not know the area and asks Mrs Y for some advice on where to do her shopping. The nearest supermarket is Asda but she has heard some things about it. What is Mrs Y's reply?

4.3 Cartoon tests

These create a highly projective mechanism by means of cartoon figures or strips, similar to those in comic books. They can be used to measure the strength of an attitude towards a particular product or brand.

The cartoon must be sufficiently interesting to encourage discussion but ambiguous enough not to disclose the nature of the research project. Clues should not be given to the character's positive or negative predisposition.

4.4 Third person techniques

Rather than asking a respondent directly what they think, it is phrased as 'your friend' or 'some people' or some other third party. Rather than ask a parent why they do not provide a nutritionally balanced breakfast, a researcher would ask, 'Why don't some parents provide their children with nutritionally balanced breakfasts?' The third-person technique is often used to avoid issues that might be embarrassing or evoke hostility if answered directly by a respondent.

4.5 Role play

Role play provides an opportunity to project one's own feelings in the safety of an assumed identity and is therefore less threatening and more likely to elicit a truthful response.

FOR DISCUSSION

Why do you think projective techniques are so called?

4.6 Quantitative data collection methodology

Quantitative research methods include: surveys and questionnaires; research panels; observation and experiments.

5 QUESTIONNAIRE DESIGN

The first step in any type of survey is the outlining of the information to be obtained. The researcher has then to develop a set of questions which can be answered correctly by the respondents.

(a) All the factors which seem to have some bearing on the problem must be set out.

(b) These factors must be discussed with people likely to have some special knowledge of the problem.

Once the list of factors is verified, questions can be drawn up and the questionnaire designed. Each question should be tested against the following criteria.

(a) What is the interviewer trying to find out by asking this question?

(b) Will all the target respondents understand the question?

(c) Will all the target respondents known how to answer?

(d) Have clear unequivocal instructions been given on the format of the answer?

(e) Having got answers to the question, can they be analysed meaningfully?

The initial draft of the questionnaire should be discussed with colleagues prior to being tested in a pilot survey.

The table **on the following page** gives examples of the types of question that can be asked.

In practice both survey design and questionnaire design are fraught with difficulties and marketing managers are well advised to seek the help of experts – preferably experienced members of the Marketing research Society.

6 ATTITUDE MEASUREMENT AND SELF-REPORTING SCALES

6.1 Definition

> An **attitude** is a learned predisposition to act in a particular way. A knowledge of attitudes may therefore enable **predictions** about likely behaviour patterns. A significant proportion of marketing research is aimed at finding out about consumer attitudes.

The measurement of behavioural factors such as attitudes and motivation has been attempted by researchers using a variety of techniques. None is fully satisfactory, the ones that are the most reliable and valid from a technical perspective are generally the most difficult and expensive.

There are several types of scaling techniques that can be used to measure attitudes. The following section illustrates a few of these.

6.2 Self-reporting scales

A scale is a set of symbols or numbers so constructed that the symbols or numbers can be assigned by a rule to the individuals (or their behaviours or attitudes) to whom the scale is applied.

A variety of measurement scales exist. However, the three key ones are the semantic differential, the staple and the Likert.

Name	*Description*	*Example*
		CLOSED-END QUESTIONS
Dichotomous	A question with two possible answers.	'In arranging this trip, did you personally phone British Airways?' Yes ☐ No ☐
Multiple choice	A question with three or more answers.	'With whom are you travelling on this flight?' No one ☐ Children only ☐ Spouse ☐ Business associates/ friends/relatives ☐ Spouse and children ☐ An organised tour group ☐
Likert scale	A statement with which the respondent shows the amount of agreement/	'Small airlines generally give better service' Strongly disagree 1 ☐ Disagree 2 ☐ Neither agree nor disagree 3 ☐ Agree 4 ☐ Strongly agree 5 ☐
Semantic differential	A scale connecting two bipolar words, where the respondent selects the point	*British Airways* Large — — — — — — — Small Experienced — — — — — — — Inexperienced
Importance scale	A scale that rates the importance of some attribute.	Good quality in flight catering is: Extremely important 1 ☐ Very important 2 ☐ Somewhat important 3 ☐ Not very important 4 ☐ Not at all important 5 ☐
Rating scale	A scale that rates some attribute from 'poor' to 'excellent'.	The check-in process was: Excellent Very good Good Fair Poor
Intention-to-buy scale	A scale that describes the respondent's intention to buy or use.	'If an inflight telephone was available on a long flight, I would' Definitely use 1 ☐ Probably use 2 ☐ Not sure 3 ☐ Probably not use 4 ☐ Definitely not use 5 ☐
		OPEN-END QUESTIONS
Completely unstructured	A question that respondents can answer in an almost unlimited number of ways.	'What is your opinion of British Airways?'
Word association	Words are presented, one at a time, and respondents mention the first word that	'What is the first word that comes to mind when you hear the following' Airline ________ British ________ Travel ________
Sentence completion	An incomplete sentence is presented and respondents complete the	'When I choose an airline, the most important consideration in my decision is ________.'
Story completion	An incomplete story is presented, and respondents are asked to complete it.	'I flew B.A. a few days ago. I noticed that the exterior and interior of the plane had bright colours. This aroused in me the following thoughts and feelings.' Now complete the story.
Picture completion	A picture of two characters is presented, with one making a statement. Respondents are asked to identify with the other and fill in the empty balloon.	
Thematic Apperception Test (TAT)	A picture is presented and respondents are asked to make up a story about what they think is happening or may happen in the picture.	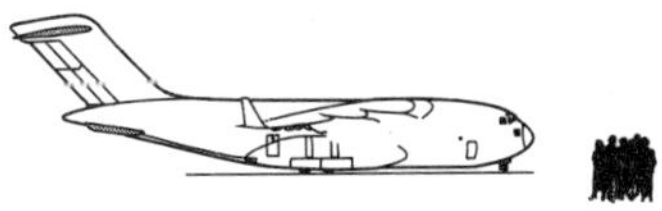

Figure 4.1: Marketing research questionnaire

6.3 Semantic differential scale

The scaling technique was developed by Osgood, Suci and Tannerbaum in 1957. The scale consists of a number of bipolar adjectival phrases and statements that could be used to describe the objectives being evaluated. Each bipolar adjective rating scale consists of seven categories, with neither numerical labels nor category descriptions other than for the anchor categories.

To remove any position bias, favourable and unfavourable objectives are randomly distributed to the left and right anchor positions. The respondent is asked to mark one of the seven categories that best describes their views about the object along the continuum implied by the bipolar object pair. An overall attitude score is calculated by summing the responses on each adjective pair. Before calculating the overall score, the response categories must be coded. Usually the categories are assigned values from 1 to 7, where 1 is assigned to the unfavourable adjectival phrase and 7 is assigned to the favourable adjectival phrase.

EXAMPLE

We would like to know what you think about our coffee shop. Below are a number of statements that could be used to describe what we offer. For each pair of adjectival phrases we would like you to mark the category that best describes your feelings about us.

Traditional	_:_:_:_:_:_:_	Contemporary
Expensive	_:_:_:_:_:_:_	Cheap
Friendly service	_:_:_:_:_:_:_	Unfriendly service
Convenient opening hours	_:_:_:_:_:_:_	Inconvenient opening hours
Slow service	_:_:_:_:_:_:_	Fast service
Attractive atmosphere	_:_:_:_:_:_:_	Unattractive atmosphere
Wide range of food and drink	_:_:_:_:_:_:_	Limited range of food + drink

6.4 Staple scale

A staple scale differs from the semantic differential in that:

(a) Adjectives or descriptive phrases are tested separately instead of simultaneously as bipolar pairs

(b) Points on the scale are identified by number

(c) There are ten scale positions rather than seven

EXAMPLE

You should select a **plus** number for words what you think describe (Bank A) accurately. The more accurately you think the word describes it, the larger the **plus** number you would choose. You would select a **minus** number for words you think do not describe it accurately. The less accurately you think a word describes it, the larger the **minus** number you would choose. Therefore, you can select any number from +5, for words that you think are very accurate, all the way to –5, for words that you think are very inaccurate.

	–5	–4	–3	–2	–1	+1	+2	+3	+4	+5
Service is courteous	☐	☐	☐	☐	☐	☐	☐	☐	☐	☐
Location is convenient	☐	☐	☐	☐	☐	☐	☐	☐	☐	☐
Hours are convenient	☐	☐	☐	☐	☐	☐	☐	☐	☐	☐
Loan interest rates are high	☐	☐	☐	☐	☐	☐	☐	☐	☐	☐

6.5 Likert attitude scales

In the Likert method a series of statements is provided and respondents are required to rate each statement on the basis of the strength of their personal feelings toward it. The numbers assigned to the responses are numerical values associated with each possible answer. When analysing the results, the signs of these numbers are reversed when a statement is unfavourable.

EXAMPLE

'Gillette is the best a man can get'

Strongly agree	Disagree	Don't know	Agree	Strongly agree
–2 ☐	–1 ☐	0 ☐	+1 ☐	+2 ☐

6.6 Guidelines for using self-reporting techniques

When administering these techniques, respondents are provided with a number of alternative choices – words, statements, numbers – and required to select the one that most closely describes their attitude toward the subject. When applying these techniques, the researcher must decide how many choices to include as well as their wording.

There is disagreement on the ideal number of choices that should be offered to respondents – four to eight choices appears to be preferred, with five the number used most often. There is also a lack of consensus on whether there should be an even or odd number of choices. An even number of choices compels the respondent to declare a position, whereas an odd number usually provides a middle position for those in situations where the respondent cannot identify their feelings. The drawback to offering a neutral position is that this choice attracts many respondents who do not have strong feelings on the issue, and hence it does not allow the researcher to distinguish between answers.

6.7 Common problems with questionnaire designs.

There are a number of problems with questionnaires in terms of their design, common pitfalls include:

- Asking two questions in one, eg Do you like and would you buy the new chocolate flavour milkshake?
- Asking leading questions, eg Do you think it is right to deprive your child of the chance to eat a healthier option?
- Using technical or inappropriate jargon
- Making the questionnaire too lengthy
- Using lots of confusing skips or jumps to different sections (especially in a self-completion survey)

Insufficient or inappropriate response options eg not including an 'other', 'don't know', 'neither' or 'not applicable' option. Some researcher use a technique known as 'forced compliance' whereby they will only offer a set number of options such as 'yes' and 'no' rather than the ability to choose 'don't know' in order to prevent respondents from 'sitting on the fence' and not committing themselves. This should only be used in carefully considered circumstances however otherwise the validity of the finding can be disputed.

7 POSTAL RESEARCH QUESTIONNAIRES

7.1 Definition

> The **questionnaire** is the primary tool of marketing research, a device for delivering questions to respondents and recording their answers.

Questionnaires are sent to respondents for self-completion. The major limitation of postal research is the low response rate. Anything higher than 10% is considered reasonably good.

Pre-coding the questionnaire makes analysis of the data more straightforward. Tick box questionnaires are easy for respondents and stand more chance of providing the researcher with a higher response.

> **Activity 1** **(10 minutes)**
>
> What do you see as the advantages and disadvantages of postal questionnaires as a way of collecting research data when compared with personal interviews?

7.2 Advantages and limitations of postal surveys

Advantages:

- low cost per response
- no interviewer bias
- questionnaire length

Limitations:

- questionnaire scope
- respondent interaction
- sampling problems
- response rate problems
- lack of control over respondents
- wrong respondents and so wrong information

FOR DISCUSSION

What do you consider to be the most appropriate applications for postal surveys?

---

8 ONLINE AND EMAIL SURVEYS

Increasingly popular, online and email surveys have a number of advantages to researchers due to the speed in which results can be obtained.

EXAMPLE

When conducting research amongst children in order to ascertain their preferences in a new range of toothbrushes, the research agency acting on behalf of Colgate were able to produce preliminary results within 24 hours. The swift nature of this feedback meant that product designers were able to implement changes to the design and work with the same group of children in order to track their responses to each modified version.

8.1 Advantages and limitation of online and email surveys

Advantages

- Low cost
- No interviewer bias
- Speed of delivery and data collection
- Ability to include complex skip patterns moving respondent to a relevant section of the survey based on their previous responses seamlessly
- Ability to integrate high quality visual materials
- Higher response rate due to the ability for respondents to participate at their convenience.
- Minimises need for manual data entry and checking
- Ability to interact with respondents virtually
- Ability to use online technology

Limitations

- Difficult to reach groups who do not have Internet access
- Larger size surveys are likely to be rejected

EXAMPLE

At Crufts 2007, The Kennel Club made use of a computerised virtual survey to conduct research at their annual dog show. Visitors were able to access the survey from an unmanned research stand at the show in order to comment on the facilities on offer.

Activity 2 **(20 minutes)**

Vovici are a provider of online survey creation software. Browse through their website http://www.vovici.com and look at the range of example surveys and case studies.

9 INTERVIEW SURVEYS

Most survey work in the UK is conducted through **face-to-face interviews**, usually by employees of a marketing research company.

9.1 Fully structured interviews/face-to-face surveys

A fully structured interview is controlled through the use of a **structured questionnaire**. The responses to a fully structured interview have been pre-determined by the research design. All respondents are given exactly the same questions and are able to exercise exactly the same responses.

9.2 Advantages of interview surveys

Their prevalence as a data collection method and the quality of the data collected are probably due to their obvious advantages.

(a) The interviewer can check the respondent is suitable before beginning the interview.

(b) The use of an interviewer ensures that *all* questions are answered in the correct order.

(c) The interviewer can check that the respondent has understood the questions and can encourage respondents to answer as fully as possible.

(d) Response rates are generally higher than with other forms of questionnaire administration.

(e) Where quotas are applied (such as 20 women under 30), the interviewer can ensure that the target number of interviews is achieved.

(f) Interviewers can attempt to persuade respondents to take part in the survey.

(g) A visual aid known as a 'showcard' can be used to show pictures, response options etc.

9.3 Types of interview survey

Interview surveys can be classified according to where they are carried out.

(a) **Store/Mall intercept surveys** are carried out in busy town centres, especially shopping centres/malls. The interviewer tends to stand in one position and approaches potential respondents as soon as the previous interview is completed, thereby eliminating time between interviews. The interviews need to be brief, however, as respondents are unlikely to want to stop for more than ten minutes.

(b) **In-house (or more accurately door-step) interviews** are part of those surveys where respondent recruitment is door to door. Interviewers may be given a list of names and addressees, or they may be limited to certain areas. Moreover, they may be given additional information such as call at every fourth house. In contrast to mall intercept interviews, in-house interviews may be prearranged by telephone. Such interview methods can be time consuming but longer interviews than in mall intercept surveys are possible (although likely to be interrupted). Often computer-assisted personal interview technology is used to improve speed and accuracy.

(c) **Hall tests** refer to interviews carried out in a pre-booked location. Recruitment is usually from a nearby street and respondents are often given refreshments. Materials, videos and displays can be used.

(d) **In-store surveys** may take place in a shop or just outside. Permission will of course be needed from the shop. Recruitment could be on the basis of people leaving or entering the store. A study of shopping intentions would require recruitment from the latter.

(e) **Business interviews** will normally take place at the interviewee's place of business but will need to be arranged in advance.

9.4 Choice of respondent

In-house interviewees can be selected using random sampling techniques from the electoral register. Interviewees for most other surveys will need to be selected using quota sampling or random location sampling. Geodemographic analysis can be applied.

9.5 Disadvantages of interview surveys

These surveys can be expensive and it is possible that interviewers interfere with objectivity by unwittingly introducing bias or by creating a particular mood when conducting the interview. For example, if the interviewer takes too light hearted an approach it may mean that the respondent treats the survey in a light-hearted way and data collected is not meaningful as a result.

FOR DISCUSSION

When training interviewers to undertake a specific personal interview survey, what kind of training is necessary?

---

10 PANEL METHODOLOGY

Consumer panel data can be gathered at the point-of-sale using bar-coding and related electronic systems, or in the home by means of home audits, diaries, and more recently, electronic scanners used in panel households.

10.1 Home audits

Home audits involve research staff visiting panel members' homes and, with their permission, physically checking household stocks of specific products surveyed by the panel. Used packaging is saved by the panel member and stored in a special container, so that these can also be checked ('dustbin check'). In addition, respondents usually answer a brief questionnaire.

10.2 Diaries

Most panels use some form of diary, which members complete with details of purchases of a range of food and other frequently purchased products. Some research organisations operate a weekly system of reporting, which is considered to result in more reliable data than if the time interval is extended, but costs are obviously a factor.

10.3 Electronic scanners

The Taylor Nelson AGB Superpanel in the UK comprises 10,000 households (33,000 individuals) who are equipped with electronic scanners, similar to those used at supermarket check-out desks, which record price, place of purchase and selected brand. This enables rapid trend analysis to be supplied to AGB's clients.

In June 1989, AC Nielsen launched the Homescan panel, which was the first panel in Europe to use in-home scanning. This consumer panel, based on 7,100 homes, derived from the Nielsen establishment survey of 80,000 households in the UK and was designed to reflect accurately household purchases of all grocery items, from fresh and pre-packed foodstuffs to household products, petfoods, toiletries, confectionery and alcohol.

Each household is provided with a small, hand-held bar-code scanner and after each shopping trip purchased items are recorded; data captured include the date, items bought, any promotional offers applicable, price, quantity and store used. On completion the information is downloaded via a modem to Nielsen's host computer.

Electronic data capture and transfer allow daily collection of purchasing data, so Nielsen clients can be provided with up-to-the-minute information and consumers' responses to marketing initiatives. Core data can vary but standard analyses include: % of households purchasing, % of expenditure, average number of visits per buyer, average spend per buyer, average spend per visit, brand comparisons, level of trial of new products, brand loyalty and demographic analyses.

Activity 3 **(10 minutes)**

A marketing research company proposes to investigate food purchasing patterns among a sample of consumers. It intends using diaries as the research instrument. Which areas of food purchasing may the diaries fail to uncover?

11 TELEPHONE RESEARCH

Telephone research is a relatively fast and low cost means of gathering data. It is most useful when only a small amount of information is required. It has been particularly useful in industrial research, although the technique has been widely used for consumer research with the growth in home telecommunications.

11.1 Disadvantages

There are a number of disadvantages to using the telephone in research, however.

(a) A **biased sample** may result from the fact that a proportion of people do not have telephones, many of those who do are ex-directory and the telephone numbers listed may be outdated.

(b) The **refusal rate** is much higher than with face-to-face interviews.

(c) The interview must be **short**.

(d) There is no way to provide visual aids.

11.2 Advantages

Advantages associated with telephone research include the following.

(a) A wide geographical area can be covered with no travel costs
(b) There is a compulsion to answer the phone
(c) Efficient call backs can be made
(d) Relatively high response rate
(e) Question modification possible

CATI (computer assisted telephone interviewing) has been used successfully by insurance services and banks as well as consumer research organisations. The telephone interviewer calls up a questionnaire on screen and reads questions to the respondent. Answers are then recorded instantly on computer.

Activity 4 **(15 minutes)**

Identify two marketing research projects for which a telephone questionnaire rather than a mail questionnaire or personal interview would be more appropriate.

12 OBSERVATION

Observation has already been discussed in some detail in Section 3 of Chapter 3.

Interviews and questionnaires depend on respondents answering questions on behaviour and attitudes truthfully. Sometimes it is necessary to **observe behaviour**, not only because respondents are unwilling to answer questions but because such questions are unable to provide the researcher with answers.

The major categories of observations are as follows.

(a) **Home audit**. Also termed indirect observation, this involves the investigation of the respondent's home, office or premises so as to determine the extent of ownership of certain products/brands. (Note that the home audit and diary panels are termed **consumer panel** research.)

(b) **Direct observation**. This involves the direct observation of the behaviour of the respondent by the researcher.

(c) **Recording devices**. Such devices record micro behaviour in laboratory settings and macro behaviour in natural settings.

  (i) Laboratory settings

    (1) **Psychogalvanometers** measure a subject's response to, say, an advertisement by measuring the perspiration rate.

    (2) **Eye cameras** are used to assess those parts of, for example, an advertisement which attract most attention and those parts which are neglected.

    (3) **Pupilometric cameras** are used in assessing the visual stimulation derived from an image.

  (ii) In **natural settings** video and movie cameras are used to record behaviour.

The use of observation as a data collection method has been stimulated by advances in electronics. EPOS systems allow firms to observe stock on hand, inflows, outflows and the speed at which stock items are moving through the store.

Observation techniques can also be qualitative in nature with common research methods including accompanied shopping, for example where the researcher goes shopping with the respondent and discusses their behaviour both before, during and after the trip.

Activity 5 **(30 minutes)**

A building society branch manager feels that staff are too reluctant to generate sales leads from ordinary investors and borrowers which may be passed on to the society's consultants in order that they can attempt to sell life insurance policies, pensions and unit trusts. You would like to understand the reasons for their reluctance. As an observer, how would you go about this?

12.1 Experiments

Experimental methods are based within the field of causal research where the relationships between factors are tested. Experiments are designed with a control group to test whether or not the factor under investigation accounts for a significant difference in opinion, behaviour or attitude of the sample respondents. An example marketing research project could be an investigation by a yoghurt manufacturer to establish the effect of an ingredient change on consumer preference. In this scenario, the researcher would conduct taste tests where one group of respondents would taste the modified yoghurt and another 'matched' group (where respondents fitted the same sampling criteria) would taste the existing recipe. Alternative experimental designs may use just one sample group but make changes to the factor under investigation over a specified time period.

13 APPROACHES TO THE ASSESSMENT OF THE VALUE AND VALIDITY OF DATA

Some approaches to this assessment are outlined below.

(a) **Commonsense.** Clearly data which is dated, which emanates from dubious sources or which is based on unrepresentative samples should be treated with extreme caution, if not totally disregarded.

(b) **Statistical approaches.** There are a variety of sampling methods for survey data as already described, which are appropriate to different situations. All of them involve some degree of risk (some probability of error). The degree of risk of statistical error can, however, be computed as we have seen.

(c) **Expert judgement.** The same data can be interpreted differently by different people – you have only to look at differences between economists or between politicians of different parties on the latest figures to see ample evidence of this. The following array – 98.7, 98.6, 98.6, 98.4, 98.1, 98.1 – might be regarded by a statistician as a declining trend but to a marketing manager the figures may represent a very steady state, especially if they were percentages of actual sales against budgeted sales for the last six years. In using this approach, therefore, the marketing manager might be wise to consult more than one expert before making a decision.

(d) **The intuitive approach.** Some people have a better feel for figures than others and seem able to judge the value and validity of data intuitively. For example, it is said that Rank Xerox ignored survey findings that there was no market for a dry copier and in doing so went on to become a world leader in this field. This approach, whilst perhaps successful for a chosen few, is not, however, recommended.

(e) **The questioning approach.** Always question the origin and the basis of the data. Ask for further information. An actual spend of 180% of budget is not important if the amount concerned is only £10. A much smaller variance on a much large amount could, however, be quite serious. Recognise that human errors occur when manipulating data, that bias can occur in questionnaire design: ask to see the questionnaire, check the figures.

13.1 The limitations of marketing research

You should be aware that research cannot supply marketers with perfect and comprehensive answers to all the questions. This may be because the research itself is badly designed (the sample populations inappropriate, the questions misleading and so on) but it can also happen because systematic research, by definition, can only ask the questions which exist in marketers' mind and elicit responses within the framework of respondents' imaginations.

As Nishikawa claims, the most important point in building marketing strategy is not logical analysis or investigative excellence, but creative action. Only proactive creativity, generating products and services *in anticipation of* customer needs and expectations, can create marketing advantage; organisations which are customer driven (as opposed to being customer focused) are invariably *reactive*. Responding to declared customer needs is acting too late for successful marketing: in order to forecast the future, organisations require creativity rather than responsiveness, challenge rather than passivity.

Nishikawa claims that marketing research linked to new products and services is especially defective, because of certain features in customer psychology.

(a) **Indifference**. Customers often provide negative responses to ideas for new products/services simply because they are indifferent to something they have not thought about or tried before.

(b) **Absence of responsibility**. People will say more or less anything when responding to research surveys, often out of a desire to please the researcher.

(c) **Conservative attitudes**. Most customers choose conventional and familiar products/services. To put it another way, only about three per cent of customers are Early Adopters.

(d) **Vanity**. Customers will try to put on a good appearance about their motives and will seldom want to admit that cheapness (for example) was the major reason for a purchase decision.

(e) **Insufficient information**. Researchers often approach customers with information and ideas seen from the seller's rather than from the customer's point of view.

One of Nishikawa's key points is that customers are most sincere when **spending rather than talking**.

13.2 Use of research data

Jobber (2007) notes the findings of two studies of Marketing Information Systems and the factors that affect usage. Systems are used more when:

- The system is sophisticated and confers prestige to its users
- Other departments view the system as a threat
- There is pressure from top management to use the system
- Users are more involved in automation

Usage of marketing research data tends to be higher if:

- Results conform to the client's prior beliefs
- The presentation of results is clear
- The findings are politically acceptable
- The *status quo* is not challenged

These findings suggest that marketing researchers need to appreciate not only the technical aspects of research and the need for clarity in report presentation but also the political dimension of information provision. It is unlikely that marketing research reports will be used in decision-making if the results threaten the *status quo* or are likely to have adverse political repercussions. The sad fact is that perfectly valid and useful information may be ignored in decision-making for reasons that are outside the technical competence of the research.

13.3 Overall research technique considerations

When designing your research there are a number decisions to be made in order to be confident that you have a reliable methodology. Everything itemised below should be included within the methodology section of a research proposal along with justified reasons for their choice.

- **Research philosophy** – Exploratory, explanatory or descriptive?
- **Availability of existing research?** – Primary, secondary or both data required?
- **Research duration?** – A longitudinal approach or an *ad hoc* piece?
- **Expected quality of the data (how detailed and contextually rich does the data need to be?)** – Qualitative, quantitative or mixed data?
- **Sampling philosophy and selection**

  Level of control of the sample that is required?
  How easy is it to access to sample?
- **Actual fieldwork data collection method** – In order to assess the suitability of a particular data collection technique, the following considerations should also be made.

  ✓ Available resources – Cost, time, personnel

  ✓ Sample characteristics

  ✓ Research questions/objectives

  ✓ Depth of questions

  ✓ Sensitivity of questions

  ✓ Extent of prior knowledge or research within the area about the topic under investigation

  ✓ Level of detailed analysis required

  ✓ Distribution issues (eg, how easy would it be to give out questionnaires etc)

  ✓ Expected quality of the data (how detailed and contextually rich does the data need to be)

  ✓ Quantity of data required (does it need to be generalisable?)

  ✓ Importance of high response rates

  ✓ Complexity versus versatility requirements in fieldwork collection

Chapter roundup

- Interviewing is a core function of marketing research and types of interview range from formal, unstructured interviews to informal discussions.
- Research directors should pay special attention to the training and monitoring of interviewers in order to keep bias to a minimum.
- Group discussions are often used at the exploratory phase of marketing research to help define the problem.
- Attitude research uses various scaling techniques and because some of these scales are versatile and relatively easy to use, care is needed to ensure that the resultant information is valid and reliable.
- The basic premise of projective techniques is that the best way to obtain the true feelings and attitudes of people is to enable them to present data indirectly about themselves by speaking through others.
- Questionnaires are a vital element of the total marketing research design but they demand experience and skill in their composition.
- Pilot testing of questionnaires is imperative and this should be undertaken with a representative sample.
- Most survey work in the UK is conducted through face-to-face interviews, usually by employees of a marketing research organisation.
- Panel or longitudinal research provides data which enable trends to be identified; panels can consist of individuals, households or organisations.
- Telephone research is low cost and fast but has the disadvantage of not being able to explore issues further as with face-to-face interviews, and true feelings about an issue can be disguised.
- Observation techniques may be employed to provide answers to some research problems. For example, observation panels are convened and measured using electronic metering devices to observe TV viewing patterns.
- There are various approaches to examining the validity and use of marketing research data. Research cannot supply marketers with perfect and comprehensive answers to all questions.

Quick quiz

1 What are the four main types of interview?

2 What are the two disadvantages of depth interviews?

3 How many respondents usually make up a focus group?

4 List three advantages of using focus groups.

5 Give two examples of situations where word association could be used?

6 Where might the third person technique be employed?

7 What does a semantic differential scale consist of?

8 How does a staple scale differ from a semantic differential?

9 How would you describe a Likert scale?

10 Name three advantages of postal surveys.

11 What are the five location types of interview survey?

12 What is the AGB Superpanel?

13 List three disadvantages of using telephone research.

14 What are the three main categories of observation?

Answers to quick quiz

1 Fully structured, semi-structured, unstructured and in-depth.

2 They are time consuming to conduct and analyse, and so are more expensive.

3 Eight to ten respondents and a moderator.

4 The group environment can be less intimidating than a one-to-one interview, group dynamics can encourage participation, differences between respondents can be highlighted.

5 Selecting brand names and developing advertising campaign themes and slogans.

6 When dealing with subjects which may be embarrassing, eg personal hygiene, or those that might evoke hostility if answered directly by the respondent.

7 The scale consists of a number of bipolar adjectival phrases and statements, each of which has seven categories.

8 It uses just one term and asks the respondent to describe how well that term describes a subject on a scale of +5 (very well) to –5 (very poorly).

9 In the Likert method a series of statements is provided and respondents are required to rate each statement on the basis of the strength of their personal feelings toward it. –2 infers strong disagreement and +2 strong agreement.

10 Low cost per response, no interview bias and the questionnaire length.

11 Mall intercept, in-house (ie door-step), hall tests, in-store and business.

12 It comprises 10,000 households who are equipped with electronic scanners to record their purchases.

13 High refusal rate, incomplete sampling frame and no opportunity to provide visual aids.

14 Home audit, direct observation and the use of recording devices.

Answers to activities

1 *Advantages*

- People may be more forthcoming if not dealing with an individual.
- Can be used to ask sensitive or potentially embarrassing questions.
- Less time-consuming for interviewers
- Standard form of question assists continuity
- Cost per person is less: can ask more people

Disadvantages

- Recipients may throw them away.
- Questions cannot be tailored to the recipient.
- May be difficult to understand responses without the scope for further questioning.

2 Your own research.

3 Spontaneous, impulse purchases eg chocolate, sweets.

- Purchased by people who are meant to be on a diet (secret purchases).
- Goods not purchased as part of the 'weekly shop' eg milk delivered to the door.
- 'Top up' purchases during the week eg fresh vegetables
- Takeaway meals.

4 Two marketing research projects for which a telephone questionnaire rather than a main questionnaire or personal interview would be more appropriate.

1. Where the impact of a TV advertising campaign was being assessed. Phone calls could be made immediately after the advertisements had run to determine who had seen it and what the impact had been.
2. Telephone questionnaires are particularly useful when time is short and the study requires a broad geographic sample. This could be useful in the prototype phase of a new product or service development.

5 The problem here is that staff behaviour may be modified and so untypical when a senior member of staff is present. Consideration could be given to using the mystery customer technique to improve the reliability of results.

Chapter 5 :
CUSTOMER SATISFACTION

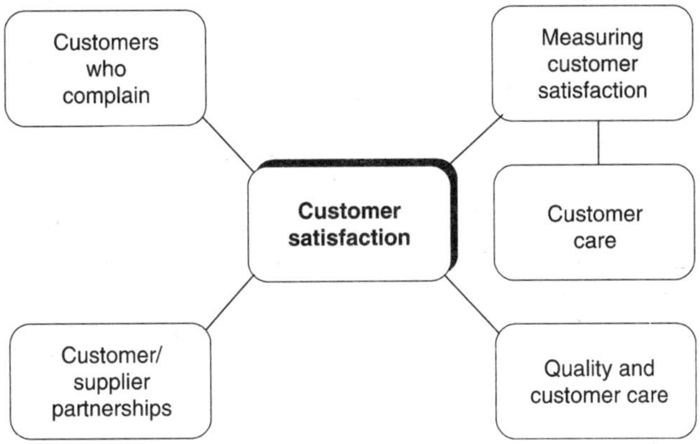

This chapter covers material relevant to both Unit 17 Marketing Intelligence and Unit 20 Sales Planning and Operations.

Introduction

This chapter is concerned with the importance of customer satisfaction within a marketing led organisation. It begins with an evaluation of the components of customer satisfaction, and the ways in which it can be obtained and measured. Customer care systems and procedures are then discussed, using examples to illustrate how organisational structure can impact on customer care management.

The relationship between quality and customer care is then explored in terms of the absolutes of quality management and the basic elements of improvement. The penultimate section is concerned with the process and management of customer complaints and their role in overall quality improvement.

The final section deals with customer/supplier relationships, which have obvious implications for customer satisfaction and retention.

Your objectives

In this chapter you will learn about the following.

(a) The principles of measuring customer satisfaction

(b) The role of effective customer care

(c) The relationship between total quality and customer care

(d) The importance of customers who complain

(e) Developments in customer/supplier partnerships

1 MEASURING CUSTOMER SATISFACTION

1.1 Fundamentals of customer satisfaction

(a) **Product/service variables**. The design of the product or service is designed to give customers benefit. Good design maximises those benefits.

(b) **Sales and promotion-related variables**. Three key variables affect customer satisfaction in this area.

   (i) **Messages** which help to shape customers' ideas about the product's benefits before they have experienced it in use.

   (ii) **Attitudes** of everyone in the organisation who comes into contact with customers: salespeople, service staff, telephone operators, and so forth.

   (iii) The use of **intermediaries** to sell on behalf of the organisation: similar selection, training and performance criteria should be applied to intermediaries as are applied to an organisation's own staff.

(c) **After-sales variables**. There are two aspects of after-sales which are especially significant for organisations.

   (i) **Support services**. Covering traditional after-sales activities like warranties, parts and service, and user training.

   (ii) **Feedback and restitution**. The way the organisation handles complaints and the level of priority attached by management to such activities.

(d) **Culture-related variables**. The crucial question here is whether the corporate culture is built around maximising customer satisfaction, or whether management merely pays lip service to it. Would it be acceptable for an employee to postpone a meeting with the managing director in order to meet a customer, for example?

EXAMPLE

Peugeot, the French carmaker, developed one of the first fuel injection engines, and its ignition system was different from conventional vehicles. This caused significant problems in the US market, where drivers were used to pumping the accelerator pedal before starting the ignition. This would put fuel into the combustion chamber and help to start the engine. When US drivers did this to a fuel injection Peugeot, the engine became flooded and would not start. Peugeot engineers were of the opinion that American drivers simply needed to be educated in how to start the cars, but others said that they needed to build an engine that operated in the way that American drivers wanted.

American drivers continued to believe that Peugeot cars were difficult to start, and eventually stopped buying them altogether. Peugeot withdrew from the US market in 1991. They had refused to listen to their customers.

1.2 Measuring customer satisfaction

Measuring whether customers have got what they wanted can be extremely problematic for a number of reasons.

(a) **Weak anecdotal evidence**, often based on single incidents, is given too much weight, especially if such evidence reinforces what people in an organisation want to hear (wishful thinking).

(b) **Single-incident disasters** may be used by one part of the organisation to attack another, rather than as an opportunity for improving performance.

(c) The views of those customers who complain, which may be **atypical**, are not counter-balanced by the views of those who do not.

(d) Many badly-served customers will not complain, but will simply **take their business elsewhere** if they can.

EXAMPLE

Word of mouth is critical to success for services because of their experiential nature.

For example, talking to people that have visited a resort or hotel is more convincing than reading holiday brochures. Promotion, therefore, must acknowledge the dominant role of personal influence in the choice process and stimulate word of mouth communication. Cowell (1995) suggests four approaches, as follows.

(i) Persuading satisfied customers to inform others of their satisfaction (eg American Express rewards customers that introduce other to its service).

(ii) Developing materials that customers can pass onto others.

(iii) Targeting opinion leaders in advertising campaigns.

(iv) Encouraging potential customers to talk to current customers (eg open days at universities).

(e) The opinions of small numbers of **highly articulate** customers, especially if of high status and personally known to top management, or expressed through the public media, will be given excessive emphasis.

(f) **Preconceptions** within the organisation about its customer-service standing and performance may be out-of-date or mistaken, especially if insufficient attention is paid to what the competition is doing.

Definition

> **Customer satisfaction** – the overall attitude a person has about a product after it has been purchased.

1.3 Customer segmentation

So far we have treated customers as if they were all alike, all wanting much the same things, all applying similar criteria when judging the product, the service, or the organisation as a whole. In practice, this is bound to be misleading, especially for organisations with a large customer base, a wide range of products, a global market, and several discrete product/brand names. Customer A may want reliability of delivery on an hourly basis; Customer B may want an unusual range of financial options; Customer C may want the highest possible standards of after-sales support; Customer D is only interested in one product; and so on.

Research shows that there are differences in customers' expectations which can be exploited by offering levels of service which match the needs of particular sectors, possibly withdrawing from some or increasing prices/charges to an economically-justified level.

1.4 Obtaining customer intelligence

Customer research survey method

One way in which customer intelligence can be gathered is via a customer (or consumer) **survey** using a questionnaire. The key steps in planning and implementing such a survey are laid out below.

Step 1 **Carry out analysis** of the organisation's customers, to decide whether they already fall into categories with differing service expectations.

Step 2 Decide whether to cover all customers or a **sample**. If the organisation only has a small group of customers, semi-structured interviews may be preferable to written questionnaires.

Step 3 **Pilot-test the questionnaire** to ensure that the questions make sense and that all potential customer concerns are being covered.

Step 4 Decide whether to conduct the survey **in person**, by **telephone** or via the **post**. Postal distribution may be unavoidable, though it will drastically reduce the response rate and may introduce bias into the sample (unless incentives are offered).

Step 5 If the survey has been well designed and administered, **analyse the results** to reveal gaps in customer-service performance.

Other methods of obtaining customer intelligence via surveys include diary panels, interviews (often known as mall intercept surveys), instore surveys and hall tests. These were all discussed in Chapter 4.

Suggestion schemes

Suggestion schemes are used to encourage customers and/or staff to come up with workable ideas on improving efficiency or quality, new marketing initiatives or solutions to problems. They are often incentivised by offering payments or prizes. There is motivational value in getting staff involved in problem-solving and planning and staff are often in the best position to provide practical and creative solutions to their work problems or the customer's needs.

Mystery shopping

Mystery shoppers are widely used to monitor service levels and the service experience provided. They eat at restaurants to check food, service and facilities, stay in hotels, drink in pubs, travel on planes and visit cinemas, health clubs and garages.

The feedback provides first hand commentary and can demonstrate the difference between the service promise and the reality of what is actually delivered. Most of the time, the focus is in the overall experience rather than individual performance, although at times staff are also the focus of attention. Normally, the mystery shopper is given a checklist of points to watch out for and they have to be skilled in classifying and memorising elements of the delivered service. To be effective, the mystery shopper must be believable and natural and thus cannot be seen with a checklist on a clipboard.

1.5 The complaints system as a research tool

It is surprising how few organisations positively encourage **complaints**, despite the fact that complaints are an essential form of feedback if properly organised. Complaints represent only a small proportion of dissatisfied customers, however: organisations never know the precise number of customers who do not complain but who simply take their business elsewhere. The number of such customers must, of course, be reduced. Equally, unless the problems are known, solutions cannot be found.

Activity 1 **(10 minutes)**

In what ways could you obtain complaints feedback?

We will be considering the impact of quality in more detail in the next section, but what is important to emphasise here is that quality has to be defined from the customer's perspective. Quality does not mean best, or even 'fit for the purpose', but means it **satisfies the needs of the customers**. Customer satisfaction is also an essential requirement of quality standards such as ISO 9001:2000 which specifies that customer satisfaction should be measured to highlight where improvements can be made.

Marketers have to avoid falling into the trap of raising a customer's expectations through glamorous promotion and elaborate packaging, because if the product fails to meet these expectations, a disappointed and dissatisfied customer may choose alternative suppliers.

Losing customers is bad news for any business; not only are **today's sales lost**, but **future potential earnings** are also sacrificed.

(a) A woman in her mid-20s spends an estimated £200 a year on cosmetics. Dissatisfied by her current brand she switches to a competitor. She remains loyal for over 20 years to the new product. Cash revenue from the lost client is worth £4,000 before the time value of money is taken into account.

(b) The car manufacturer who estimates an average driver will buy seven cars in his or her lifetime is looking at perhaps £100,000 in lost custom if the salesperson fails to provide the service or approach needed to convert the buyer into a driver loyal to the brand.

But besides the lost value from that customer, bad service or products will generate bad word of mouth publicity. This can be very persuasive and can cost the company even more in lost customers or potential customers.

Activity 2

Over the next two weeks keep listening for word of mouth publicity about products or services. Keep a note of the relative proportions of good and bad messages. How much credibility do they have? Do they influence your behaviour?

You will find they come up in many forms.

- Have you tried that new restaurant?
- Did you see the latest film?
- What is the service like?

Try actively eliciting comments by asking for advice on a new car purchase or holiday destination.

Look for websites which provide negative publicity concerning organisations, such as www.mwr.org.uk and www.essentialaction.org.

1.6 Datamining

Datamining is the process of analysing basic data to reveal important and previously unsuspected relationships. The classic example is the store that discovered a group of men whose typical purchase was a pack of disposable nappies and a pack of beer. This particular sub-segment was subsequently catered to by placing beer and nappies in close proximity.

Sophisticated software can be used to analyse website traffic in similar ways. Customers reveal their interests and concerns by the specific use they make of websites, both in the things they do and in the things they do not do. Analytic software can establish such things as number of new and repeat visits, page popularity and the success of advertising banners. Such analysis can be used to amend website design, follow up leads and improve the conversion rate of visits.

FOR DISCUSSION

"The customer is always right." Do you agree?

1.7 Customer retention

Retaining existing customers is more profitable than acquiring new customers for several reasons.

(a) Customer expenditure increases over time

(b) Repeat customers often cost less to service

(c) Sales, marketing and set-up costs are amortised over a longer customer lifetime

(d) Satisfied customers may be prepared to pay a premium price.

(e) Satisfied customers provide referrals

The starting point for developing customer retention strategies and programmes is research. Encouraging customers not to leave the relationship but to stay and buy more, requires a in-depth understanding of both what causes customers to leave and what motivates customers to buy from one company rather than its competitors.

It should be noted that not every customer is equally attractive (and hence important to retain). The 80/20 rule is in evidence so it makes sense to ensure that retention rates are highest among the 20% of customers who provide the company with 80% of their profit.

If customer retention strategies are to be successful, they should focus on customer defection and customer loyalty. If these can be successfully managed, then the probability of an improved customer retention rate will almost certainly increase.

2 CUSTOMER CARE

Inevitably things will go wrong from time to time. Most customers, however, are less concerned with the mishap than how the issue is rectified. This is where **customer care** is relevant. Customer care has been very much in the forefront of management thinking in both the public sector (with the Citizens' Charter etc) and private sector over recent years. Whilst it is easy to scoff, the Citizens' Charter, Patients' Charter, Rail Users' Charter and so on have all tried to specify the level of service users are entitled to expect and compensation if this is not delivered. This start at quantification is an excellent beginning. From these benchmarks improvements can be developed, implemented and monitored.

In *Perfect Customer Care* (2003), Dr Ted Johns, argues that 'The majority of customer complaints will not directly relate to the quality of the service/product, but to the peripheral issues. Quality in the eyes of the customer is always supposedly much more than the quality of the product or basic service offered'.

Most complaints are apparently peripheral to the actual product/service offered, and relate to telephone courtesy, delivery, availability of product, user instructions and so forth. **Customer care programmes** are devoted to maximising the benefits a customer receives within the operating constraints of the business. This means, effectively, that the operations staff who deliver service should do so with a **marketing philosophy** in mind.

In other words, the service should be designed as far as possible with the customer in mind, rather than the procedural conveniences of the company. Although the old adage 'you can't please all of the people all of the time' may still be true, it is still important to put in place systems, procedures and practices to minimise customer dissatisfaction.

Activity 3 **(10 minutes)**

Assume that you have ordered two fencing panels from a local DIY store. For a small extra charge, the panels will be delivered (as they are too big to fit into your car). On the appointed day, a delivery is made – but only one of the panels you purchased is delivered, not two. You phone up; delivery is promised the following day, but fails to arrive. You phone up again and speak to a senior manager, who apologises for his staff. Delivery is made, and you are given a third extra panel to compensate for the inconvenience. The fencing panels themselves are fine. What customer care lessons can you learn from this example?

For organisations, one of the key components of service excellence is **process alignment**, ie making sure that the organisation serves the customer rather than the other way round. In the words of Accenture (the global management consultants), it is 'deliberately designing and modifying business processes so that **every activity is geared to meeting the customer's wants**'.

Chris Daffy in his book, *Once a Customer, Always a Customer* (2000), argues that an organisation structure that is totally customer-focused would have just two layers.

The customer-focused company

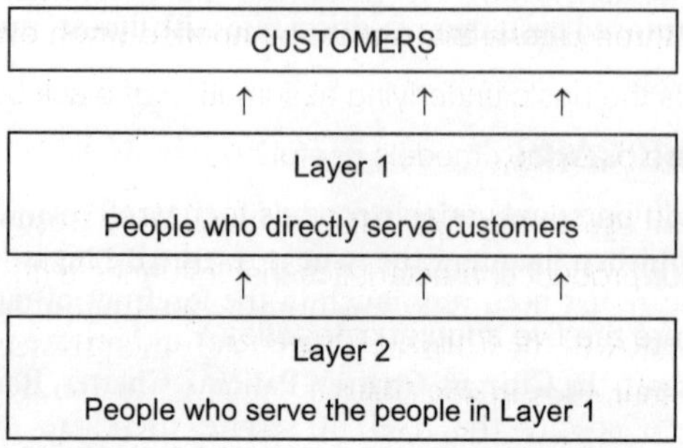

FOR DISCUSSION

The organisations which are most effective at dealing with customers are typically those which have radically changed their structures in order to make them less hierarchical. Why do you think that this is the case?

EXAMPLES

(a) **The Automobile Association**

The AA has gone through a major delayering exercise, cutting the number of levels between its front-line employees (the patrolmen) and the Chief Executive from twelve to five, and delegating much more responsibility at lower levels.

(b) **Cigna Services UK (health insurance)**

Cigna now operates almost totally on the basis of multi-functional teams. The customer is assigned to a team and that team, rather than separate functional groups within the organisation, deals with very aspect of that customer's business with Cigna.

(c) **Hamilton Acorn (paintbrush manufacturer)**

Acorn's customer services department now draws together in a single unit a number of functions that had previously been done separately: warehousing and distribution, customer queries, data input, sales administration and export. The company has also reorganised the factory floor into cells or small teams, each with its own supervisor, and each responsible for a product form start to finish. This manufacturing re-organisation was vital if the improvements demanded by customers were actually going to happen: as the company's Operations Director has said, 'You can't just put a sign up and say, 'Hooray, now we've got a customer services department, now we're going to be great', because they can't do a damned thing unless they've got the back-up from the manufacturing side all the way through.'

2.1 Get it right, first time

One of the basic principles of Total Quality Management (TQM) is that the **cost of preventing mistakes is less than the cost of correcting them** once they occur. The aim should therefore be to **get things right first time.**

For instance, a 1:3:8 ratio is used in shipbuilding. A defect corrected when it occurs only costs one unit; if it has to be corrected at a subsequent inspection it costs three units; but if it has to be corrected after delivery to the customer it costs eight units. Arguably the figure of eight units could be even higher.

EXAMPLES

Birmingham Midshires Building Society

Until recently, a major source of complaint from the customers of the Birmingham Midshires Building Society concerned delays and errors. In response, the Society has adopted a 'right first time' philosophy throughout the organisation. They recognise that 'Re-work is costly, complaints are costly, and to recover properly from complaints about errors is a drain on business resources. Therefore we need to make sure that we've got the right measures and mechanisms in place to start providing a timely, high quality service'.

TNT Express (deliveries and distribution)

According to the Managing Director of TNT Express UK Limited: 'Some people believe that quality actually adds to cost. We do not agree. Our experience in the recession (of the early 1990s) reinforced our view that quality reduces costs. A get-it-right-first-time approach is reducing the often significant cost of correcting mistakes in our business.'

2.2 The Ted Johns blueprint for customer service excellence: the twelve pillars of performance (2003)

Ted Johns has created the following framework for:

(a) Specifying the desirable mix of internal, external and strategic components needed by an organisation which majors on service as a source of competitive advantage

(b) Evaluating the actions needed by organisations if they seek to establish themselves as 'contenders' or 'world class' players.

The framework involves three major dimensions: your **strategy**, your **people** and your **customers**. Each in turn has four sub-dimensions. None of the twelve factors is optional, and none is more important than the others (though without the **strategy** impetus, it is very unlikely that anything significant will happen).

Dimension 1: Your strategy

Commitment	Customer service is a key **corporate scorecard indicator**. (Xerox seeks customer delight, satisfaction and retention as key parameters for progress, arguing that profitability will follow from the achievement of these measures.) • **A clear and shared vision** from the top, rooted in the customer. • Sustained top-management **commitment** to change • Visible **role-modelling** by senior managers • Employee **involvement and engagement** • Motivation via **customer-linked rewards and recognition** systems • **Training** • Bold goals for **performance improvement** • **Benchmarking,** Xerox is always prepared to **learn from other organisations.**
Credibility	Your customers must have good grounds for believing your promises. Even when an organisation is trusted by its customers, it must continue to work hard to ensure that its reputation remains intact.
Classification	You segment your customers, periodically review your segmentation profiles and vary your product/service offer across segment boundaries.
Concentration	You focus your marketing efforts on your most profitable customers. Many companies disseminate their marketing efforts without any regard to **customer profitability potential, segment profitability potential,** or even **product/service profitability potential**.

Dimension 2: Your people

Capability	All your people, whether in the front line or not, are recruited and trained against a customer service competency blueprint. Many of the most successful Japanese companies pay much attention, when recruiting people, to possession of the right attitudes (ie customer focus, flexibility, enthusiasm for change, teamworking readiness).
Continuity	You have retention, reward and recognition strategies which encourage your people to remain. The *Reichheld* service/profit cycle shows the enormous benefits which are likely to accrue from employee retention.
Courtesy	Your people are polite, considerate, tolerant and friendly when dealing with customers.
Creativity	Your people produce ideas for service innovations and improvements. After all, employees at the front line are often the first to notice that customers are asking for different things and are beginning to complain about elements in the product/service package.

Dimension 3: Your customers

Consistency	**Customers like to know what to expect** from have called organisational routines, ie various predictable ways of operating that ultimately help to create customer confidence through familiarity and experience. This does not mean, however, that customer expectations remain static: they are constantly rising.
Communication	Your customers understand what you say to them; equally, you actively promote opportunities for **two-way** dialogue.
Comfort	Your customers feel comfortable with everything which collectively comprises the **company reputation**. Recent surveys on **electronic commerce** have strongly endorsed the argument that customers are much more willing to enter into transactions if they feel they are dealing with a **reputable brand** or organisation.
Contact	You offer customer service at times to suit your customers. Increasingly, customers expect service to be available 24 hours a day, seven days a week. They also expect the person on the other end of the telephone to be able to give them information and solutions.

3 IMPROVING QUALITY AND CUSTOMER CARE

For marketing service managers, the 'quality control' and 'engineering' of the interactions which take place between customers is a key strategic issue. Customers are often, in the course of service delivery, interacting with other customers to gather information, and form views about the nature and quality of the service of which they are contemplating purchase. Minimising exposure to negative feedback, and promoting the dissemination of positive images and messages about the value of the service, and the quality of customer responses to it, are important objectives here.

Activity 4 **(10 minutes)**

All levels of staff must be involved in customer service. To achieve this end, it is vital for senior management consciously to promulgate values of customer service constantly, in order to create and build a culture of customer service within the company. How do you think that this might be achieved?

3.1 Basic elements of quality improvement

(a) **Determination**, or the commitment of management

(b) **Education**, which involves staff training

(c) **Implementation**, which should clearly specify the process whereby quality is to be established within the organisation.

The power of quality claims is most evident when they are not fulfilled, as when a company's product fails. Here, consumers' expectations are not realised and dissatisfaction results. In these situations marketers immediately take steps to reassure customers.

FOR DISCUSSION

When the company confronts the problem effectively, consumers often are willing to forgive and forget, as was the case with Perrier, when traces of benzene were found in the water. When a company appears to be acting slowly or attempting a cover-up, consumer resentment is likely to grow. Try to think of some recent examples.

3.2 Total quality and total customer orientation

A **customer orientation**, seeking to satisfy the customer, is pursued in marketing by recognising that customers buy 'the sizzle, not the steak' – products are bought for the benefits they deliver; how customers can use the product to accomplish the things they want to do.

Definition

> **Total quality management** is defined as:
>
> '... the total composite product and service characteristics of marketing, engineering, manufacture and maintenance, through which the product and service in use will meet the expectations by the customer'.

What constitutes a 'quality product or service' must, it seems, be related to what the customer wants. Indeed, quality would have no commercial value otherwise. The customer must be the final arbiter of the quality which a product possesses.

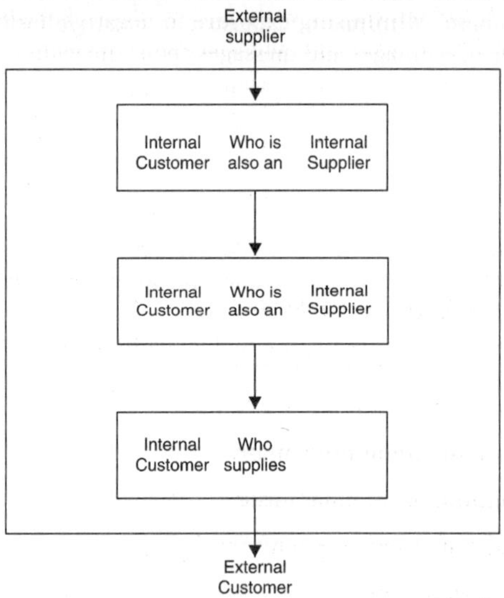

Figure 5.1: Customer involvement in quality chain

John Oakland (2003) argues that **meeting customer requirements** is the main focus in a **search for quality**. While these requirements would typically include aspects such as availability, delivery, reliability, maintainability and cost effectiveness, in fact the first priority is to establish what customer requirements **actually are**.

(a) If the customer is **outside the organisation,** then the supplier must seek to set up a marketing activity to gather this information, and to relate the output of their organisation to the needs of the customer.

(b) **Internal customers** for services are equally important, but seldom are their requirements investigated. The quality implementation process requires that all the supplier/customer relationships within the **quality chain** should be treated as marketing exercises, and that each customer should be carefully consulted as to their precise requirements from the product or service with which they are to be provided. Each link in the chain should prompt the following questions.

Of customers

- Who are my immediate customers?
- What are their true requirements?
- How do or can I find out what the requirements are?
- How can I measure my ability to meet the requirements?
- Do I have the necessary capability to meet the requirements? (If not, then what must change to improve the capability?)
- Do I continually meet the requirements? (If not, then what prevents this from happening, when the capability exists?)
- How do I monitor changes in the requirements?

Of suppliers

- Who are my immediate suppliers?
- What are my true requirements?
- How do I communicate my requirements?
- Do my suppliers have the capability to measure and meet the requirements?
- How do I inform them of changes in the requirements?

4 CUSTOMERS WHO COMPLAIN

If a person is unhappy with a product or service then essentially they have three courses of action open to them:

1. **Voice response** – a verbal complaint to the retailer in person or to the manufacturer by phone
2. **Private response** – negative word of mouth and/or boycott the retailer or manufacturer
3. **Third party response** – take legal action, write to an MP/newspaper, register a complaint with the local authority

A number of factors influence which route is taken. The consumer may in general be assertive or passive.

FOR DISCUSSION

Action is more likely to be taken for expensive products such as household durables, cars and clothing than for inexpensive products.

Also, if the consumer does not believe that the store will respond positively to a complaint, the person will be more likely to switch brands than fight. Marketers should encourage consumers to complain to them as people are very likely to spread the word about unresolved negative experiences to their friends.

The propensity of customers to complain has changed radically over the past few years. The availability of instant communication (such as Internet chat rooms and other social sites) has facilitated far more information sharing. Not only are customers much **more willing to make a noise** about their grievances, but they will also **tolerate much less** by way of restitution and delays – and, moreover, they will (as organisations see it) **fight dirty** more quickly, using threats of disclosure to television programmes and/or litigation in order to achieve their objectives.

(a) Technically, one has to argue that if customers are more prepared to tell you about their dissatisfaction, then this means that the organisation will secure **more reliable, representative and comprehensive customer feedback** than it ever did when it relied on a situation where only one in ten of the customers who were dissatisfied bothered to tell you about it. The remaining nine either quietly took their business elsewhere, or bided their time until the moment when they could do so.

(b) Of course, **not all companies see the complaint process as an opportunity.**

   (i) Some still have **no proper complaint-handling mechanism** at all, which means that customers have some initial communication barriers to overcome; it may also mean that the **treatment of complaining customers is erratic**, with some receiving generous restitution whilst others have their complaints ignored or dismissed.

   (ii) Some organisations **don't keep records of the complaints received** – indeed, they may have **no clear definition** of the term 'complaint' so that, for example, someone telephoning to ask for a copy of assembly instructions accidentally omitted from a flatpack furniture product may find that their call has been classified as 'information request' rather than 'complaint', especially if there is corporate pressure to minimise the number of 'complaint' items.

   (iii) Yet more organisations, receiving complaints, will respond **defensively** and seek to imply, if they can, that there is **something wrong with the complainant**, eg they washed the item of clothing in the washing machine when the instructions clearly said that it should only be dry-cleaned.

   (iv) Several will hope, apparently, that if they simply **ignore** complaints then most of them will go away: thus correspondence does not stimulate replies, telephone calls are not returned and customer service managers are consistently unavailable.

In fact complaints are part of the marketing process.

(a) If you actively **encourage** your customers to complain, you demonstrate **faith in your product/service** offer.

(b) **Analysing the nature of each complaint**, as well, will show where design, manufacturing, delivery and functionality resources need to be concentrated.

(c) If complaints are handled efficiently, expeditiously and sympathetically, then potentially defecting customers can be tied to you even more closely than before: they will rather **tell others about the wonderful way in which you handled their complaint** than tell them about what was wrong in the first place.

When customers walk into a shop, or phone the customer complaints line, they want the company's employees to **own the problem**. They do not want to be **passed around** and they do not want to be told about the **organisation's difficulties** ('we're very short-staffed at the moment' or 'the computer's down' or 'she's at lunch').

Ownership of the problem needs to be reinforced by the ability to give an **immediate response.**

(a) **Front-line staff** must be **empowered** to deal with complaints quickly: for most customers, time is of the essence, and if they are kept waiting, or transferred through several departments, then the original complaint rapidly escalates into rage.

(b) **Managers** find empowerment very difficult: they **worry excessively** about what customer-facing people will do if **left to their own devices**. What seems to happen, in effect, is that organisations devote all their energies to designing **procedures** which will prevent recovery and restitution systems from being **abused**, by either customers or employees: they forget that 99 per cent of all complaints are genuine, and 99 per cent of all employees are trying to do their best.

The ability to **empathise** is a key component in the effective handling of customer complaints, yet, typically, organisations are **reluctant to look at 'problems' from the customer's perspective**. If they did then much more attention would be given to creating procedures which lean over backwards to ensure that the complaining customer is mollified.

Activity 5 **(20 minutes)**

Can you give examples from your own experiences of good and bad service encounters?

EXAMPLE

A regular airline customer wrote to the company, complaining that its in-flight golf magazine catered only for Americans. His recommended solution was for the airline to supply equivalent golf magazines for British passengers. The airline wrote back to say that this was not practicable, but that as he was a regular flyer then they had arranged for him to have a year's subscription to the British magazine he had mentioned. The subscription cost the airline around $30, but every time the magazine landed on the customer's doormat it would remind him positively of the company.

Training staff on how to deal with customers, then **letting them get on with it**, are two fundamental elements in the complaints management process.

Why should a business embrace **customer service** as a source of competitive advantage? The simple answer is that **if you don't, someone else will** – and, all other things (price, availability or whatever) being equal in the eyes of the consumer, better service or customer care will lead the consumer to choose your competitor's product.

5 CUSTOMER/SUPPLIER PARTNERSHIPS AND AGREEMENTS

5.1 Relationships with suppliers

Increasingly, companies are looking to develop **long-term relationships with suppliers** they can trust and with whom they can tackle problems and develop opportunities. This symbiotic approach, advocated by those pursuing a total quality approach to management, is the basis of relationship marketing. While relationship marketing is concerned with customers, long-term business relationships can be built up with **favoured suppliers**. There are several factors behind this trend.

(a) Some firms have relationships with favoured suppliers rather than a free-for-all of suppliers competing for business on the basis of price.

(b) Just-in-time production methods, whereby supplies are delivered often and in small quantities, require a relationship of trust between supplier and customer.

(c) Relationships with favoured suppliers are encouraged by the total quality movement.

Supplier relationships can be built up in a number of ways, for example:

(a) Staff secondments
(b) Joint research and development projects

The end result of the relationship approach from the company's point of view is a **reduction in vulnerability to changing customer and supplier demands**: the bargaining powers of customers and suppliers are effectively managed in a marketing network.

5.2 Partnership sourcing and partnership marketing

Partnership sourcing and **partnership marketing** are other concepts which you may be asked to compare. The emphasis is on working together with all members of a value chain (suppliers, wholesalers, retailers and so on) to make sure that customer's needs are met profitably.

Definition

> From the perspective of a manufacturer, **partnership sourcing** implies a company seeking co-operation as it works back through the value chain. By contrast, **partnership marketing** implies co-operation as it works forwards through its value chain.

Essential features of partnership sourcing

- Joint involvement in new product development
- Joint solution of distribution problems
- Emphasis on long-term price stability
- Quality standards which are consistent and to an agreed level

Implications of partnership marketing

- Joint **promotional activity** shared by a manufacturer and its wholesalers and retailers
- Joint **research** to assess customers needs
- Joint **monitoring** of quality standards
- Joint **new product development** which is focused on meeting customers' identified needs

Another type of arrangement is the **co-maker agreement**.

EXAMPLE

The basic product and process know-how within a company is no longer the key factor in achieving an effective and efficient product development process. Rather, the number and complexity of technologies in today's products require a wide range of technological capabilities and competencies and huge investments in human, technological and financial resources. These investments are both too large and too risky to be undertaken by a single company.

Rather, companies prefer to establish a network of relationships that allows them to share costs, benefits and risks when a new product must be designed and launched. Know-how and knowledge is provided by people who contribute to product development either as single individuals or as a team. The way these teams and individuals are organised to carry out product development is critical to business growth.

Given these various changes, all companies in the car industry are continuously seeking new ways to address competitive pressures. Recognising the need to shorten development cycles, improve quality and increase productivity has historically led these companies to collaborative relationships – relationships that can be facilitated and supported by the implementation of information and communication technologies.

This increasing collaboration has in turn changed the industry's competitive structure, so that the competition is increasingly between groups of companies rather than between individual companies. These groups of companies, organised as networks, are composed of both competitors and suppliers.

The agreements linking network members may take various forms – partnerships, joint ventures, co-maker relationships and so on. Within a network, various inter-organisational projects are established to strengthen and leverage trust and openness relationships.

Against this background, at the end of the '80s Magneti Marelli changed its mission and organisation from product supplier to strategic partner capable of providing complete high-tech solutions. Recognising the importance of collaborative relationships, the company has formed and participated in several networks and network-related projects. In September 2009 Magneti Marelli signed an agreement with FAAM to develop, produce and sell lithium batteries. Magneti Marelli is a leader in automotive systems and components with a high electronics content. FAAM is one of the most successful companies in Italy in the field of lead batteries and electric vehicles production.

Chapter roundup

- Customer satisfaction is the overall attitude a person has about a product or service after it has been purchased.
- Measuring customer satisfaction can be extremely problematic for a variety of reasons including inaccurate customer preconceptions, single incident disasters and weak anecdotal evidence.
- One way in which customer intelligence can be gathered is via a customer survey.
- Complaints are an essential form of feedback when properly organised.
- Customer care has been very much in the forefront of management thinking in both the public sectors (eg the Citizens' and Patients' Charters) and private sector (eg Rail Users' Charter) over recent years.
- The twelve pillars of performance framework have three major dimensions, strategy, people (ie employees) and customers.
- The power of quality claims is most evident when they are not fulfilled, as when a company's product or service fails.
- Total quality management is defined as the total composite product and service characteristics of marketing, engineering, manufacture and maintenance, through which the product or service in use will meet the expectations of the customer.
- Complaints are an essential part of the marketing process and a key component in the effective handling of customer complaints is the ability to empathise.
- Partnership sourcing implies a company seeking co-operation as it works back through the value chain.
- Partnership marketing implies co-operation as it works forward through its value chain.

Quick quiz

1. What are the four fundamentals of customer satisfaction?
2. What are the key problems in measuring customer satisfaction?
3. List five methods of gathering customer intelligence.
4. What does the term process alignment mean in the context of effective customer care?
5. What are the customer dimensions of the twelve pillars of performance?
6. What are the basic elements of quality improvement?
7. What three courses of action are open to a dissatisfied customer?
8. List three factors behind the trend in developing customer/supplier relationships.
9. Name four essential features of partnership sourcing.

Answers to quick quiz

1 Product/service variables, sales and promotion-related variables, after-sales variables and culture-related variables.

2 Weak, anecdotal evidence; single incident disasters; lack of counterbalance with positive comments; many simply go elsewhere.

3 Survey, diary panels, interviews, in-store surveys and hall tests.

4 It means making sure that the organisation serves the customer rather than the other way round.

5 Consistency, communication, comfort and contact.

6 Management commitment, organisational education and implementation.

7 Voice response, private response and third party response.

8 The move towards favoured suppliers, just in time production methods and the fact that relationships with favoured suppliers are encouraged by the total quality movement.

9 Joint involvement in new product development, joint solution of distribution problems, emphasis on long-term price stability and quality standards which are consistent and to an agreed level.

Answers to activities

1 Provide a telephone complaints number (preferably freephone).
Positively request that complaints are sent in.
Advertise an incentive eg a free prize for respondents.
Provide a named person to whom complaints should be addressed.

2 The result of, or answer to, this activity will depend on your findings.

3 Check orders before despatch.

Follow up re-deliveries which have been booked.

Offer a useful form of compensation: an extra panel may be useless to the customer.

Apologies help soothe anger and frustration.

Poor service detracts from a good product.

4 Senior management are seen to participate in customer service.

Staff training.

Monitoring (eg incoming calls).

Constantly stress the importance of customer service.

Stress the importance from the recruitment stage onwards.

Respond quickly and effectively to customer complaints.

5 The response will depend on personal experience.

Part B

Marketing Planning

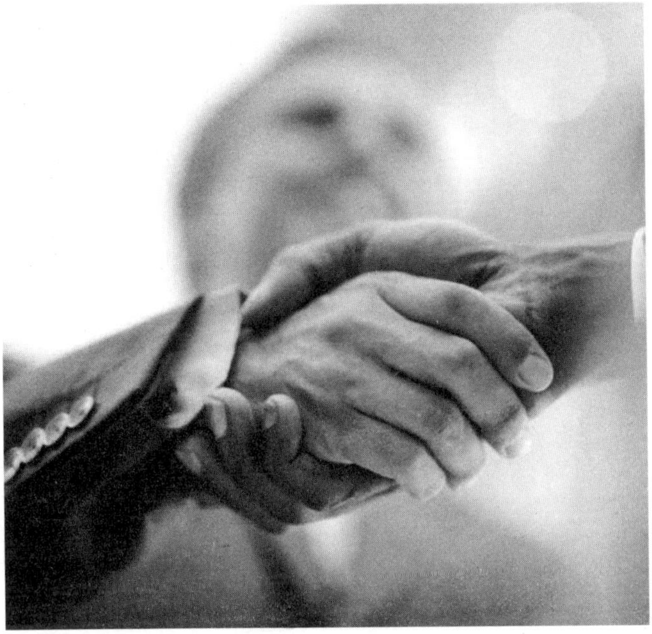

Chapter 6:

MARKETING PLANNING AND MARKETING VISION

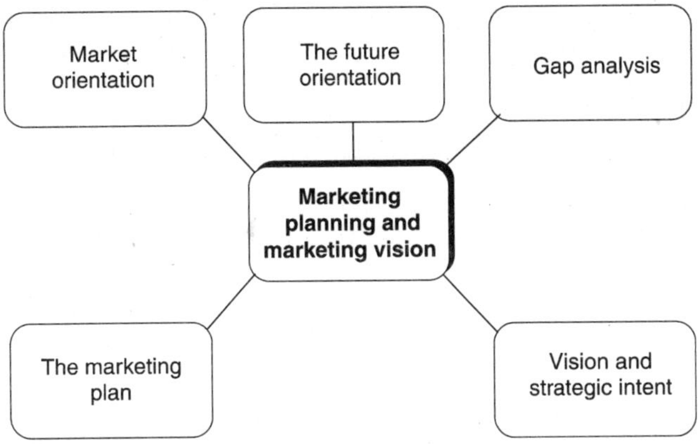

Introduction

This chapter covers market orientation and discusses how organisations can plan for the future, using marketing analysis and strategy.

Your objectives

In this chapter you will learn about the following.

(a) What market orientation and a market-led organisation are

(b) The role of marketing in market-led organisations

(c) How organisations can plan for the future

(d) The importance of developing effective marketing plans

(e) The role of marketing in the strategic planning process

(f) How to produce marketing plans

(g) Barriers to marketing planning

1 MARKET ORIENTATION

A 'market' is a group of customers. 'Marketing' is a process or activity.

Definition

(a) **Marketing** is the management process responsible for identifying and satisfying customers' needs profitably. (Chartered Institute of Marketing)

(b) The American Marketing Association's definition is: 'The process of planning and executing the conception, pricing, promotion, and distribution of ideas, goods and services to create exchanges that satisfy individual and organisational goals.'

Many industries are 'knowledge'-based industries. The ability to tap knowledge and create ideas can be instrumental in corporate success, as is the ability to communicate these ideas. Ideas can include information that will help customers determine whether the product will, in fact, be able to satisfy their needs. Marketing therefore encompasses many of the qualities that businesses need to have in order to survive. Ideas can be intellectual property, such as software and so forth, which can be sold as products.

'Marketing' can also refer to a department within an organisation, with its own professional staff with specialist expertise.

FOR DISCUSSION

If you have a good product or service you don't need marketing. It will sell itself.

1.1 Marketing-led and market-led orientation

Given that marketing is a process, an organisational function, and an academic discipline, it is worth going back to first principles. A **market** is a customer or group of customers.

Definition

Market orientation is characteristic of those companies which 'focus on customer needs as the primary drivers of organisational performance.'

(*Jobber* 2007))

A **marketing-led organisation is led by the marketing department.** Marketing orientation might just refer to increased power for marketing personnel.

In a company with a market orientation, by contrast, the aim of providing superior customer value dominates **all** thinking.

- What the business is
- Which markets to service
- Investments and acquisitions
- Which people to employ and how to promote them

In **market-led** organisations, the marketing department is **not** in a world of its own. Customer value is designed and created by **multi-function** product teams supporting **all the business functions**. In this type of organisation everyone is responsible for putting the customer's needs at the forefront of their actions.

> **Activity 1** **(10 minutes)**
>
> Think of a company which is market-led. What characteristics does it have? How is it set apart from the competition?

1.2 Market-led strategic change

Market-led strategic change rests on the following assumptions.

Assumptions

- All organisations must follow the dictates of the market to survive.
- Organisational effectiveness can be pursued by being market-led, focusing on the customer.
- Barriers to being market-led come, not from ignorance of customer characteristics, but from the way organisations are run.
- Becoming market-led often needs an upheaval.
- A deep seated strategic change is not just a matter of hiring a marketing executive.

In short the pursuit of **customer satisfaction** is at the heart of the market-led company. Piercy (2001) makes a distinction between '**marketing**' and '**going to market**'. Markets are more important than marketing, per se, and markets and customers are important for everyone in a company (not just the marketing department). '**Going to market** is a process owned by everyone in the organisation ... the context for marketing should be the **process** of going to market, not the marketing department.'

The process of going to market needs to be **managed**. Piercy highlights the key elements of this.

(a) Strategies are based on customers and markets.

(b) Internal programmes and external actions are driven by such strategies.

(c) The entire company must 'get its act together' in order to deliver its strategy into the market.

(d) Cross-functional teams cross organisational boundaries to get the job done.

(e) New types of relationships are created.

(f) New ways of doing business are supported by a new information technology infrastructure.

1.3 Challenges for the market-led organisation

Four broad issues arise for the market-led organisation.

Issue	Comment
Sophisticated customers	• Rising expectations: customers exposed to world class service will expect it everywhere • Customers can see through marketing-speak, and want transparency • Increased cynicism about marketing
New competitors	• From overseas • Reinventing the business (eg Direct Line Insurance)
New type of organisation	• Outsourcing arrangements • Collaboration arrangements • Alliances (eg airlines) • Stakeholder influences
New ways of doing business	• Customer-specific marketing • Databases are used to develop profiles of individual customers to entice them into a **relationship** • Internet marketing: buyers and sellers can conduct a dialogue as the Internet is interactive • Customer co-operatives: Internet newsgroups and chatrooms enable customers to get together perhaps to negotiate discounts or to share experience of a brand

FOR DISCUSSION

The Internet will take over as the main marketing medium.

1.4 Role of 'marketing' in market-led firms

What might be the role of marketing and marketing management in this particular context? The role of 'marketing' has changed significantly, but it has also become much more important to the activities of many firms.

(a) **From staff to line**. Marketing thinking and action are better integrated into the day-to-day decisions of managers running important parts of the business. In other words, instead of a separate, 'staff' marketing department going its own sweet way and putting a promotional gloss on what the organisation does, marketing is more involved in line decisions, such as segment or product management.

(b) **From specialist to strategic**. Marketing has evolved beyond its traditional focus. Tasks once exclusively associated with marketing, such as market assessment, are now only a part of a far more integrated marketing process that may include other functions such as product development or distribution.

(c) **From isolated to widespread**. Marketing has become more diffused within the organisation, and is no longer the concern of the few.

2 THE FUTURE ORIENTATION

EXAMPLE

'Some management teams were simply more foresightful than others. Some were capable of imagining products, services and entire industries that did not exist and then giving them birth. These managers seemed to spend less time worrying about how to position the firm in existing competitive space and more time creating fundamentally new competitive space.' *(Hamel and Prahalad*,1996)

There are two 'approaches' to the future.

- The future will be similar to the present.
- The future will be radically different.

In *Competing for the Future (1996)* Hamel and Prahalad suggest that:

- The future is not just something that 'happens' to organisations
- Organisations can 'create' the future

In practice, there is truth in both perspectives.

(a) Some trends are likely to continue indefinitely. In the physical environment, global warming will continue for the long term. In terms of demography, other than wars or famine, it is relatively easy to predict population trends.

(b) Other developments are harder to determine.

   (i) In 1900, a long-term investor would have invested in railway shares.

   (ii) In 1947, it was assumed that demand for computers would be no more than five worldwide.

   (iii) Even now, nobody really knows which inventions or innovations will succeed.

Activity 2 **(10 minutes)**

Think back to five years ago. What events that have had an impact on business organisations have occurred? Which could have been foreseen?

Hamel and Prahalad suggest, however, that **some companies are more 'prepared' to shape the future** than others, and that this **future-oriented stance is somehow embodied in the corporate culture**. Hamel and Prahalad offer a 'diagnostic' to indicate how future-oriented a company is.

Diagnostic statement	Protect the past	Create the future
Senior management's viewpoint about the future is ...	Conventional, reactive	Distinctive, far-sighted
Senior management spend most of their time on ...	Re-engineering current processes	Regenerating core strategies
Within the industry, the company ...	Follows the rules	Makes the rules
The company is better at ...	Operational efficiency	Building new

Diagnostic statement	Protect the past	Create the future
		businesses
To what extent does the company pursue competitive advantage by …	Catching up with competitors?	Creating new sources of competitive advantage?
How is the company's agenda for change actually set?	By competitors	By a vision of the future
Are managers	Engineers of the present?	Architects of the future?
Are employees	Anxious?	Hopeful?

Activity 3 **(30 minutes)**

Undertake this diagnostic test for your own company. Carry it out alone and then get another member of staff to do it – from another department if possible.

3 GAP ANALYSIS

Strategic planners must think about the extent to which new strategies are needed to enable the organisation to achieve its **objectives**. One technique whereby this can be done is **gap analysis.** Gap analysis is based on establishing:

(a) What are the **organisation's targets for achievement** over the planning period?

(b) What would the organisation be expected to achieve if it **did not** develop any new strategies, but **simply carried on in the current way** with the same products and selling to the same markets?

There will be a difference between the targets in (a) and expected achievements in (b). New strategies will then have to be developed which **will close this gap**, so that the organisation can expect to achieve its targets over the planning period.

Definition

Gap analysis is 'the comparison of an entity's ultimate objective with the sum of projections and already planned projects, identifying how the consequent gap might be filled'.

A forecast or projection based on existing performance: F_0 forecasts

The **F_0 forecast** is a forecast of the company's future results assuming that it **does nothing new**. The company is expected to continue to operate as at present without any changes in its products, markets, organisation, assets, human resources, research spending, financial structure, purchasing and so forth. Preparation of an F_0 forecast entails the following.

- The analysis of revenues, costs and volumes
- Projections into the future based on past trends

- Other factors affecting profits and return (eg in the environment, strikes, competitors)
- Finalising the forecast

The purpose of the F_0 forecast and gap analysis is to determine the **size of the task** facing the company if it wishes to achieve its target profits.

Forecasts can never be completely accurate. If possible, the error should be quantified in either of the following two ways.

(a) **Estimating likely variations.** For example 'in 2008 the forecast profit is £5 million with possible variations of plus or minus £2 million'.

(b) **Providing a probability distribution for profits.** For example 'in 2008 there is a 20% chance that profits will exceed £7 million, a 50% chance that they will exceed £5 million and an 80% chance that they will exceed £2½ million. Minimum profits in 2008 will be £2 million.'

The profit gap

The **profit gap** is the difference between the target profits (according to the overall corporate objectives of the company) and the profits on the F_0 forecast. Other forms of gap analysis (eg for sales revenue) can be developed.

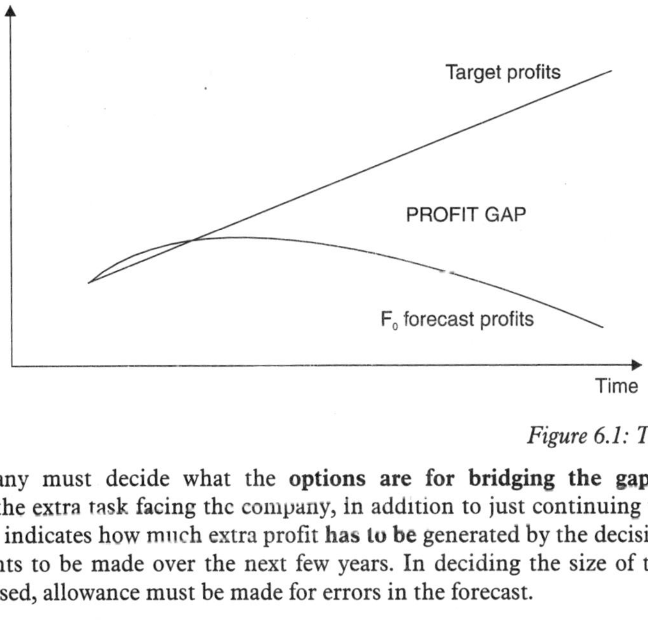

Figure 6.1: The profit gap

The company must decide what the **options are for bridging the gap.** This gap represents the extra task facing the company, in addition to just continuing the existing business. It indicates how much extra profit **has to be** generated by the decisions and the commitments to be made over the next few years. In deciding the size of the gap that must be closed, allowance must be made for errors in the forecast.

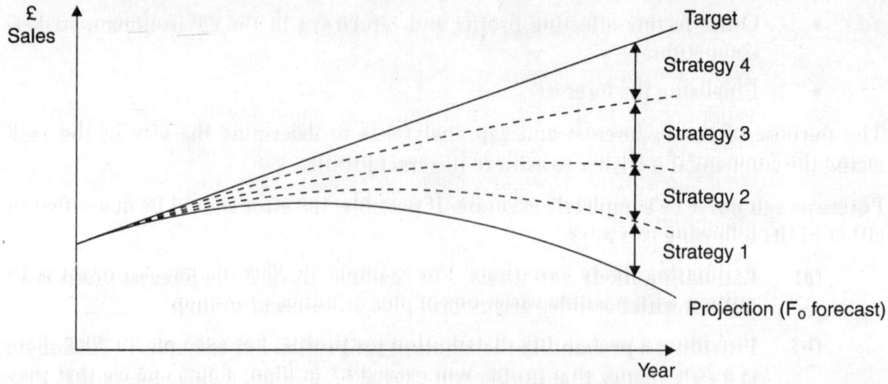

Figure 6.2: Strategies for bridging the profit gap

According to McDonald (2007) the gap can be filled in several ways.

(a) Improved productivity (eg reduce costs, increase prices)
(b) Market penetration (increased market share)
(c) New products and/or new markets
(d) New strategies (eg a joint venture)

The method chosen should be **consistent** with the company's **capabilities and strengths**. It is usually better to attempt to increase profits from **existing products and markets** at first, as this is the least risky.

4 VISION AND STRATEGIC INTENT

A strategic thinker should have a **vision** of:

- What the business is now
- What it could be in an ideal world
- What the ideal world would be like

A vision gives a general sense of direction to guide the company, even if there is not too much attention to detail.

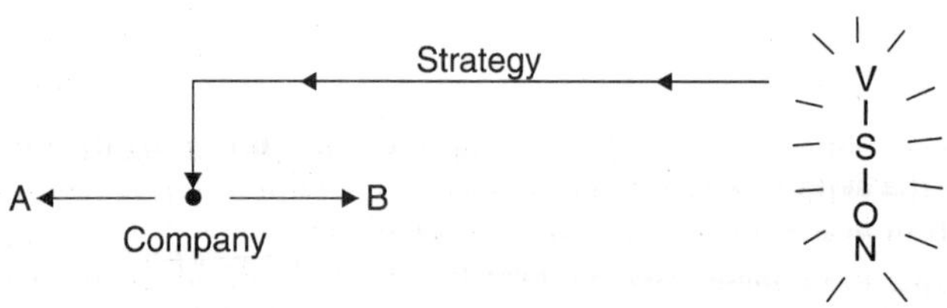

A company with two choices would move to 'B' rather than 'A'. The strategy draws on the vision. A vision might provide the 'boundaries' for the firm's direction.

Problems with vision

- It ignores real, practical problems.
- It can degenerate into wishful thinking on the part of managers, blinding them to reality.

4.1 Strategic intent

Strategic intent is similar to vision.

(a) 'A **dream** that energises a company' (Hamel and Prahalad 1994). It has an **emotional** core.

(b) It implies a '**stretch**' for the organisation, even if current resources will not satisfy the aspirations of the vision. It is more than just matching resources with objectives.

(c) Sense of **direction**. It is a long-term ambition, which enables the integration of complex skills within the firm.

(d) Sense of **discovery**: strategic intent offers a new destination for employees to work towards.

(e) It gives **coherence** to strategic plans.

'Strategic intent' aims to enthuse employees with the company's business goals, as if they are fighting a war. (**Values** in the long-term are possibly more motivating.)

5 THE ROLE OF THE MARKETING PLAN

5.1 Corporate strategy and business strategy

Definition

> **Corporate strategy** is concerned with identifying the scope of activities and markets with which the company wishes to be associated.

The direction in which a company will move forward will be dependent upon a number of factors.

(a) The nature of the **changing environment**

(b) The existing and future **resource capabilities** of the organisation

(c) The strategies adopted by **competitors**

(d) The **expectations and values** of the management and workforce

(e) The maintenance of a **competitive position** within the market

One way of looking at this is from the perspective of the three main players, as in the 'strategic triangle', so called by Japanese management consultant Kenichi Ohmae (1983).

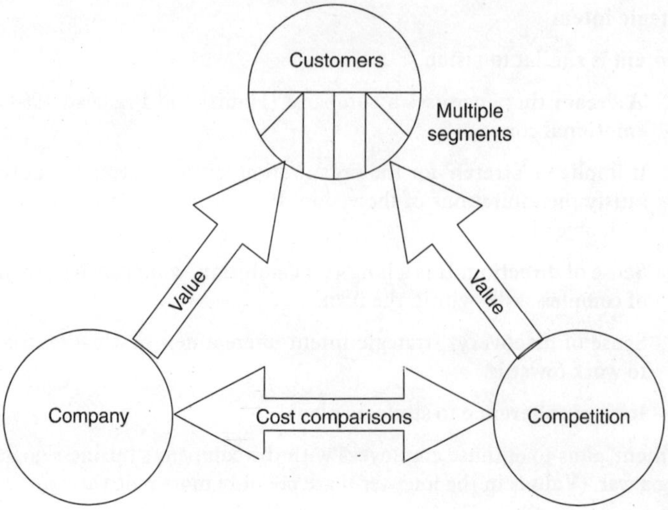

Figure 6.3: *Strategic triangle*
Source: *Ohmae* (1983)

Once the corporate strategy has been decided, this may then be translated into a **business unit strategy**. Business unit strategy is concerned with how individual strategic business units will compete within their chosen market.

Functional strategies (or operational strategies) encompassing marketing, finance, production and personnel will then be created to support the corporate or individual business unit strategy.

Within the marketing strategy, there will also be a breakdown at product group or brand level.

5.2 The role of marketing planning in the strategic planning process

Definition

> **Marketing planning** is the 'logical sequence and series of activities leading to the setting of marketing objectives and the formulation of plans for achieving them.' (*McDonald*, 2007)

Figure 6.4 below illustrates the relationship between corporate objectives and operational objectives at the functional marketing level.

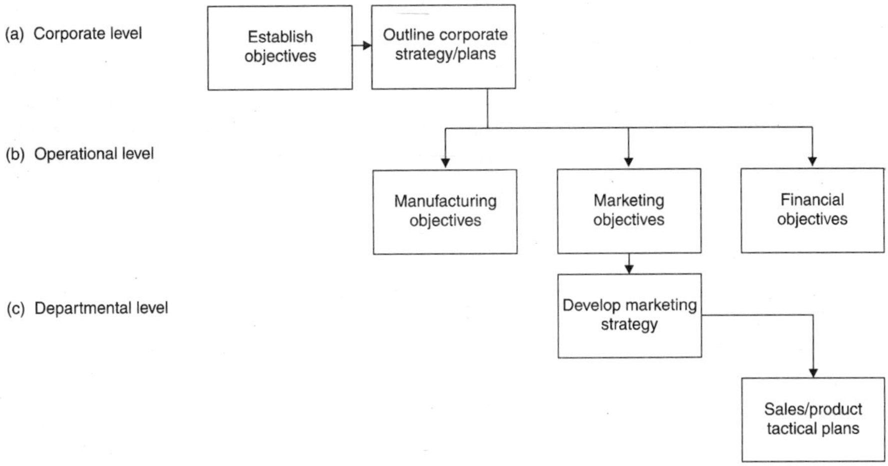

Figure 6.4: Relationship between corporate and operational objectives

Unless an organisation is so small that it is a single unit, without functional departments, the overall objectives of the organisation must indicate different requirements for different functions. While some corporate goals cannot be stated in quantifiable terms, subsidiary objectives must be very clear cut, so that performance can be measured. The SMART criteria are often used to ensure that objectives are adequately stated.

(a) **Specific.** Vague generalities must be avoided.

(b) **Measurable.** Desired outcomes must be quantified so that clear measures of performance can be set.

(c) **Attainable.** A pious hope is useless for controlling performance or motivating staff.

(d) **Results-oriented.** Objectives should be stated in terms of **outcomes** rather than inputs.

(e) **Time-bounded.** A time by which the objective is to be achieved should be set.

Marketing objectives should be clear statements of where the organisation wants to be in marketing terms. They describe what the organisation expects to achieve as a result of its planned marketing actions. Remembering the SMART criteria, examples of marketing objectives might look like this:

(a) 'To increase market share from the current X% to Y% by 2010.'

(b) 'To achieve a sales revenue of £X million at a cost of sales not exceeding 80% in 2010.'

Objectives can be set for overall achievement as above, or for elements of the strategic plan.

EXAMPLE

For example, if one of the strategies to achieve a profitable increase in sales revenue was to increase awareness of the product, then an advertising objective (a marketing sub-objective) might be: 'To increase product awareness in the target market from V% to W% in 2010.'

When developing a strategy, a company is seeking a **match with its operating environment**. This may mean adjusting the company's strategy to fit into the existing market environment. Overall, the strategy must enable the company to meet the specific needs of its consumers and to do so more efficiently than its competitors.

As we have already seen, strategies develop at a number of levels. To reiterate, **corporate strategy** is concerned with the overall development of an organisation's business activities, while **marketing strategy** is concerned with the organisation's activities in relation to the markets which it serves.

5.3 Marketing plans and other functional plans

Marketing plans are formulated to show how marketing can contribute to the corporate plan.

Marketing makes a particularly important input to corporate planning decisions. Information inputs from marketing to the **corporate** planning decisions perform a double duty in that they also provide the bases for deciding marketing objectives and strategies. **Marketing research** is vital to **all stages** of the marketing plan, hence the need for an **effective marketing information system.**

Aspect	Comment
The environmental audit	Reviews the organisation's position in relation to changes in the external environment (social/cultural, legal, economic, political and technological) and provides information which directly affects the setting of corporate objectives. The market place is, by definition, part of the 'environment'.
Competitor analysis	Provides competitor intelligence, competitor response models and so on which again influence corporate objectives, strategy and contingency planning.
The customer audit	Assesses the existing and potential customer bases to provide information as to whether to develop new markets.
Product portfolio analysis	Provides input for decisions as to whether to drop particular products and/or add new ones.
The sales forecast	Provides the basis for all other functional activities as well as marketing.

Activity 4 **(30 minutes)**

Consider the company you work for, or your college. Your brief is to undertake an environmental audit and competitor analysis for the industry, or college sector.

The **marketing plan** uniquely is concerned with **products** and **markets**.

(a) These are typically stated in terms of market share, sales volume, levels of distribution and profitability.

(b) Decisions might be taken as to the type of products sold to particular customer groups.

Objectives of other departments

(a) The marketing manager's plans are often frustrated by other people in the organisation. These 'blockers' can be people in the marketing department but are more likely to be people in other departments.

(b) The less an organisation is truly market-oriented, the more likely it is that marketing plans are ineffective. Each functional area has its own particular concerns and constraints and, at strategic level, marketers have to take these into account if they want to achieve anything.

What other departments do

Department	**Activity**
Production	Purchasing, acquiring resources and forming them into products/services the firm can offer.
Human resources	Obtaining the right number of people at the right level of skills. This is vital in **service industries** for successful marketing plans – people are integral to the service marketing mix because they act as 'front-line' marketers as representatives of the face of the organisation.
Finance	The need to remain profitable, raising and distributing money and maintaining a healthy cash-flow.
Research and development	May be independent of either production or marketing.
Information Technology (IT)	In firms where **information** is a key resource, there might be separate plans and strategies for information technology. Financial services firms such as banks pay particular attention to IT. **Database marketing** depends on effective use of IT.

All these functional plans exist in the wide framework of the corporate plan. In practice all these plans are interrelated.

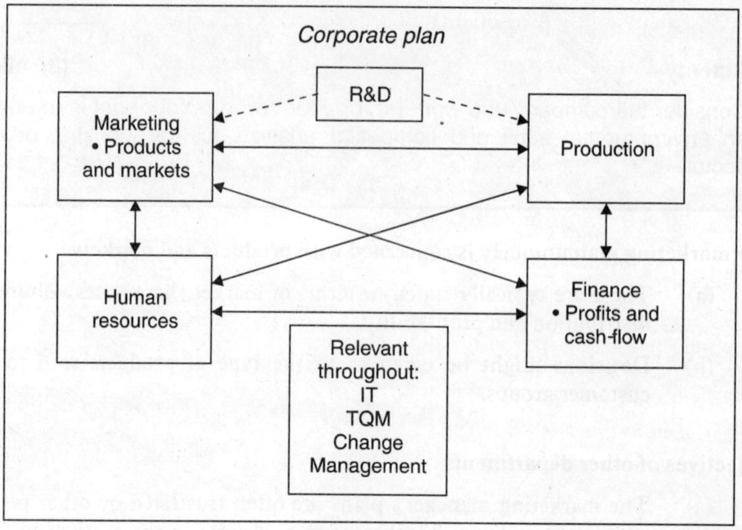

Figure 6.5: Interrelationships of functional plan

5.4 Activities crossing functional boundaries

Certain activities cannot be really packaged into 'functional plans'.

(a) **Total quality management (TQM)** is relevant to the whole organisation.

  (i) **Marketing**: quality means satisfying customer needs.

  (ii) **Production**: TQM employs a very specific set of production techniques to reduce variation in the physical process of manufacture and to enhance quality.

  (iii) **R&D**: TQM requires precise attention to the design of both products and processes.

  (iv) **Human resources**: TQM requires a change in the way people work, so that continuous improvement can be made to manufacturing processes.

  (v) **Finance**: TQM supporters believe that the cost of preventing mistakes is less than the cost of rectifying them.

(b) **Change management** programmes affect every function within the organisation. Examples include change to the organisation structure and radical new approaches to business such as **business process re-engineering**.

(c) **Research and development.** This requires input from marketing and production.

At strategic level, marketing cannot be managed in a vacuum. Marketing directors and managers cannot take strategic decisions on their own without reference to the managing director and the directors of other functions – ie corporate management as a team.

5.5 The marketing plan in outline

There is no standard template of contents for a marketing plan. Different organisations will find it appropriate to consider different things at different times in their development. Here is a broad outline.

The marketing plan – an outline

Situation analysis	**See Chapter(s)**
• PESTEL	8
• SWOT	10
• Market analysis	8, 9
Marketing strategy	
• Objectives	6
• Tactics	6
• Marketing mix	10, 11
Numerical forecasts/budget	
• Sales • Expenses	} 12
Controls	
• Marketing organisation	7
• Performance measures	12

On page 163 we present a diagram of the **concise** framework for the marketing plan.

5.6 Strategic and tactical decisions in marketing

It is also worthwhile considering the difference between a **strategic marketing plan** and a **tactical marketing plan**.

(a) **Strategic marketing plan**

- (i) Three to five or more years long.
- (ii) Defines scope of product and market activities.
- (iii) Aims to match the activities of the firm to its distinctive competences.

(b) **Tactical marketing plan**

- (i) One-year time horizon
- (ii) Generally based on existing products and markets
- (iii) Concerned with marketing mix issues

EXAMPLE

Here is the Coca-Cola Company's mission statement for Stakeholders which is published in Jeffrey Abrahams' book, 101 Mission Statements From Top Companies (Ten Speed Press, 2007): "The Coca-Cola Promise: The Coca-Cola Company exists to benefit and refresh everyone it touches. The basic proposition of our business is simple, solid, and timeless. When we bring refreshment, value, joy and fun to our stakeholders, then we successfully nurture and protect our brands, particularly Coca-Cola. That is the key to fulfilling our ultimate obligation to provide consistently attractive returns to the owners of our business."

5.7 Content of marketing plan

Kotler identifies the formulation of **marketing plans** as follows.

Section	**Content**
The executive summary	This is the finalised planning document with a summary of the main goals and recommendations in the plan.
Situation analysis	This consists of the SWOT analysis and forecasts.
Objectives and goals	What the organisation is hoping to achieve, or needs to achieve, perhaps in terms of market share or 'bottom line' profits and returns.
Marketing strategy	This considers the selection of target markets, the marketing mix and marketing expenditure levels.
Action programme	This sets out how these various strategies are going to be achieved.
Budgets	These are developed from the action programme.
Controls	These will be set up to monitor the progress of the plan and the budget.

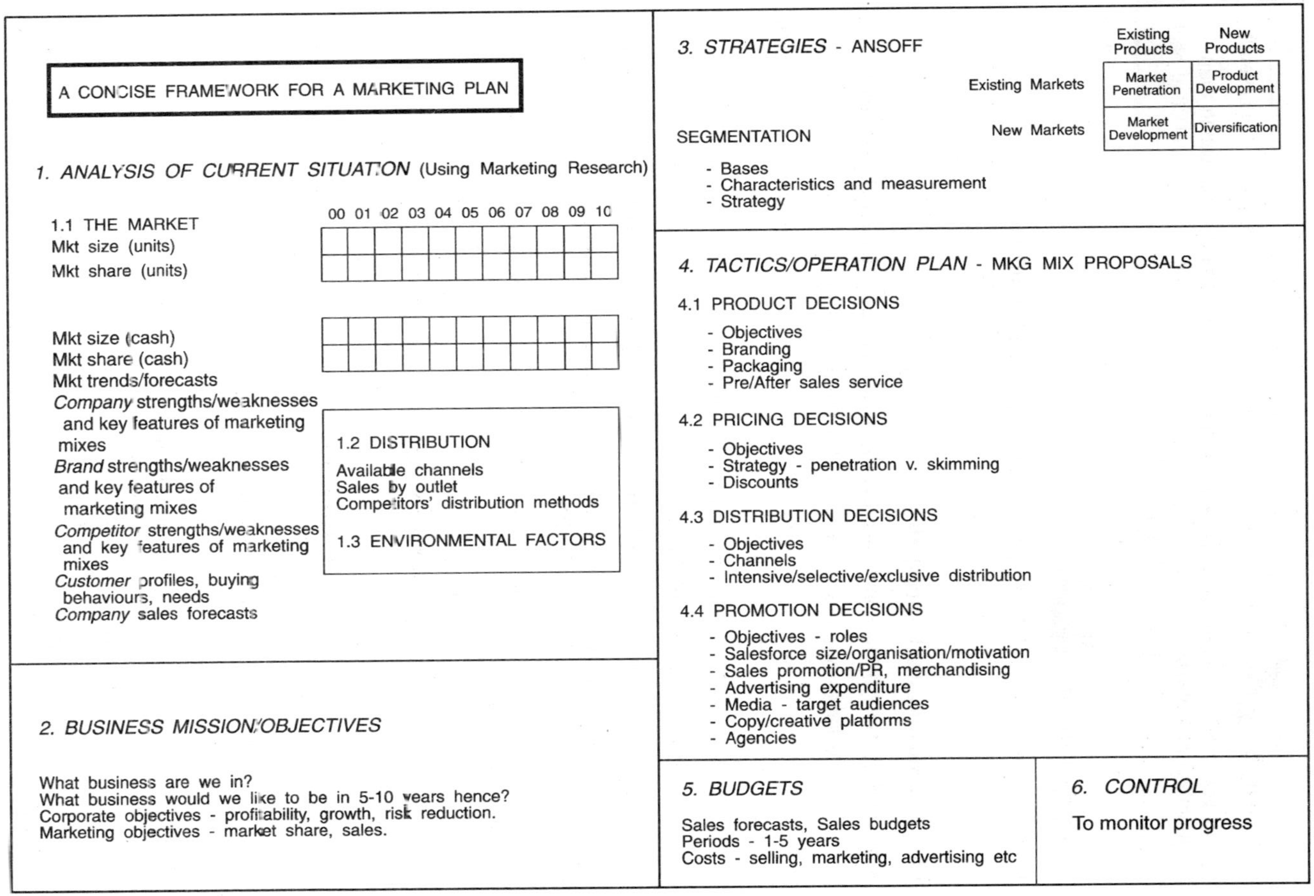

Figure 6.6: Example of a marketing plan

Activity 5 **(1 hour)**

For your own company or college undertake section 2 of the marketing plan – business objectives.

FOR DISCUSSION

'Control' is the most neglected aspect of the marketing planning process.

5.8 Formulating marketing strategy

A **marketing strategy** is a plan to achieve the organisation's objectives by specifying.

(a) What resources should be allocated to marketing.

(b) How those resources should be used to take advantage of opportunities which are expected to arise in the future.

In the context of applying the **marketing concept**, a marketing strategy would:

(a) **Identify target markets** and customer needs in those markets

(b) Plan products which will **satisfy the needs** of those markets

(c) **Organise marketing resources**, so as to match products with customers in the most efficient and effective way possible.

The strategic concepts of **segmentation** and **product positioning** should be at the heart of modern marketing planning.

Analyse and describe market segments

↓

Test segments for (commercial) validity

↓

Choose a competitive segmentation strategy

↓

Develop a market positioning/product positioning strategy

FOR EXAMPLE

According to McDonald (2007) the most frequently cited problems arising from a lack of marketing planning are:

1 Lost opportunities for profit
2 Meaningless numbers in long-range plans
3 Unrealistic objectives
4 Lack of actionable market information

5 Interfunctional strife
6 Management frustration
7 Proliferation of products and markets
8 Wasted promotional expenditure
9 Pricing confusion
10 Growing vulnerability to environmental change
11 Loss of control over the business

5.9 The marketing action plan: marketing mix proposals

The link between the formulation and the implementation of marketing strategy is the **marketing action plan,** which identifies how the mix will be deployed. The mix represents the **controlled** use of a firm's resources allocated to the marketing budget.

(a) The marketing mix may be simplified into the four Ps plus three Ps for service.

  (i) **Product:** quality, features, fashion, packaging and branding, after sales service, guarantees, durability etc.

  (ii) **Price:** the level of price, credit terms, discounts guarantees.

  (iii) **Place:** factors here include the location of sales outlets and the number and type of sales outlets (shops, supermarkets etc), the location of service departments, stock levels and transportation and delivery services.

  (iv) **Promotion** advertising, sales promotion, selling, PR.

  (v) **People**: courtesy, competence of the people delivering the service.

  (vi) **Processes**: how the service is delivered.

  (vii) **Physical evidence**: the environment of the service encounter.

(b) **Different marketing mixes** will appeal to different **market segments** in any particular market.

(c) The marketing mix for a product must be **planned** in advance. It should also be **reviewed** in the light of experience and, if product sales have not been as good as expected, managers might take **control action** by should be given to changing the mix, for example, lowering product quality, reducing price and spending more on advertising.

> **Activity 6** **(1 hour)**
>
> Following on from your environmental and competitor audit (Activity 4) in your chosen industry or college, investigate what the main market leaders' approach to segmentation and marketing mix are.

5.10 Barriers to marketing planning

Not all businesses use a marketing planning approach. Indeed, not all businesses use any kind of formal planning at all. Even in quite large and successful organisations, including some that claim to be market or customer oriented, the marketing planning process is of limited effectiveness. There are a number of reasons for this: these are sometimes called **barriers to marketing planning**, or barriers to implementation.

The barriers

(a) **Confusion of objectives, strategy and tactics** arises when managers concentrate on short-term objectives, such as sales targets and annual budgets and ignore the need for longer-term strategic direction of the firm's activities. Too many senior managers believe they are planning strategically when they are actually managing a short-term tactical operation.

(b) **Isolation of the marketing function** arises when a firm attempts to introduce a marketing orientation but thinks this can be done simply by creating a marketing department. For the necessary transformation to occur, the other functions must all alter their mode of operation in order to put the customer at the centre of the business. Where prices are set by the finance department, product development in the hands of technical staff, distribution is organised by logistics experts and sales dealt with by a separate sales department, for example, it is unreasonable to expect the most capable marketer to achieve anything.

(c) **Organisational barriers** can exist in isolation, but where there is more than one, they are likely to interact.

   (i) **Cultural** barriers exist when there is a lack of acceptance by influential people in the organisation that planning and marketing are important.

   (ii) **Change management** barriers are similar to cultural barriers and exist when there is a need for change that is not accepted by the people running the organisation.

   (iii) **Behavioural** barriers can exist even when the need for planning is accepted but top management do not provide the support that is needed or there is a lack of involvement by key figures in other organisational functions.

   (iv) **Cognitive** barriers arise when the knowledge and skill required to implement planning are unavailable.

   (v) **Systems and procedures** may be inadequate or inappropriate or they may be a lack of data.

   (vi) **Resources**, such as money, staff and time, may be scarce

(d) **Competitor strategy and activity** may be sufficiently vigorous and creative to cause management to concentrate on countering them; this attention to immediate operational priorities distracts marketing managers from the priorities and processes of marketing planning, leading to a failure to plan for the longer-term.

McDonald (2007) discusses barriers to marketing planning in some detail, and presents what he terms the '**Ten S' approach** to overcoming them. The following table has been adapted from this.

Barrier	How to overcome it
1 **Confusing marketing tactics and strategy**	**'Strategy before tactics'** Develop a three year strategic plan first, before the lower level operational plan. Tactics need to be directive and demonstrate how jointly they will contribute to achieve the strategy.
2 **Isolation of the marketing function**	**'Situate marketing within operations'** Marketing needs to be close to the customer.
3 **Confusing marketing 'function' with 'concept'**	**'Shared values about marketing'** It should be a 'market-focused' state of mind throughout the whole organisation, rather than being regarded purely as a set of activities.
4 **Organisational barriers**	**'Structure around markets'** Organisation structure should reflect the marketplace (eg customer groups) rather than functional departments.
5 **Lack of in-depth analysis**	**'Scan the environment thoroughly'** Undertake an effective marketing audit.
6 **Confusion between process and output**	**'Summarise information in SWOT analyses'** The process of gathering information (or marketing intelligence) will lead to the marketing plan.
7 **Lack of knowledge and skills**	**'Skills and knowledge'** Ensure that the relevant people have them.
8 **Lack of a systematic approach**	**'Systematise the process'** Have a set of written procedures so that all issues are covered in all areas of the business.
9 **Failure to prioritise objectives**	**'Sequence objectives'** According to their impact on the organisation and the resources required.
10 **Hostile corporate cultures**	**'Style and culture'** Needs the participation and support of the leaders of the organisation.

In summary, here are some pointers for successful marketing planning

(a) A bureaucratic approach must be avoided.
(b) All functions must contribute to the process.
(c) The chief executive and top management must give their support.
(d) The planning process must be integrated with operations.

Chapter roundup

- Marketing as a business orientation is being customer-focused on customer needs. It is also a business function often with a department in an organisation.
- Key elements to manage market-led strategic change are:
  - Strategies are based on customers and markets
  - Internal programmes and external actions are driven by such strategies
  - The company must 'get its act together' in order to deliver its strategy. This involves more than the marketing department
  - Cross-functional teams cross organisational boundaries to get the job done
  - New type of relationships are created
  - New ways of doing business are supported by a new information technology infrastructure
- Challenges to the future centre around:
  - Sophisticated customers
  - New competitors
  - New types of organisation
  - New ways of doing business
- The future can be better understood by using Hamel & Prahalad's diagnostic test in Section 2.
- Gap analysis shows any differences between an organisation's targets and its expectations of achievement if the current strategy is pursued.
- Strategies can then be developed to 'fill' the gap, but they must be consistent with the organisation's capabilities and strengths.
- A vision gives general strategic direction to an organisation.
- Marketing plans are designed to contribute to the corporate plan, being clear statements of where the organisation wants to be in marketing terms.
- Marketing plans will include information on the following.
  - An environmental audit
  - Competitor analysis
  - A customer audit
  - Product portfolio analysis
  - Sales forecasts
- A marketing plan will consist of:
  - Analysis of current situation (market, distribution and environment)
  - Business mission/objective
  - Strategies
  - Tactics (operational plan)
  - Budgets
  - Control
- Strategies should take account of market segmentation and product positioning.
- The operational plan should cover all aspects of the extended marketing mix.
- Barriers to marketing planning can be overcome using McDonald's 'Ten S' approach.

Quick quiz

1. What is meant by market orientation?
2. What are the four main challenges according to Piercy for the market-led organisation?
3. How can a company determine how 'future-oriented' it is?
4. What is 'gap analysis'?
5. Why should organisations develop marketing plans?
6. What type of information does a company need to develop a marketing plan?
7. Give an example of a business activity that crosses functional boundaries.
8. Outline the steps in developing a marketing plan.
9. What is the extended marketing mix (7 Ps)?
10. What are the barriers to marketing planning?

Answers to quick quiz

1. The organisational culture where creating superior customer value is the main business objective.
2. Sophisticated customers, new competitors, new types of organisation, new ways of doing business.
3. A company could undertake Hamel and Prahalad's diagnostic test.
4. A comparison of an organisation's ultimate objective with the sum of projections and already planned projects, identifying how a gap could be filled.
5. To contribute to the organisation's corporate planning process to enable the organisation to plan strategies for the future.
6. Information on the environment, on competitors, on customers, on sales and products.
7. Could be TQM, change management programmes or research and development.
8. Analysis
Objectives
Strategies
Tactics
Control
9. Product, Price, Place, Promotion, People, Processes, Physical evidence.
10. See paragraph 5.10.

Answers to activities

1 The answer to this will depend on the company you have chosen.

2 The rapid advance of e-commerce: probably the speed of the advance could not be foreseen.

Greater customer willingness to complain; could not be foreseen.

Economic peaks and troughs: should be foreseeable.

New financial services legislation: not foreseeable five years ago.

Changes of government: probably foreseeable.

3 The answer to this will depend on the company you have chosen.

4 The answer to this will depend on the company you have chosen.

5 The answer to this will depend on the company you have chosen.

6 The answer to this will depend on the company you have chosen.

Chapter 7:
ORGANISATIONAL CAPABILITY

Introduction

A look at the internal environment of an organisation is a way of identifying strengths and weaknesses. The other functions of the organisation effectively act as constraints over what marketing personnel can achieve.

A company needs to evaluate its ability to compete and satisfy customer needs. The firm's resources, once identified, must be harnessed to a market orientation to ensure that those resources are directed at satisfying those needs.

There are a number of approaches to be taken with regard to corporate capability. In this chapter we conduct an overview of resources in the context of organisational effectiveness. The key issues are what resources the organisation has and how they are deployed.

Your objectives

In this chapter you will learn about the following.

(a) How resources and limiting factors can affect business operations

(b) The importance of the marketing audit process

(c) The difference between marketing efficiency and effectiveness

(d) How the PLC concept can be used for marketing planning

(e) How BCG and value chain analysis can be used for strategic planning

1 RESOURCES AND LIMITING FACTORS

An analysis of corporate/marketing resources covers:

- What the organisation currently has or owns
- What the organisation has access to, even if it currently does not own the resources
- How effectively it **deploys** its resources

1.1 Resource audit

A **resource audit** is a review of the organisation resources which can be grouped into these categories (*Hooley, Saunders and Piercy* (2003)).

Resource	Comment
Technical resources	• Technical ability • Processes for NPD • Ability to convert new technology into new marketing products
Financial standing	Firms with a good financial standing find it easier to raise money
Managerial skills	An effective management is a key organisation resource in planning activities, controlling the organisation and motivating staff.
Organisation	Organisation structure can be a resource for marketers, for example product divisionalisation or brand management control at brand level. The organisation structure should facilitate communication and decision-making.
Information systems	Information systems have a strategic role.

Resources are of no value unless they are organised into systems, and so a resource audit should go on to consider how well or how badly resources have been utilised, and whether the organisation's systems are **effective** and **efficient** in meeting customer needs profitably.

Activity 1 **(30 minutes)**

Review the above resource audit using the example of either your company or your college.

1.2 Limiting factors

Every organisation operates under resource **constraints**.

Definition

A **limiting factor** or **key factor** is 'a factor which at any time or over a period may limit the activity of an entity, often one where there is shortage or difficulty of supply'.

EXAMPLES

Possible limiting factors

- A shortage of production capacity
- A limited number of key personnel, such as salespeople with technical knowledge
- A restricted distribution network
- Too few managers with knowledge about finance, or overseas markets
- Inadequate research design resources to develop new products or services
- A poor system of strategic intelligence
- Lack of money
- A lack of staff who are adequately trained

Once the limiting factor has been identified, the planners should:

- **Short-term,** make best use of the resources available
- **Long-term,** reduce the limitation

1.3 Resource use

Resource use is concerned with the **efficiency** with which resources are used, and the **effectiveness** of their use in achieving the planning objectives of the business.

Distinctive competences

A strategic approach involves identifying a firm's **competences.** Members of organisations develop judgements about what they think the company can do well – its core competence. These competences may derive from:

- **Experience** in making and marketing a product or service
- The talents and potential of individuals in the organisation
- The **quality of co-ordination**/distribution

Definition

> The **distinctive competence** of an organisation is what it does well, or better, than its rivals.

Tests for identifying a core competence

(a) It provides potential **access to a wide variety of markets.** GPS of France developed a 'core competence' in 'one-hour' processing, enabling it to process films and build reading glasses in one hour.

(b) It **contributes significantly to the value enjoyed** by the customer. For example, in GPS in (a) above, the waiting time restriction was very important.

(c) It should be **hard for a competitor to copy,** if it is technically complex, involves specialised processes, involves complex interrelationships between different people in the organisation or is hard to define.

In many cases, a company might choose to **combine competences.**

Bear in mind that relying on a competence is no substitute for a strategy. However, **distinctive competences are an important support for competitive positioning.**

FOR DISCUSSION

Skoda has been successful in changing its image. What do you consider its core competences?

EXAMPLE

"Rentokil Initial plc employs over 78,000 people in over 50 countries, offering the strengths and experience of a multi-national organisation, whilst retaining the agility and characteristics of a local company. Services include: pest control, package delivery, interior landscaping, catering, cleaning, washroom solutions and textiles." Exposure to cyclical business is minimal, and it has expanded into all the major developed economies.

Head office is lean and mean and there are no functional hierarchies. Rentokil is run through a branch structure whereby every manager has their own budget and profit centre and is incentivised according to their own success. There are no big ad budgets: marketing is embedded in the way everyone does their job, and decision making is influenced by a true 'customer needs first' orientation. Market intelligence is facilitated by the fact that most employees have daily contact with their customers. Not only is profit responsibility devolved as far as possible down the organisation, but the businesses are run geographically rather than by business stream. What's more, all Rentokil's services are presented and marketed in the same way in every country where they operate.

http://www.rentokil-initial.com

---

2 MARKETING AUDITS AND MARKETING EFFECTIVENESS

2.1 Marketing audits

Definition

> A **marketing audit** is an examination of a company's marketing environment and activities with a view to determining problem areas and opportunities and recommending a plan to improve performance.'

A marketing audit does not exist in the compulsory formal sense that an external financial audit does. For proper strategic control, however, a marketing audit should have the following features.

(a) **Regular**. It should be conducted **regularly,** for example once a year.

(b) **Comprehensive**. It should take a **comprehensive** look at every product, market, distribution channel, ingredient in the marketing mix etc. It should not be restricted to areas of apparent ineffectiveness (for example an unprofitable product, a troublesome distribution channel, low efficiency on direct selling etc).

(c) **Systematic**. It should be carried out according to a set of predetermined, specified procedures.

(d) **Independence**. A consultant might be appointed, or someone else within the organisation.

FOR DISCUSSION

An outside independent consultant is the best person to undertake a marketing audit.

2.2 The audit procedure

A marketing audit should consider the following areas.

- The macro- and micro-marketing environments
- Marketing strategies
- Marketing systems
- Marketing organisation
- Marketing function

The marketing environment

(a) **Micro**. What are the organisation's major markets, and what is the segmentation of these markets? What are the future prospects of each market segment?

(i) Who are the customers, what is known about customer needs, intentions and behaviour?

(ii) Who are the competitors, and what is their standing in the market?

(b) **Macro**. Have there been any significant developments in the broader environment (for example economic, or political changes, population or social changes etc)?

Activity 2 **(30 minutes)**

Choose a magazine you are familiar with. Undertake a short analysis of the micro- and macro-factors of its marketing environment.

Marketing strategy audit

(a) What are the organisation's marketing objectives and how do they relate to overall objectives? Are they reasonable?

(b) Are enough (or too many) resources being committed to marketing to enable the objectives to be achieved? Is the division of costs between products, areas etc satisfactory?

Marketing systems. What are the procedures for formulating marketing plans and management control of these plans? Are they satisfactory?

Marketing organisation. Does the organisation have the structural capability to implement the plan?

Marketing functions. A review of the effectiveness of each element of the mix (eg advertising and sales promotion activities) should be carried out.

(a) A review of **sales and price levels** should be made (for example supply and demand, customer attitudes, the use of temporary price reductions etc).

(b) A review of the **state of each individual product** (ie its market 'health') and of the product mix as a whole should be made.

(c) A critical analysis of the **distribution system** should be made, with a view to finding improvements.

Marketing productivity. How profitable and cost-effective is the marketing programme?

Advantages of a marketing audit

- It should reduce the need for crisis management
- It should identify information needs
- A formal process forces people to think

2.3 Efficiency and effectiveness of marketing

Definitions

> (a) **Efficiency**: gaining maximum output for a minimum input and is normally used relatively (ie in comparison to a standard or norm, to competitors, to industry norms, or the PIMS database).
>
> (b) **Effectiveness**: doing the right things rather than doing things right. A firm can be incredibly efficient in producing widgets at the lowest cost but if no one will buy them it is all to no effect and it will soon be out of business.

A company that is both efficient and effective will prosper. A company that is inefficient but effective will survive, at least in the short term. A company that is both inefficient and ineffective will die quickly. Let us put this on a grid.

Efficiency \ Effectiveness	High	Low
High	THRIVE	DIE SLOWLY
Low	SURVIVE	DIE QUICKLY

Figure 7.1: Efficiency: effectiveness grid
Source: *Wilson, Gilligan, Pearson*

FOR DISCUSSION

Effectiveness is more important than efficiency.

2.4 The importance of marketing effectiveness

Although it is obviously true that marketing effectiveness is a vital component of organisational effectiveness, it is not always easy to measure precisely, especially as marketing 'assets' are hard to measure and value.

EXAMPLE

Major tasks facing those responsible for marketing campaign effectiveness

(a) Who should receive messages
(b) What the messages should say
(c) What image of the organisation/brand receivers should retain
(d) How much is to be invested in the process
(e) How the messages are to be delivered
(f) What actions receivers should take
(g) How the whole process should be controlled
(h) How to determine what was achieved

The marketing excellence framework

In *Manufacturing: the Marketing Solution,* the Chartered Institute of Marketing (CIM) developed a framework for evaluating companies' marketing operations. A sample of 44 companies from the UK's manufacturing sector was taken, and each company's marketing activities were assessed and scored on a marketing excellence framework. Then, the marketing excellence score was compared with financial results.

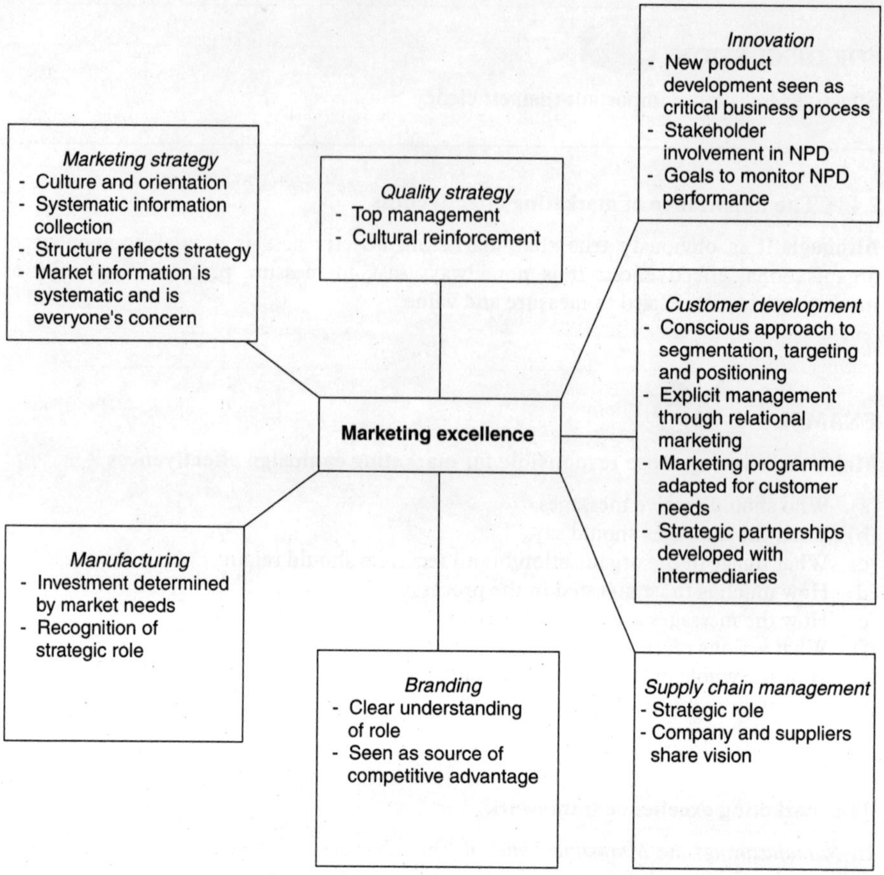

Figure 7.2: Marketing excellence

Measuring marketing capability

Kotler has developed the thinking on marketing effectiveness into a general purpose rating tool based upon the following fifteen questions, as adapted in the table opposite.

Marketing effectiveness rating

Customer philosophy

1 To what extent does management recognise the need to organise the company to satisfy specific market demands?

2 To what extent is the marketing programme tailored to the needs of different market segments?

3 Does management adopt a systems approach to planning, with recognition being given to the interrelationships between the environment, suppliers, channels, customers and competitors?

Marketing organisation

4 To what extent does senior management attempt to control and integrate the major marketing functions?

5 What sort of relationship exists between marketing management and the management of the R&D, finance, production and manufacturing functions?

6 How well organised is the new product development process?

Marketing information

7 How frequently does the company conduct marketing research studies of customers, channels and competitors?

8 To what extent is management aware of the sales potential and profitability of different market segments, customers, territories, products and order sizes?

9 What effort is made to measure the cost-effectiveness of different levels and types of marketing expenditure?

The strategic perspective

10 How formalised is the marketing planning process?

11 What is the quality of the thinking that underlies the current marketing strategy?

12 To what extent does management engage in contingency thinking and planning?

Operational efficiency

13 How well is senior management thinking on marketing communicated and implemented down the line?

14 Does marketing management do an effective job with the resources available?

15 Does management respond quickly and effectively to unexpected developments in the market-place?

Each question can be answered on three levels.

(a) Question 1 could have answers:

1.1 To no extent
1.2 To some extent
1.3 To a very high extent

(b) Question 5 could have answers:

5.1	Extremely poor, antagonism exists, marketing regarded as being too demanding
5.2	Normally satisfactory although there is an underlying attitude that each department is basically self-serving
5.3	Extremely good with all departments working together to serve the customer

(c) Each of these three levels is then allocated a score of 0, 1, or 2:

Poor = 0
Satisfactory = 1
Excellent = 2

(d) Each manager works his way through the fifteen questions in order to arrive at a score. The scores are then aggregated and averaged. The overall measure of marketing effectiveness can then be assessed against the following scale.

0 – 5	=	None	Firm's survival in doubt
6 – 10	=	Poor	
11 – 15	=	Fair	Opportunity to improve
16 – 20	=	Good	
21 – 25	=	Very good	
26 – 30	=	Superior	Beware complacency

EXAMPLE

According to Schultz *et al.* (*Integrated Marketing Communications – Putting it Together and Making it Work, 2000*):

'What exists in the mental network of the consumer or the prospect is truly where marketing value resides. [It] is what people believe, not what is true. [It] is what people want, not what is available; what people dream about, not what they know that really differentiates one product from another in a parity marketplace. That is why...communications is rapidly becoming the major marketing force of today and certainly tomorrow.'

So the proper co-ordination of all marketing messages becomes extremely important. What the marketer says about a product must fit with whatever information the customer has already collected.

3 THE PRODUCT LIFE CYCLE

Many firms make a number of different products or services. Each product or service has its own financial, marketing and risk characteristics. The combination of products or services influences the attractiveness and profitability of the firm.

The profitability and sales of a product can be expected to change over time. The **product life cycle (PLC)** is an attempt to recognise distinct stages in a product's sales history. Marketing managers distinguish between product class, form and brand.

Definitions

(a) **Product class:** this is a broad category of product, such as cars, washing machines, newspapers, also referred to as the generic product.

(b) **Product form:** within a product class there are different forms that the product can take, for example five-door hatchback cars or two-seater sports cars, twin tub or front-loading automatic washing machines, national daily newspapers or weekly local papers etc.

(c) **Brand:** the particular type of the product form (for example Ford Fiesta, Vauxhall Astra; *Financial Times*, *Daily Mail*, *Sun* etc).

3.1 Stages

The product life cycle applies in differing degrees to each of the three cases. A product-class (eg cars) may have a long maturity stage, and a particular make or brand **might** have an erratic life cycle (eg Rolls Royce) or not. Product forms however tend to conform to the 'classic' life cycle pattern, commonly described by a curve as follows.

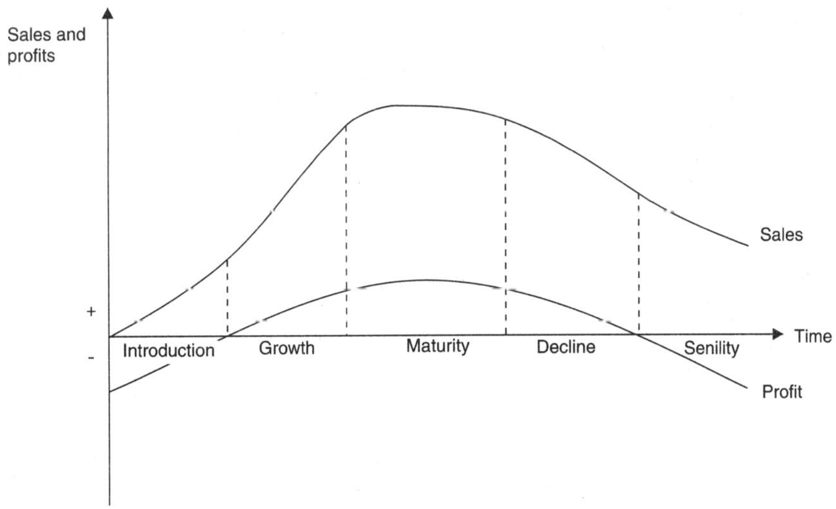

Figure 7.3: The product life cycle

Introduction

(a) A new product takes time to find acceptance by would-be purchasers and there is a slow growth in sales. Unit costs are high because of low output and expensive sales promotion.

(b) There may be early teething troubles with production technology.

(c) The product for the time being is a loss-maker.

Growth

(a) If the new product gains market acceptance, sales will eventually rise more sharply and the product will start to make profits.

(b) Competitors are attracted. As sales and production rise, unit costs fall.

Maturity

(a) The rate of sales growth slows down and the product reaches a period of maturity which is probably the longest period of a successful product's life.

(b) Most products on the market will be at the mature stage of their life.

(c) Profits are good.

Decline

(a) Some products reach a stage of decline, which may be slow or fast.

(b) Eventually, sales will begin to decline so that there is over-capacity of production in the industry.

(c) Severe competition occurs, profits fall and some producers leave the market.

(d) The remaining producers seek means of prolonging the product life by modifying it and searching for new market segments.

(e) Many producers are reluctant to leave the market, although some inevitably do because of falling profits.

Activity 3 **(5 minutes)**

What would the PLC curve look like for a 'fad' product such as the Big Billy Bass singing fish?

The PLC is not the same shape for every product; fad items for example are often a spike shape. It is also true to say that the concept suggests that marketers are powerless to alter the shape of the PLC. This is clearly not true with the long established and famous example of Johnson & Johnson baby lotion. When the lotion entered the decline phase, the company sought a new market and successfully reversed the downward trend with their slogan ' best for baby – best for you' targeting women as users of the product. It is essential therefore that the marketer regards the PLC as a tool to help identify the stage of a product or brand life rather than an inevitable pattern of sales which they should simply accept.

3.2 The PLC and marketing planning

It is essential that firms plan their portfolio of products to ensure that new products are generating positive cash-flow before existing 'earners' enter the decline stage.

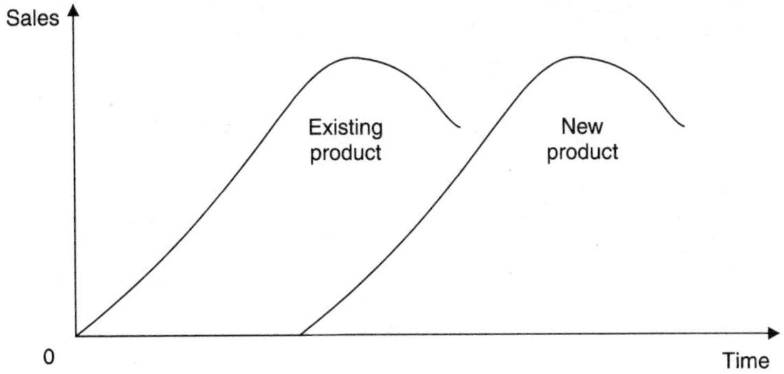

In the situation above the company is likely to experience cash-flow problems.

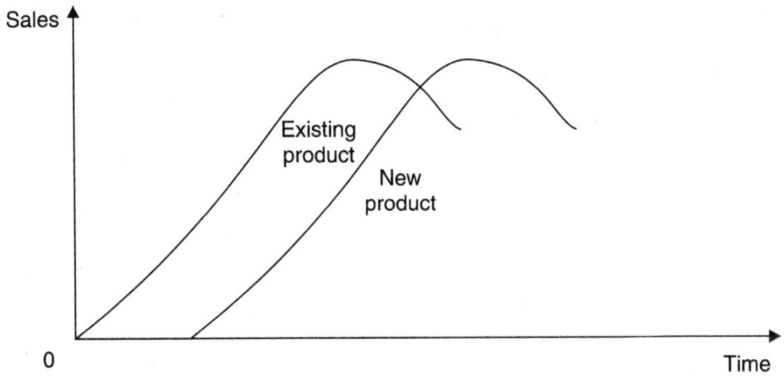

Figure 7.4: PLC and cash flow

By considering the product life cycle of the existing product when planning the timing for launch of a new product cash-flow problems can be avoided.

It is perhaps easy enough to accept that products have a life cycle, but it is not so easy to sort out how far through its life a product is, and what its expected future life might be.

(a) There ought to be a **regular review** of existing products, as a part of marketing management responsibilities.

(b) **Sources of PLC predictions**

- (i) An analysis of past sales and profit trends
- (ii) The history of other products
- (iii) Marketing research
- (iv) If possible, an analysis of competitors
- (v) A review of technological developments

(c) The future of each product should be estimated in terms of both sales revenue and profits.

Decisions for each product

(a) **Continue selling,** with no foreseeable intention yet of stopping production.

(b) **Prolong the product's life,** perhaps by adjusting the mix or finding new customers.

(c) **Stop producing** the product.

The possible implications of each stage are shown in the table opposite.

3.3 The product life cycle and the marketing orientation

Does the PLC promote a 'product-oriented' focus when in fact a 'market-oriented' focus is necessary? Ansoff extended the PLC concept to encompass the **demand/technology life cycle** (DLC), and the technology life cycle (TLC). The diagram below illustrates how a **demand life cycle** is made up of a number of **technology life cycles** which in turn are composed of PLCs.

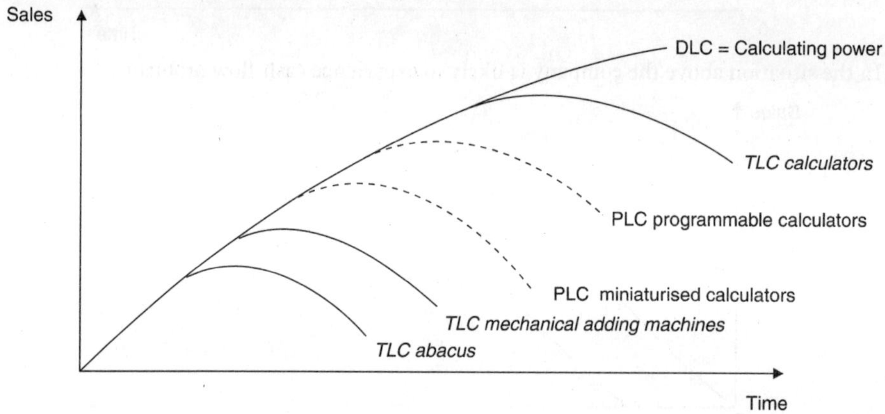

Figure 7.5: Technology lifecycles

For example, 'calculating power' represents a human demand that is probably in the growth stage of the DLC. This has been composed of a number of TLCs – finger counting, abacuses, slide rules, adding machines, calculators, computers. Each new technology usually satisfies the **generic need** in a **superior way**.

The TLC indicates that for many products, death will eventually transpire through **technology** and **competitive innovation.**

Activity 4 **(10 minutes)**

You are a marketing manager for a company manufacturing 'All Bright' toothpaste. Recently sales have been falling for the product, which has been established for a number of years. What type of marketing strategies could you consider to improve sales?

		Phase		
	Introduction	*Growth*	*Maturity*	*Decline*
1 *Products*	Initially, poor quality. Product design and development are a key to success. No standard product and frequent design changes (eg microcomputers in the early 1980s).	Competitors' products have marked quality differences and technical differences. Quality improves. Product reliability may be important.	Products become more standardised and differences between competing products less distinct.	Products even less differentiated. Quality becomes more variable.
2 *Customers*	Initial customers willing to pay high prices. Customers need to be convinced about buying.	Customers increase in number.	Mass market. Market saturation. Repeat-buying of products becomes significant. Brand image also important.	Customers are 'sophisticated' buyers of a product they understand well.
3 *Marketing*	High advertising and sales promotion costs. High prices possible.	High advertising costs still, but as a % of sales, costs are falling. Prices falling.	Markets become segmented. Segmentation and extending the maturity phase of the life cycle can be key strategies.	Less money spent on advertising and sales promotion.
4 *Competition*	Few or no competitors.	More competitors enter the market. Barriers to entry can be important.	Competition at its keenest: on prices, branding, servicing customers, packaging etc.	Competitors gradually exit from the market. Exit barriers can be important.
5 *Profit margins*	High prices but losses due to high fixed costs.	High prices. High contribution margins, and increasing profit margins. High P/E ratios for quoted companies in the growth market.	Falling prices but good profit margins due to high sales volume. Higher prices in some market segments.	Still low prices but falling profits as sales volume falls, since total contribution falls towards the level of fixed costs. Some increase in prices may occur in
6 *Manufacturing*	Over-capacity. High production costs. High labour skill content in manufacture.	Under capacity. Move towards mass production and less reliance on skilled labour.	Optimum capacity. Low labour skills.	Over-capacity because mass production techniques are still used.
7 *Distribution*	Few distribution channels.	Distribution channels flourish and getting adequate distribution channels is key to marketing success.	Distribution channels fully developed, but less successful channels might be cut.	Distribution channels dwindling.

4 PORTFOLIO ANALYSIS

Portfolio planning analyses the current position of an organisation's products on SBUs in their markets, and the state of growth or decline in each of those markets. Several matrices have been developed over the years to analyse market share, market growth and market position.

Definition

> **Portfolio:** A collection of products/SBUs reporting to one entity. Each product SBU can be separately identified for decision-making and performance measurement.

4.1 Market share, market growth and cash generation: the Boston classification

The **Boston Consulting Group** (BCG) developed a matrix, based on empirical research, which classifies a company's products in terms of potential cash generation and cash expenditure requirements. This is related to **market share relative to competitors**.

You should also note that BCG analysis can be applied to:

- Individual products
- Whole strategic business units (SBUs)

To illustrate how to evaluate a portfolio a simulated company example will be provided. An industrial equipment company has five products with the following sales and market characteristics.

Product	*Sales £m*	*£m sales Top 3 firms*			*Market growth rate %*	*Relative share*
A	0.5	0.7	0.7	0.5*	15%	0.71
B	1.6	1.6	1.6*	1.0	18%	1.0
C	1.8	1.8*	1.2	1.0	7%	1.5
D	3.2	3.2*	0.8	0.7	4%	4.0
E	0.5	2.5	1.8	1.7	4%	0.2

* Company sales within the market

This information can then be plotted on to a matrix. The circles indicate the contribution the product makes to overall turnover. The centre of circles indicates their position on the matrix:

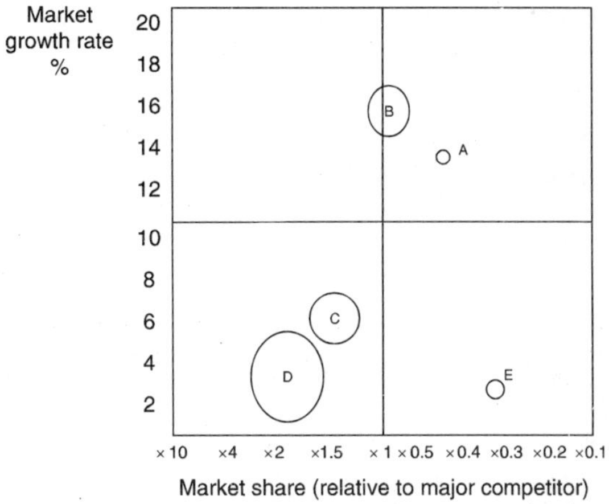

Figure 7.6: BCG analysis

This growth/share matrix for the classification of products into cash cows, cash dogs, stars and question marks is known as the **Boston classification** (or the **Boston Matrix**).

(a) **Stars** are products with a high share of a high growth market. In the short term, these require capital expenditure in excess of the cash they generate, in order to maintain their market position, but promise high returns in the future.

(b) In due course, stars will become **cash cows,** with a high share of a low-growth market. Cash cows need very little capital expenditure and generate high levels of cash income. Cash cows generate high cash returns, which can be used to finance the stars.

(c) **Question marks** are products in a high-growth market, but where they have a low market share. Do the products justify considerable capital expenditure in the hope of increasing their market share, or should they be allowed to 'die' quietly as they are squeezed out of the expanding market by rival products? Because considerable expenditure would be needed to turn a question mark into a star by building up market share, question marks will usually be poor cash generators and show a negative cash flow.

(d) **Dogs** are products with a low share of a low growth market. They may be ex-cash cows that have now fallen on hard times. Dogs should be allowed to die, or should be killed off. Although they will show only a modest net cash outflow, or even a modest net cash inflow, they are 'cash traps' which tie up funds and provide a poor return on investment, and not enough to achieve the organisation's target rate of return.

There are also **infants** (ie products in an early stage of development), **warhorses** (ie products that have been cash cows in the past, and are still making good sales and earning good profits even now) and even **cash dogs,** which are dogs still generating cash.

The evaluation and resulting strategic considerations for the company in the diagram above are these.

(a) There are two cash cows, thus the company should be in a cash-positive state.

(b) New products will be required to follow on from A.

(c) A is doing well (15%) but needs to gain market share to move from position 3 in the market – continued funding is essential. Similar for B.

(d) C is a market leader in a maturing market – strategy of consolidation is required.

(e) D is the major product which dominates its market; cash funds should be generated from this product.

(f) E is very small. Is it profitable? Funding to maintain the position or selling off are appropriate strategies.

Activity 5 **(10 minutes)**

The marketing manager of Juicy Drinks Ltd has invited you in for a chat. Juicy Drinks Ltd provides fruit juices to a number of supermarket chains, which sell them under their own label. 'We've got a large number of products, of course. Our freshly squeezed orange juice is doing fine – it sells in huge quantities. Although margins are low, we have sufficient economies of scale to do very nicely in this market. We've got advanced production and bottling equipment and long-term contracts with some major growers. No problems there. We also sell freshly squeezed pomegranate juice: customers loved it in the tests, but producing the stuff at the right price is a major hassle: all the seeds get in the way. We hope it will be a winner, once we get the production right and start converting customers to it. After all the market for exotic fruit juices generally is expanding fast.'

What sort of products, according to the Boston classification, are described here?

The **product life cycle** concept can be added to a market share/market growth classification of products, as follows.

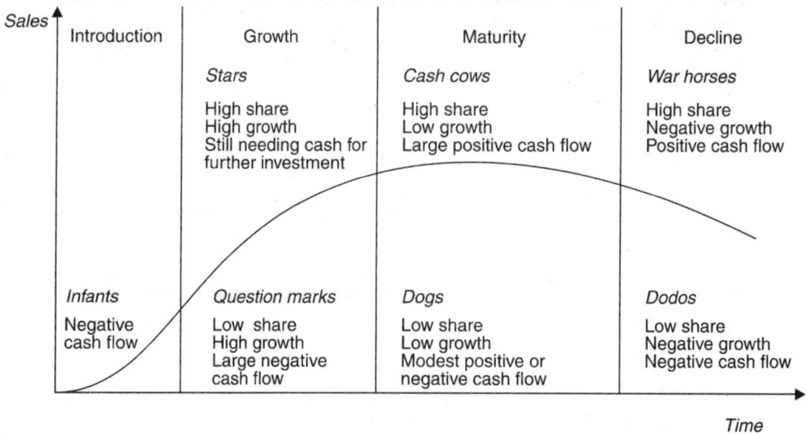

Figure 7.7: Product life cycle and market share

The BCG portfolio analysis is useful because it provides a framework for planners to consider and forecast potential market growth and to evaluate the competitive dimension through an evaluation of market share and the likely changes in cash flow.

4.2 Competitiveness of products

As a result of some of these weaknesses in the BCG model variations have evolved. Johnson and Scholes cite **General Electric's Business Screen** which compares market attractiveness with business strength.

(a) Determinants of industry/market attractiveness

- Market factors (eg size, growth)
- Competitors
- Investment factors
- Technological change
- Other PEST factors

(b) Determinants of business strength

- Product quality
- Distribution
- Brand reputation
- Production capacity
- Management skill

(c) These factors can then be scored and weighted. For example, a market with a low size and intense competition based on price might receive a lower weighting than a market with high growth and limited competition. The GE matrix is based on Return on Capital Employed.

(d) Business strengths and market attractiveness are thus plotted on a grid, and a strategy appropriate to each can be considered.

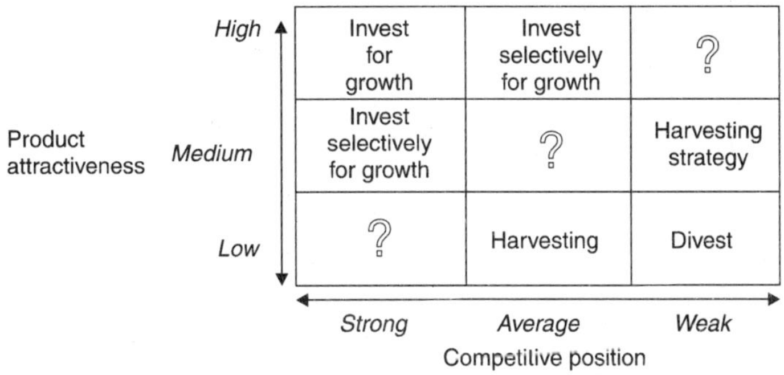

Figure 7.8: General Electric's Business screen

Each 'cell' requires a different management approach.

(a) Each SBU can be plotted in one of the cells and the appropriate management approach adopted.

(b) It is possible that SBUs might move around the matrix. Changes in PEST factors may change an industry/market's attractiveness.

(c) The matrix ignores the possibility of **knowledge generation** and **competence** sharing between SBUs. Applications in one SBU may be of value elsewhere.

The advantage and disadvantages of portfolio planning

Advantage

Portfolio planning provides an excellent framework for analysis, and a starting point for developing a product-market mix strategy.

Drawbacks

(a) Portfolio models are simple: they do not reflect the uncertainties of decision-making.

(b) BCG analysis, in particular, does not really take risk into account.

(c) They ignore opportunities for creative segmentation or identifying new niches.

(d) They assume a market is 'given' rather than something that can be created and nurtured. After all, industries may be 'unattractive' because customer needs have not been analysed sufficiently.

(e) A great deal of complicated analysis is needed to come up with relevant data. How do you decide whether an industry is attractive or not?

FOR DISCUSSION

What type of data is needed for adequate analysis for portfolio planning?

---

5 THE VALUE CHAIN

The **value chain** model of corporate activities, developed by Michael Porter (*Competitive Advantage*, 2004), offers a bird's eye view of the firm and what it does. Competitive advantage, says Porter, arises out of the way in which firms organise and perform **activities**. (In other words, this describes **how** an organisation uses its inputs and transforms them into the outputs that customers pay for.)

Definition

Activities are the means by which a firm creates value in its products. (They are sometimes referred to as **value activities**.)

Activities incur costs, and, in combination with other activities, provide a product or service which earns revenue.

Let us explain this point by using the example of a **restaurant**. A restaurant's activities can be divided into buying food, cooking it, and serving it (to customers). There is no reason, in theory, why the customers should not do all these things themselves, at home. The customer however, is not only prepared to **pay for someone else** to do all this but also **pays more than the cost of** the resources (food, wages etc). The ultimate value a firm creates is measured by the amount customers are willing to pay for its products or services above the cost of carrying out value activities. A firm is profitable if the realised value to customers exceeds the collective cost of performing the activities.

(a) Customers '**purchase**' **value**, which they measure by comparing a firm's products and services with similar offerings by competitors.

(b) The business '**creates**' **value** by carrying out its activities either more efficiently than other businesses, or combine them in such a way as to provide a unique product or service.

Porter (2004) grouped the various activities of an organisation into a **value chain.** Here is a diagram to explain the theory.

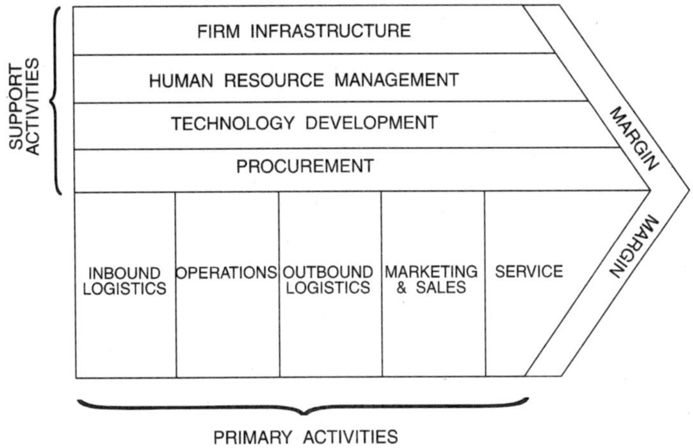

Figure 7.9: The value chain

The **margin** is the excess the customer is prepared to **pay** over the **cost** to the firm of obtaining resource inputs and providing value activities.

Primary activities are directly related to production, sales, marketing, delivery and service.

Activity	Comment
Inbound logistics	Receiving, handling and storing inputs to the production system (ie warehousing, transport, stock control etc).
Operations	Convert resource inputs into a final product. Resource inputs are not only materials. 'People' are a 'resource' especially in service industries.
Outbound logistics	Storing the product and its distribution to customers: packaging, warehousing, testing etc.
Marketing and sales	Informing customers about the product, persuading them to buy it, and enabling them to do so: advertising, promotion etc.
After sales service	Installing products, repairing them, upgrading them, providing spare parts and so forth.

Support activities provide purchased inputs, human resources, technology and infrastructural functions to support the primary activities.

Activity	Comment
Procurement	Acquire the resource inputs to the primary activities (eg purchase of materials, subcomponents equipment).
Technology development	Product design, improving processes and/or resource utilisation.
Human resource management	Recruiting, training, developing and rewarding people.
Management planning	Planning, finance, quality control: Porter believes they are crucially important to an organisation's strategic capability in all primary activities.

Linkages connect the activities of the value chain.

(a) **Activities in the value chain affect one another**. For example, more costly product design or better quality production might reduce the need for after-sales service.

(b) **Linkages require co-ordination**. For example, just-in-time requires smooth functioning of operations, outbound logistics and service activities such as installation.

EXAMPLE

Amazon.com, one of the most celebrated website enterprises, aims to become the Internet's first one-step store, and has already diversified from its original bookshop business into such fields as electronic consumer products, mobile telephones, cars, leisure, gardening equipment, holidays, travel and toys. Its diversification programme has undoubtedly given it substantial breadth, helping to reduce the likelihood that its customers will feel the necessity to go elsewhere for some of their needs.

On the other hand, there are considerable cost burdens involved, not least in delivery. If customers order a variety of product items, it is likely that they will be delivered separately, from separate locations, with shipping expenses that vastly exceed the cost when goods are sent all at once. It is also relevant to note that, in Amazon's experience, it takes an average of 3.67 attempts before customer orders can be successfully delivered, because customers are themselves out during conventional delivery hours, and so forth. The necessity for repeat visits is a further cost-creating scenario.

Among Amazon's major assets is a massive customer database (29 million people) and an almost unparalleled level of information and insight into customer preferences and behavior patterns. Cross-selling opportunities are accordingly impressive, and the company has embarked upon a number of co-branding arrangements with complementary retailers.

Since expanding into offering a wider range of products, Amazon also has actively competed with ebay to offer the opportunity for customers to buy and sell their second-hand items as well as providing a shop window for independent Amazon approved retailers. Both independent retailers and individual sellers are solely responsible for postage of items and cannot utilise Amazon's distribution facilities. The e-tailer is also clear within its website that customers are dealing with a third party.

Overall, such trends are creating **pressure** for companies. As Gary Hamel has said, 'The main threat facing companies is that prices will be driven down by consumers' ability to shop around using the Internet'. This phenomenon, dubbed 'frictionless capitalism' by Bill Gates, will make it harder for companies to make money using traditional business models.

Value system

Activities that add value do not stop at the organisation's **boundaries**. For example, when a restaurant serves a meal, the quality of the ingredients – although they are chosen by the cook – is determined by the grower. The grower has added value, and the grower's success in growing produce of good quality is as important to the customer's ultimate satisfaction as the skills of the chef. A firm's value chain is connected to what Porter calls a **value system**.

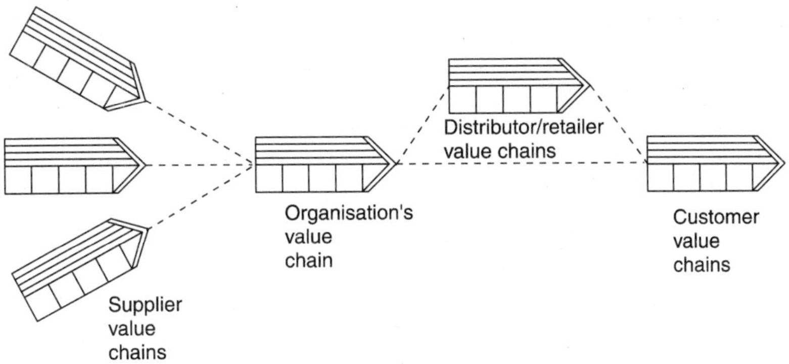

Figure 7.10: Value system

Using the value chain. A firm can secure competitive advantage by:

- Inventing new or better ways to do activities
- Combining activities in new or better ways
- Managing the linkages in its own value chain
- Managing the linkages in the value system

EXAMPLE

Companies are drifting downstream. That is, they are gradually losing interest in how they make their products, and focusing more on how those goods and services reach their ultimate customer.

The car industry's new obsession with what happens to its products once they leave the factory arises in part because it has already cut the costs of production substantially. So it is planning to take an axe to distribution costs, too. Ford is the company that is reshaping itself most radically.

It is handing over more of the responsibility for manufacturing to sub-contractors. But at the same time it is acquiring automotive servicing companies, such as the UK's Kwik-Fit and a Florida-based car recycling business.

The trend is visible in other industries, too. Personal computer manufacturers have delegated most of the important technical decisions that shape their products to component suppliers such as Intel and Microsoft. They increasingly delegate the mundane task of making their products to third-party manufacturers.

But they are following Dell Computers in seizing back customer relationships from distributors and dealers. Indeed, by offering customers free Internet access or free online training, they seek to infiltrate themselves into the customer's life.

Peter Martin, Financial Times

> **Activity 6** **(10 minutes)**
>
> Sana Sounds is a small record company. Representatives from Sana Sounds scour music clubs for new bands to promote. Once a band has signed a contract (with Sana Sounds) it makes a recording. The recording process is subcontracted to one of a number of recording studio firms which Sana Sounds uses regularly. (At the moment Sana Sounds is not large enough to invest in its own equipment and studios.) Sana Sounds also subcontracts the production of recordings and CDs to a number of manufacturing companies. Sana Sounds then distributes the discs to selected stores, and engages in any promotional activities required.
>
> What would you say were the activities in Sana Sounds' value chain?

The examples below are based on two supermarket chains, one concentrating on low prices, the other differentiated on quality and service. See if you can tell which is which.

(a)

	INBOUND LOGISTICS	OPERATIONS	OUTBOUND LOGISTICS	MARKETING & SALES	SERVICE
Firm infrastructure	Central control of operations and credit control				
Human resource management	Recruitment of mature staff	Client care training	Flexible staff to help with packing		
Technology development		Recipe research	Electronic point of sale	Consumer research & tests	Itemised bills
Procurement	Own label products	Prime retail positions		Adverts in quality magazines & poster sites	
	Dedicated refrigerated transport	In store food halls Modern store design Open front refrigerators Tight control of sell-by dates	Collect by car service	No price discounts on food past sell-by dates	No quibble refunds

(b)

	INBOUND LOGISTICS	OPERATIONS	OUTBOUND LOGISTICS	MARKETING & SALES	SERVICE
Firm infrastructure	Minimum corporate HQ				
Human resource management		De-skilled store-ops	Dismissal for checkout error		
Technology development	Computerised warehousing		Checkouts simple		
Procurement	Branded only purchases big discounts	Low cost sites			Use of concessions
	Bulk warehousing	1,000 lines only Price points Basic store design		Low price promotion Local focus	Nil

Figures 7.11 and 7.12: Value chains for supermarket chains

The two supermarkets represented are based on the following.

(a) The value chain in (a) above is based on Marks & Spencer foods, which seeks to differentiate on quality and service. Hence the 'no quibble' refunds, the use of prime retail sites, and customer care training.

(b) The value chain in (b) above is similar to that of Lidl, a 'discount' supermarket chain which sells on price, pursuing a cost leadership, or perhaps more accurately, a cost-focus strategy. This can be seen in the limited product range and its low-cost sites.

Chapter roundup

- An organisation's resources can be audited. These will include technical, financial, managerial, organisational and information resources.
- An organisation's activities can run into difficulties due to limiting factors.
- Distinctive competences are what organisations do well.
- Marketing audits review the company's overall marketing operation.
- Companies should strive to be both efficient and effective in their marketing operations. Marketing effectiveness can be measured using the table developed by Kotler.
- Product life cycle analysis looks at the stages in a product's sales history.
- PLCs vary between product class, form and brands.
- Each stage of the PLC has characteristics and strategic implications.
- Portfolio analysis looks at the products or SBUs an organisation has and their markets.
- The Boston Consulting Group (BCG) matrix relates a company's product or SBU market share and market growth.
- Products or SBUs can then be put into categories of stars, dogs, cash cows or question marks.
- General Electric's Business Screen compares market attractiveness and business strength.
- The value chain was developed by Porter to give an overall view of the firm and what it does.

Quick quiz

1 What are 'limiting factors' to an organisation's strategy?

2 From where might a company derive distinctive competences?

3 How often should a company undertake a marketing audit?

4 What should a marketing audit investigate?

5 What is the difference between marketing effectiveness and efficiency?

6 Why might the PLC be different for a product category and a brand?

7 If the rate of sales growth has slowed but profits are still made what stage of the PLC is the product in?

8 BCG analysis can only be used on products. True or false?

9 What 'primary activities' are included in value chain analysis?

Answers to quick quiz

1 Factors that limit the organisation's activities such as shortage of money.

2 Production, marketing, human resources, integration/coordination or distribution.

3 About once a year.

4 The marketing environment (micro and macro)
Marketing strategy
Marketing systems

5 Efficiency – maximum output for minimum input
Effectiveness – making sure the organisation is doing the right things

6 Brands will usually have a shorter PLC than the product category, eg coffee (the category) will have a longer PLC than Gold Blend (a brand).

7 Maturity.

8 False – can be for strategic business units.

9 Inbound logistics, operations, outbound logistics, marketing and sales and service.

Answers to activities

1 The answer will depend on the precise circumstances of your company or college.

2 The answer will depend on the magazine you have chosen.

3

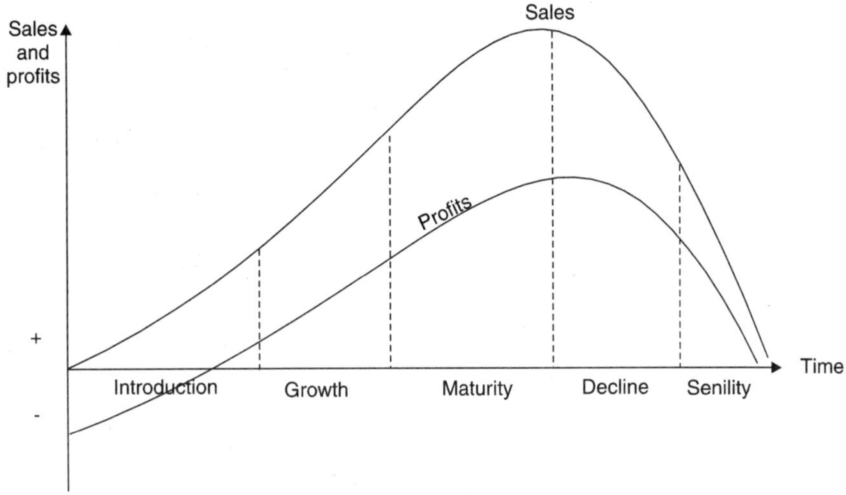

4 New packaging and a relaunch
Link product with dental research
Aim at a specific sector eg children, housewives, the elderly
Free toothbrush attached
Money off coupons
'Buy one get one free'

5 Freshly squeezed orange juice: cash cow
Pomegranate juice: probably a question mark; might become a star

6 *Primary activities*

- Inbound physical distribution. Sana Sounds do not manufacture 'products' as such, but the acquisition of bands can be placed in this section. Inventory and warehousing of manufactured CDs will also be included here.
- Outbound physical distribution – the delivery of manufactured CDs to outlets.
- The marketing of the bands.
- Service to both 'customers' – ie bands and retail outlets.

Support activities

- The rise of technology in terms of general IT facilities and in procurement aspects ie which recording studios to use.
- Human resource management issues will be vital, to keep the bands from taking their business elsewhere.
- Firm's infrastructure will consist of general management of the business, planning and finance.

Chapter 8 :
EXTERNAL ENVIRONMENTAL ANALYSIS

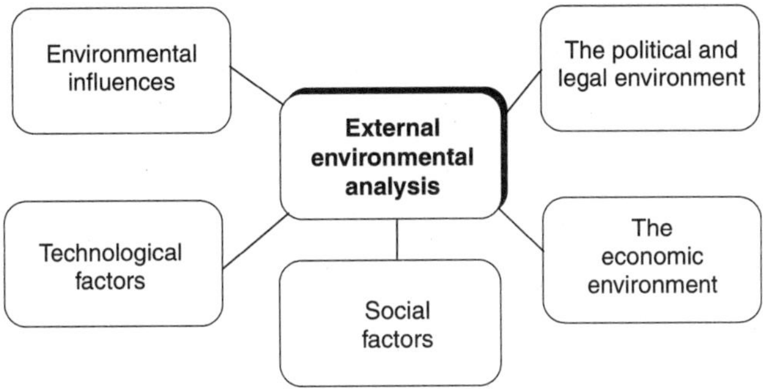

Introduction

Business plans cannot be produced in a vacuum. They must be developed within the context of the wider environment in which the organisation is operating. They need to take into account the opportunities and threats which are emerging as these external factors change. These are the issues this chapter will be covering.

A key issue to keep in mind is **environmental change**. Some organisations face more complex and changing environments than others; the fashion industry is in a 'fast-moving' environment, but this speed of environmental change does not exist for all industries.

Your objectives

In this chapter you will learn about the following.

(a) The factors that make up the external environment

(b) Aspects of the political and legal influences

(c) The importance of economic factors

(d) The importance and diversity of social aspects

(e) The impact technology has on business enterprises

1 ENVIRONMENTAL INFLUENCES

As we have seen earlier, planning is a central part of the management task wherever you are working in the organisation and the first stage should always be to clarify the current position.

(a) **Controllable.** Different managers need to review different aspects of the business. The factors which can be controlled by the **marketing** manager can be primarily represented by the 7P's of the marketing mix.

(b) **Not controllable.** Issues of production capacity and sources of supply are of interest and of indirect importance to the marketing manager, but outside the area of direct control. That said, marketing mix decisions and marketing activities do have a significant impact on these other departments.

Activity 1 **(30 minutes)**

Choose a business/market with which you are familiar. How has it changed over the last five years? Produce a list of all the external factors (things which the organisation cannot control) which have had a significant impact on the organisation in that time. Refine your list as you work through the rest of this chapter.

Definition

The **environment** of an organisation is everything outside its boundaries. All the factors affect the organisation's performance, but the organisation cannot control them.

FOR DISCUSSION

There is no real point in assessing the external environment when an organisation cannot do anything about it.

Organisations have a variety of relationships with the environment

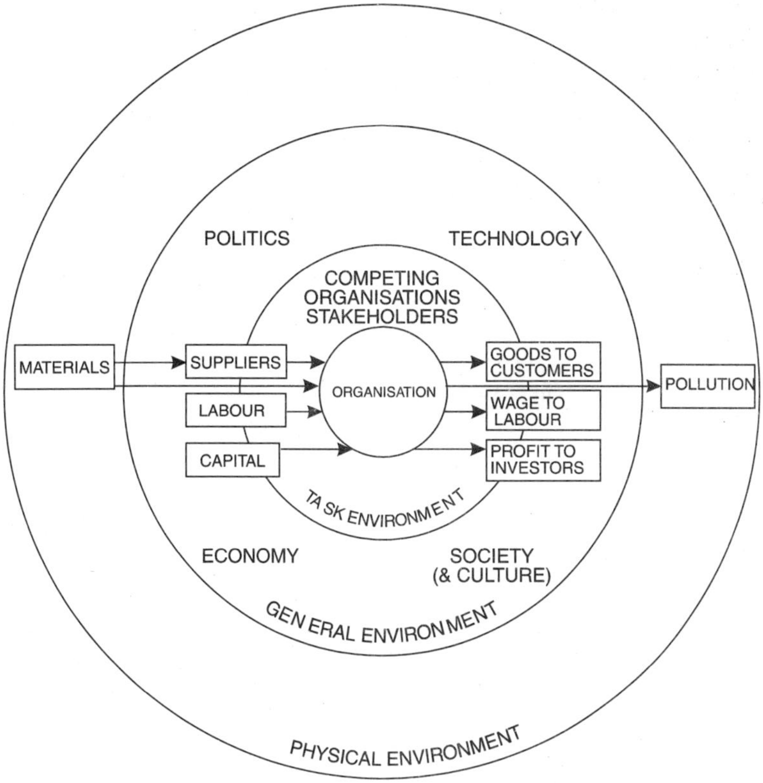

Figure 8.1: External environment

1.1 Classifying the environment

(a) The **micro environment** is of immediate concern, and is uniquely configured for each organisation: no organisation has a network of suppliers, customers, competitors or stakeholders identical to another's.

(b) The **macro environment** relates to factors in the environment affecting all organisations.

- Political-legal factors
- Economic factors
- Social and cultural factors
- Technological factors

(PEST)

The acronym **PEST** is often expanded to **PESTEL**, which gives the **legal** aspect its own heading and introduces a heading for **environmental protection**. Other versions include **SLEPT**, in which the environmental protection aspect is folded into the other five and **STEEPLE**, where the extra E stand for **ethics**.

EXAMPLE

Smoking was banned in New York's bars and restaurants from 1 April 2003. At about the same time a tax increase raised the price of a packet of Camels from $6 to $7.50 – a 25% price rise.

John Kirkwood, Chief Executive of the American Lung Association expected at the time that New York's attack on smoking would inspire similar legal moves across the USA. Meanwhile, he forecast that cigarette consumption in New York would decline markedly.

Anti-smoking groups are promoting four attacks on the tobacco industry.

(a) Increased local taxes
(b) Smoking bans
(c) Anti-smoking advertising
(d) Education and smoking cessation programmes

In the UK when a smoking ban took effect in July 2007, from January the government actively used high volume anti-smoking advertising and increased availability of smoking cessation programmes to prepare the public for the ban and to promote the message that it was a socially desirable policy. Manufacturers of smoking cessation products capitalised on the likely increased demand for their products by running widespread promotional activity during the end of June and July.

The smoking ban raises an interesting point regarding the organisations', macro-environment. For many marketers it is very difficult to distinguish between PEST factors. This example demonstrates why because owing to the complexities of the situation you could describe the smoking ban in terms of each of the four factors for many industries. A pub chain for example would need to consider the ban in terms of each PEST factor.

Political/legal factors – Government-based policy making it illegal to smoke within enclosed public areas.

Economic factors – Anticipated downturn in initial trade with smokers expected to remain at home more often.

Social and cultural factors – Significant change in the social behaviours of smokers, significant emphasis on outside space especially in the short term, likely change in lifestyle and habits of customers, changed social and demographic composition of pub-goers, increased number of family groups as customers.

Technological factors – Within the first few weeks of the ban, reports were published of the need for improved fragrance technologies. Previously the smells of stale beer, sweat and flatulence had been masked by tobacco odour; demand for specialised commercial fragrances to be pumped into pubs increased dramatically.

Activity 2 **(30 minutes)**

Choose an industrial product, a consumer durable, a fast moving consumer good and a service business. For each of them identify *how* you think the environmental factors identified in the following paragraphs might affect a business operating in that market.

1.2 Environmental uncertainty

Strategic decisions are made in partial ignorance, as we have seen, because the environment is uncertain. Uncertainty relates to the **complexity and dynamism** of the environment.

(a) **Complexity** arises from:

(i) The **variety of influences** faced by the organisation. The more open an organisation is, the greater the variety of influences. The greater the number of markets the organisation operates in, the greater the number of influences to which it is subject.

(ii) The amount of **knowledge** necessary. All businesses need to have knowledge of the tax system, for example, but only pharmaceuticals businesses need to know about mandatory testing procedures for new drugs.

(iii) The **interconnections** of environmental influences. Importing and exporting companies are sensitive to exchange rates, which themselves are sensitive to interest rates. Interest rates then influence a company's borrowing costs.

(b) **Dynamism**. Stable environments are unchanging. Dynamic environments are in a state of change. The computer market is a dynamic market because of the rate of technological change.

It is not always easy to detect which environmental factors will be relevant in the future.

EXAMPLE

Back in 1998, P&G brand's Sunny Delight drink was one of the most successful product launches ever, leaping into the top 20 almost from the outset. Its initial launch strategy – a reassuring 'better for you' message for mums and a 'great taste' message for children – was spot on.

The trouble started when pressure groups and the media rubbished P&G's good-for-you claims – highlighting the low levels of juice (two per cent) and the fact that its main ingredients were water and corn syrup. This generated a backlash against the brand.

According to a BBC News report, the negative publicity escalated when a Sunny Delight ad showing a snowman turning orange was released at about the same time as reports of a girl who turned orange (due to the UK product's use of Beta Carotene for color) after drinking too much Sunny Delight.

The backlash cost P&G dearly. Sales sagged – down ten per cent in 2001 – wiping tens of millions of pounds off the brand's value. At its peak, the business was worth about £150m. Now it's closer to £70m. But how could such an expert marketer as P&G make such a hash of things? There is no single reason. Rather, it's a combination of factors.

Perhaps, for instance, P&G focused 'too much' on its existing consumers. P&G has a habit of researching its products to death – the phrase 'our consumers tell us' is never far from brand managers' lips – but the crucial influence in this case was not loyal consumers, but sceptics.

The drink was redesigned and re-launched in 2003 as 'SunnyD'. In the UK the new SunnyD contains 70% fruit juice with no artificial ingredients or added sugar.

FOR DISCUSSION

Information needs for assessing environmental factors are diverse and complex.

Activity 3 **(5 minutes)**

How do you consider that the Johnson and Scholes model can be applied to attitudes about genetically modified foods?

2 THE POLITICAL AND LEGAL ENVIRONMENT

We will outline in **general** terms some key issues to keep in mind. Laws come from common law, parliamentary legislation and government regulations derived from it, and obligations under EU membership and other treaties.

2.1 Legal factors affecting all companies

Factor	Example
General legal framework: contract, tort, agency	Basic ways of doing business; negligence proceedings
Criminal law	Theft; insider dealing; bribery; deception
Company law	Directors and their duties; reporting requirements; takeover proceedings; shareholders' rights; insolvency
Employment law	Trade Union recognition; Social Chapter provisions; minimum wage; unfair dismissal; redundancy; maternity; Equal Opportunities
Health and Safety	Fire precautions; safety procedures
Data protection	Use of information about employees and customers
Marketing and sales	Laws to protect consumers (eg refunds and replacement, 'cooling off' period after credit agreements); what is or isn't allowed in advertising
Environment	Pollution control; waste disposal
Tax law	Corporation tax payment; Collection of income tax (PAYE) and National Insurance contributions; VAT

Some legal and regulatory factors affect **particular industries**, if the public interest is served. For example, electricity, gas, telecommunications, water and rail transport are subject to **regulators** (Offer, Ofgas, Oftel, Ofwat, Ofrail) who have influence over:

- Competition and market access
- Pricing policy (can restrict price increase)

This is because either:

- The industries are, effectively, monopolies, and/or
- Large sums of public money are involved (eg in subsidies to rail companies)

EXAMPLE: GAS DEREGULATION

Government policy. Gas used to be a state monopoly. The industry was privatised as one company, British Gas. Slowly, the UK gas market has been opened to competition: now about twenty suppliers compete with British Gas.

Regulators. Ofgas regulates the gas industry. Ofgas has introduced a Code of Conduct requiring gas suppliers to train sales agents, allow for a cooling off period and so on.

Contracts. British Gas is vulnerable to competitors because of its prices. When it was privatised, it inherited 'take or pay contracts' requiring it to buy gas at a specific price from gas producers. Since that time, gas prices have fallen, and competitors have been able to benefit from this.

New markets. Government policy has also deregulated the electricity market, so that companies such as British Gas can now sell electricity.

2.2 Anticipating changes in the law

- The governing party's election **manifesto** is a guide to its political priorities, even if these are not implemented immediately.
- The government often publishes advance information about its plans (**green paper** or **white paper**) for consultation purposes.
- The **EU's single market programme** indicates future changes in the law.

The general political environment will have implications for business because of the attitudes to business and support for business and/or trade unions and related legislation.

EXAMPLE

There are many examples of products in the UK that have caused a furore when they are not recognised by the EU. Examples such as chocolate and ice cream have different regulations in terms of content and labelling in various EU countries.

FOR DISCUSSION

The political and legal environment is influenced by socio-cultural factors.

3 THE ECONOMIC ENVIRONMENT

The economic environment is an important influence at local and national level.

3.1 Influence of the economic environment

Factor	Impact
Overall growth or fall in gross domestic product	Increased/decreased demand for goods (eg dishwashers) and services (holidays).
Local economic trends	Type of industry in the area. Office/factory rents. Labour rates. House prices.
National economic trends:	
• Inflation	Low in most countries; distorts business decisions; wage inflation compensates for price inflation
• Interest rates	How much it costs to borrow money affects **cash flow**. Some businesses carry a high level of debt. How much customers can afford to spend is also affected as rises in interest rates affect people's mortgage payments.
• Tax levels	Corporation tax affects how much firms can invest or return to shareholders. Income tax and VAT affect how much consumers have to spend, hence demand.
• Government spending	Suppliers to the government (eg construction firms) are affected by spending.
• The business cycle	Economic activity is always punctuated by periods of growth followed by decline, simply because of the nature of trade. The UK economy has been characterised by periods of 'boom' and 'bust'. Government policy can cause, exacerbate or mitigate such trends, but cannot abolish the business cycle. (Industries which prosper when others are declining are called **counter-cyclical** industries.)

The **forecast state of the economy** will influence the planning process for organisations which operate within it. In times of boom and increased demand and consumption, the overall planning problem will be to **identify** the demand. Conversely, in times of recession, the emphasis will be on cost-effectiveness, continuing profitability, survival and competition.

3.2 Impact of international factors

Factor	Impact
Exchange rates	Cost of imports, selling prices and value of exports; cost of hedging against fluctuations
Characteristics of overseas markets. Different rates of economic growth and prosperity, tax etc	Desirable overseas markets (demand) or sources of supply
Capital, flows and trade	Investment opportunities, free trade, cost of exporting

FOR DISCUSSION

Information on foreign markets is notoriously difficult to gather and assess.

EXAMPLE: MARKETING RESEARCH IN CHINA

With its accession to the World Trade Organisation, China is widely perceived as the world's greatest marketing opportunity. But while it is easy to be dazzled by a population of 1.3 billion, the reality is that less than ten per cent of Chinese citizens have incomes that can afford Western products. And for high-end goods, such as luxury cars, the market is more akin to that of a small EU state.

As foreign investors scramble to take advantage of China's untapped potential, one group of Western businesses looks set to prosper: international marketing research agencies. Some agencies have been locally established since the Chinese government embarked on economic reform in the Eighties. But are these Western-owned agencies – armed with a battery of imported techniques – qualified to help incoming businesses acquire the deep cultural insights that they need to make their brands appealing to Chinese consumers?

The issue of whether marketing research techniques can cross cultures extends beyond the specific case of China. With the growth in international business, research agencies favour common methodologies that can be applied globally, allowing clients to compare markets. What this has demonstrated is that Western techniques, particularly those that use projection and visual imagery, can work well in most cultures. But there must be scope for local adaptation. *Alicia Craig, Marketing Week, 28 February 2002*

3.3 The single European currency

Most countries in the EU now account fully in euros. Interest rates are set by the European Central Bank whose goal is price transparency. The implications of the introduction of the euro are:

(a) **Price transparency**: it is obvious that prices differ in various markets. Cars are known to be priced higher in the UK than elsewhere. Markets may become harder to segment.

(b) **Interest rates** are set for the whole of the eurozone, not by country.

4 SOCIAL FACTORS

These were covered comprehensively in Chapter 1 on Buyer Behaviour.

4.1 Different social factors

Factor	Comment
Growth	The rate of growth or decline in a national population and in regional populations.
Age	Changes in the age distribution of the population. In the UK, there will be an increasing proportion of the national population over retirement age. In developing countries there are very large numbers of young people. • Elderly people have unique needs • As a segment they will become increasingly powerful.
Geography	The concentration of population into certain geographical areas.
Ethnicity	In the UK, about 5% come from ethnic minorities, although most of these live in London and the South East.
Household and family structure	A household is the basic social unit and its size might be determined by the number of children, whether elderly parents live at home etc. In the UK, there has been an **increase in single-person households** and lone parent families. Obviously, this impacts on the relevance of models such as the **family life cycle**.
Social structure	The population of a society can be broken down into a number of subgroups, with different attitudes and access to economic resources. Social class, however, is hard to measure (as people's subjective perceptions vary). • Social classification systems cover occupations closely: 1 Higher managerial and professional; 2 Lower managerial and professional; 3 Intermediate; 4 Small employers and own account workers; 5 Lower supervisory craft and related occupations; 6 Semi-routine occupations; 7 Routine occupations • Social status generally passes from generation to generation, despite evidence of social mobility in individual cases.

Factor	Comment
Employment	Many people believe that there is a move to a casual flexible workforce; factories will have a group of **core employees,** supplemented by a group of **peripheral employees,** on part-time or temporary contracts, working as and when required. Some research indicates a 'two-tier' society split between '**work-rich**' (with two wage-earners) and '**work-poor**' households. However **most employees are in permanent, full-time employment.**
Wealth	Rising standards of living lead to increased demand for certain types of consumer good. This is why developing countries are attractive as markets.

Activity 4 **(20 minutes)**

Club Fun is a UK company which sells packaged holidays. Founded in the 1960s, it offers a standard 'cheap and cheerful' package to resorts in Spain and, more recently, to some of the Greek islands. It was particularly successful at providing holidays for the 18 to 30 age group. What do you think the implications are for Club Fun of the following developments?

(a) A fall in the number of school leavers.

(b) The fact that young people are more likely now than in the 1960s to go into higher education.

(c) Holiday programmes on TV which feature a much greater variety of locations.

(d) Greater disposable income among the 18 to 30 age group.

4.2 Business ethics

The conduct of an organisation, its management and employees will be measured against **ethical standards** by the customers, suppliers and other members of the public with whom they deal.

Types of ethical problems a manager may meet with in practice:

(a) **Production practices**. Attempts to increase profitability by cutting costs may lead to dangerous working conditions, inadequate safety standards in products or reprehensible practices (eg child labour). This is a problem for firms which outsource production to low-cost factories overseas.

(b) **Gifts**. There is a fine line to be drawn between gifts, accepted as part of a way of doing business, and bribes. The company BAE has been involved in a great deal of controversy over its arms deals with Saudi Arabia, which allegedly involved the payment of bribes to Saudi officials.

(c) **Social responsibility**: companies are being held to account for pollution and human rights issues.

(d) **Competitive behaviour**. There is a distinction between competing aggressively and competing unethically and illegally.

FOR DISCUSSION

If a business practice is operating overseas it should only concern itself with local business practices, not what it would do in its home country.

5 TECHNOLOGICAL FACTORS

Technology refers to:

(a) Apparatus or equipment: eg a TV camera.

(b) Technique: eg how to use the TV camera to best effect, perhaps in conjunction with other equipment such as lights.

(c) Organisation: eg the grouping of camera-operators into teams, to work on a particular project.

Technology contributes to overall economic growth. Technology can increase total output, by enabling gains in productivity (more output per units of input), reduced costs (eg transportation technology, preservatives) and new types of product.

The term technology when applied within PEST analysis should be used in the widest context and not just with reference to IT developments. For example improvements in the development of packaging materials is an important technological issue. When TetraPak launched their new packaging solution, many food brands were able to use the improved materials and better meet consumer needs.

EXAMPLE

One of the biggest technological discoveries in recent years has been Aerogel, sometimes referred to as 'frozen smoke'. Scientists expect it to become a wonder material and see it as a discovery as important as Bakelite and silicone have been. Originally invented in 1931, the material was far too costly and brittle to be used for any purpose outside the lab but in 2002, Nasa-owned company Aspen Aerogel developed a cheaper, lighter and more flexible version which is said to have a plethora of uses ranging from providing extreme weather insulation, filtering polluted water or protection from bomb blasts. Developmental work has already begun for the future everyday uses of the product, and includes new style jewellery, more powerful squash and tennis rackets and hydrogen-based fuels.

Dunlop and Hugo Boss were some of the first brands to make use of Aerogel. Hugo Boss launched a range of extra warm but lightweight winter jackets with an Aerogel lining. The line had to be withdrawn, however, because customers complained that they were too hot!

5.1 Effects of technological change on organisations

(a) The type of products or services that are made and sold.
(b) The way in which products are made (eg robots, new raw materials).
(c) The way in which services are provided.

EXAMPLE: MAIL ORDER/INTERNET

(a) Companies selling easily transportable goods were first to make use of mail order and then the Internet – for instance, books and CDs – can offer much **greater consumer choice** and are enjoying considerable success – nowadays virtually anything can be found for sale using this medium.

(b) **The way in which markets are identified.** Database systems make it much easier to analyse the market place. We explore database marketing in brief below and information bought through agencies is available much faster.

(c) **The way in which firms are managed.** IT encourages 'delayering' of organisational hierarchies, homeworking, and better communication.

(d) **The means and extent of communications with external clients, via Website, e-mail etc).**

EXAMPLE

Merlin Stone of IBM, in an article entitled *Marketing Management – has it changed that much?* asks how information technology has affected the marketer. He believes that it has affected the entire cycle:

(a) Objective setting
(b) Environmental analysis
(c) Strategy definition
(d) Planning
(e) Implementation
(f) Measurement
(g) Control
(h) Feedback

He identifies what he sees as key features of the marketing environment in the technological age.

(a) Other functions in the organisation such as **logistics** and **human resources** have changed to meet growing **customer expectations** of service, as technology shortens elements of the cycle such as delivery times. Such functions continue to support the marketer's role, but are growing in importance as companies realise that recruiting good staff, for example, is key to maintaining **quality**. The increased focus on corporate **governance** and **business ethics** is also relevant here.

(b) Innovations do not last – the design to delivery cycle is now shorter, as mentioned above. Companies are increasingly willing to **outsource** some of their functions, including IT departments. With outsourcing, **information flows** are quicker, so new **marketing** initiatives can be deployed almost instantly rather than having to wait for an in-house IT department to put new systems in place.

(c) **Interactive** and **direct marketing** is now far more common. Customer loyalty schemes provide an example. These are not universal, however – the low cost airlines, for example, have dispensed with relationship marketing in favour of concentrating on what improves their yield.

(d) All the aspects of dealing with the customer (from initial order to post-sales service and follow-up) have become integrated into **customer relationship management schemes** aided by powerful **databases**, rather than being regarded as a set of distinct functional activities.

(e) The customer relationship cycle of **recruit/retain/develop** is much less firm now. Customers can switch between different companies very easily and are much more able to **compare offers**. Just by looking at the Internet, they can become their own 'expert' on a range of matters from medical queries to cheap flights to better deals on international phone calls. They can even customise the exact product that they want – luxury cars being an often-quoted example.

(f) The new technology has made massive **data sets** available, although companies **often** struggle with how best to analyse and manage the mountains of customer data that often threatens to overwhelm rather than inform.

(g) Customers are able to influence each other very readily, through **e-mail** and **websites.**

(h) New communication channels such as **texting** via mobile phones, especially amongst younger consumers, have opened up new avenues for marketing communicators. Younger customers have their own access to marketing information and are choosing for themselves rather than leaving it to their parents.

(i) Thanks to the ease of access to information, the **decision cycle** for customers (both consumers and organisations) has become much quicker. Offers can be compared on the Internet on a Saturday morning and the purchase made in the afternoon, rather than spending several weekends searching the shops.

(j) **Feedback** arrives much more quickly for the same reason – companies may find themselves having to change their policies much more rapidly. The **cost effectiveness** of marketing initiatives is becoming more important, and the knowledge of costs is more complete.

(k) It is true that new sets of strategies are possible, focusing on **individual customers**. However, it is also true that it is **quality implementation** of those strategies that differentiates, because plans have become far more detailed and focused and need close control.

The impact of **recent** technological change also has potentially important social consequences, which in turn have an impact on business.

(a) **Homeworking.** Whereas people were once collected together to work in factories, home working will become more important.

(b) **Intellective skills.** Certain sorts of skill, related to interpretation of data and information processes, are likely to become more valued than manual or physical skills.

(c) **Services.** Technology increases manufacturing productivity, releasing human resources for service jobs. These jobs require **greater interpersonal skills** (eg in dealing with customers).

Chapter roundup

- The environment in which an organisation operates is made up of non–controllable factors.
- The environment can be subdivided into micro (specific to the organisation) and macro (affecting all organisations within the industry).
- *Johnson and Scholes* have developed a framework for auditing environmental influence.
- The political and legal environment will include all aspects of law (criminal and commercial law) and European and other agreements.
- The economic environment includes local, national and international trends.
- Social factors include demographic social and cultural aspects. Business ethics can also be considered within social factors.
- Technological factors can be thought of in terms of equipment, techniques or organisation.

Quick quiz

1. What are the main categories of external influences which affect the organisation?
2. What is the source of environmental complexity?
3. How does the legal framework potentially affect an organisation?
4. Give two examples of national economic trends which companies need to monitor.
5. Give two examples of international economic factors which companies operating overseas (or wishing to) should monitor.
6. How has the changing age structure affected business plans?
7. What ethical problems might a business organisation face, especially when expanding abroad?
8. In what three ways does technological change affect business?

Answers to quick quiz

1 Political, Economic, Social, Technological.

2 Variety of influences, amount of knowledge needed, interconnections of influences.

3 In many ways – the general legal framework, health and safety law, environmental and marketing legislation, treaties and EU regulations. All regulate the way businesses are conducted.

4 Can include inflation, taxes, interest rates, government spending, the business cycle.

5 Can include exchange rates, economic characteristics, growth, tax, wealth, capital aspects, interest rates.

6 The profile of customers or potential customers may change. Segments may become more/less attractive as might certain products/services.

7 Can be examples of production practices, gifts, social responsibility and competitive behaviour.

8 (a) Type of products/services that are made/sold.
(b) Way in which products are made.
(c) Way in which services are provided.

Answers to activities

1 The answer will depend on the business or market which you have chosen.

2 The answer will depend on the products chosen.

3 Johnson and Scholes' approach to change will indicate that the pressure from consumers, consumer groups and the media means that GM producers and users will have to take notice of the cultural change that has damaged the image of GM food.

Decisions would have to be made over whether to use GM products or produce them at all, or whether the customer could/should be 'educated' to use them.

According to the Johnson and Scholes model this might include the training and management style of staff to allow for strategic change. It may be that the organisation's culture will have to change because of the challenge of the GM food issue.

4 (a) Fewer potential customers
Fewer potential staff, as they are presumably recruited from the same age group

(b) Less disposable income among the target age group
Greater expectations among the target group
Greater desire for long haul, backpacking travel

(c) Greater choice
Greater expectations from holidays
Club Fun's locations perceived as cheap, boring or mundane

(d) A greater number of potential customers, but also the risks that they will travel further afield, be prepared to spend more and avoid 'cheap and cheerful' holidays

Company may have to improve the quality of the product

Chapter 9:
COMPETITOR ANALYSIS

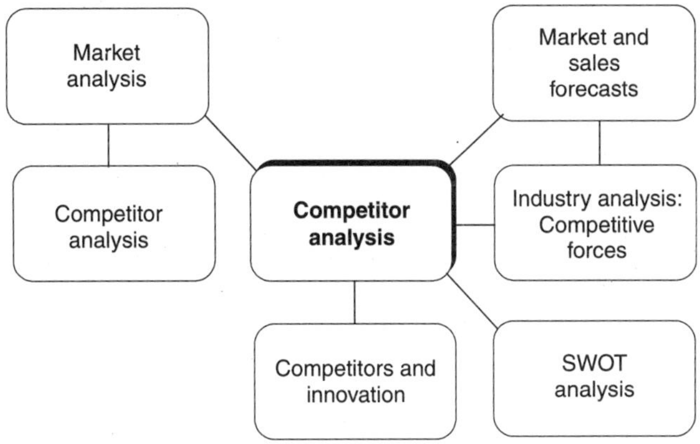

Introduction

The chapter begins by considering the components and importance of market and sales forecasts, along with a discussion concerned with estimating market demand.

The second section reviews the competitive forces which can impact on industries and need to be analysed if we are to understand the nature of competition. Porter's Five Forces model is illustrated and explained. The following section notes the challenges of undertaking a market analysis as a range and variety of inputs can be included.

The next section identifies the key aspects of competitor analysis. This includes who they are, their goals, their strategies, their strengths and weaknesses and how they are likely to respond.

The importance of innovation in competition and as well as illustrating how value can be created through innovation is covered in the penultimate section; it lists the characteristics of innovators.

The final section looks at the concept of SWOT analysis. SWOT analysis not only considers competitors but rather all strengths, weaknesses, opportunities and threats faced by the organisation. It is placed here as it should be used as a summary for the complete marketing audit.

Your objectives

In this chapter you will learn about the following.

(a) The importance of market and sales forecasts

(b) The scope of competitive forces

(c) The principles of market and competitor analysis

(d) Competitors and innovation

(e) How to undertake a SWOT analysis

Strictly speaking, the content of this chapter is included in Unit 17, Marketing Intelligence. However, it is also of relevance in the consideration of Marketing Planning, and so is included here.

1 MARKET FORECASTS AND SALES FORECASTS

Market forecasts and sales forecasts complement each other. The market forecast should be carried out first of all and should cover a longer period of time.

Definition

> **Market forecast.** This is a forecast for the market as a whole. It is mainly involved in the assessment of environmental factors, outside the organisation's control, which will affect the demand for its products/services.

(a) Components of a **market forecast**

(i) The **economic review** (national economy, government policy, covering forecasts on investment, population, gross national product, etc).

(ii) **Specific market research** (to obtain data about specific markets and forecasts concerning total market demand).

(iii) Evaluation of **total market demand** for the firm's and similar products, for example profitability, market potential etc.

(b) **Sales forecasts** are estimates of sales (in volume, value and profit terms) of a product in a future period at a given marketing mix.

1.1 Research into potential sales

Definition

> **Sales potential** is an estimate of the part of the market which is within the possible reach of a product.

Factors governing sales potential

- The price of the product
- The amount of money spent on sales promotion
- How essential the product is to consumers
- Whether it is a durable commodity whose purchase is postponable
- The overall size of the possible market
- Competition

Whether sales potential is worth exploiting will depend on the cost which must be incurred to realise the potential.

EXAMPLE

Market research has led a company to the opinion that the sales potential of product X is as follows.

	Sales value	*Contribution earned before selling costs deducted*	*Cost of selling*
either	£100,000	£40,000	£10,000
or	£110,000	£44,000	£15,000

In this example, it would not be worth spending an extra £5,000 on selling in order to realise an extra sales potential of £10,000, because the net effect would be a loss of £(5,000 – 4,000) = £1,000.

1.2 Estimating market demand

Estimating market demand is not necessarily as straightforward as you might at first think. Imagine you are the marketing manager of a company producing sports footwear. What is your market demand? Is it the volume of shoes purchased in the UK, or Europe, or the whole world? Should you be considering tennis shoes as well as running shoes? Shoes for children or only adults? And should you be forecasting demand for next year or over the next five years? The permutations seem endless. *Kotler* (2008) identifies 90 possible combinations of market demand definitions based on product level, geographic area and time horizon.

A demand function is simply an expression which shows how sales demand for a product is dependent on several factors. These demand variables can be grouped into two broad categories.

(a) **Controllable variables or strategic variables.** These are factors over which the firm's management should have some degree of control, and which they can change if they wish. Controllable variables are essentially the marketing mix.

(b) **Uncontrollable variables.** These are factors over which the firm's management has no control.

  (i) **Consumer variables** depend on decisions by consumers, or the circumstances of consumers (for example, their wealth).

  (ii) **Competitor variables** depend on decisions and actions by other firms, particularly competitors.

  (iii) **Other variables.** These include decisions by other organisations (for example the government) or factors which are outside the control of anyone (for example, weather conditions, or the total size of the population).

A demand function can be set out as follows.

$$Q_a = f(P_a, A_a, D_a, O_a;\ I_c, T_c, E_c;\ P_b, A_b, D_b, O_b;\ G, N, W ...)$$

P_a, A_a, D_a, O_a	I_c, T_c, E_c	P_b, A_b, D_b, O_b	G, N, W ...
Strategic variables	Consumer variables	Competitor variables	Other variables
Controllable variables	Uncontrollable variables		

where Q_a is quantity demanded of a product A per period
- P_a is price of product A
- A_a is advertising and sales promotion for product A
- D_a is the design or quality of product A
- O_a is the number of retail outlets or other outlets for distribution of product A
- I_c is incomes of consumers/customers
- T_c is the tastes and preferences of consumers
- E_c is the expectation of consumers about future prices etc
- P_b is the prices of related goods (substitutes, complements)
- A_b is advertising/promotion for related goods
- D_b is design and quality of related goods
- O_b is the number of outlets for distribution of related goods
- G is government policy
- N is the number of people in the economy/potential market
- W represents the weather conditions

The demand function set out above is little more than commonsense. But what firms should want to estimate or forecast is what future demand is likely to be. To do this, **an attempt should be made to quantify the relationship between demand for a product and the significant demand variables.** For example a demand function might be measurable as

$$Q_a = 3{,}000 - 0.032\ P_a + 240\ A_a + 0.05\ O_a + 0.35\ P_b - 320\ A_b - 0.02\ O_b + 36\ I_b$$

There are two problems with measuring a demand function in this way.

(a) **Measurement.** There is the problem of deciding how to measure variables, especially qualitative variables such as product design, and consumer tastes.

(b) **Valuation.** Then there is the mathematical problem of putting values to the 'constants' or coefficients for each variable. This might be done using **regression analysis**.

Follow a few simple guidelines in choosing forecasting methods:

1. Use the simple methods you understand rather than complex methods that few people do
2. Simple methods are often as good as complicated ones
3. Use different methods and combine them
4. Expensive does not necessarily mean good
5. Before making decisions based on forecasts, be aware of the way they are produced, as well as the limitations and risks involved
6. Don't forget that sales forecasting is both an art and a science.

FOR DISCUSSION

If the environment is uncertain, flexibility, not forecasting, is the key!

EXAMPLE

The UK summer of 2007 was a complete washout for many industries, especially for those that based their sales predictions on experience from the previous summer. It is clear why organisations dealing in ice cream, BBQs and domestic holidays would be impacted, but unpredictable weather influences a surprising range of industries. One soft drinks manufacturer was down by £3m, directly due to the poor summer of 2007. Fresh soup manufacturers on the other hand reported sales higher than expected as consumers sought comforting warm meals.

Cinema attendance was 28% higher during the summer in 2007 compared to 2006, and much of this was accounted for by the poor weather .

2 INDUSTRY ANALYSIS: THE COMPETITIVE FORCES

In discussing competition Porter (2004) distinguishes between factors which characterise the nature of competition:

(a) **In one industry compared with another** (eg in the chemicals industry compared with the clothing retail industry) and make one industry as a whole potentially more profitable than another (ie yielding a bigger return on investment).

(b) **Within a particular industry.** These relate to the competitive strategies that individual firms might select.

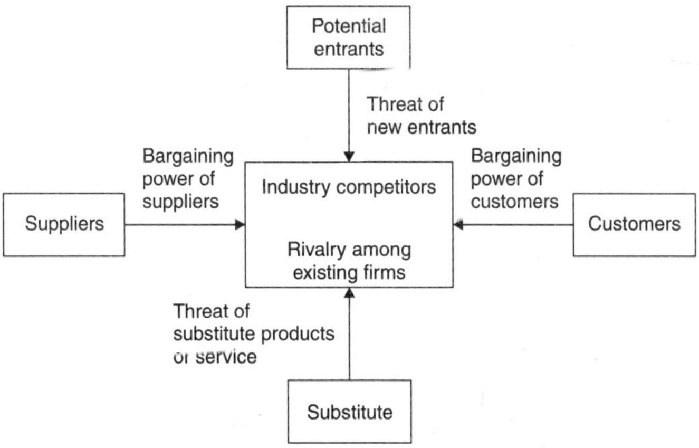

Figure 9.1: Porter's five forces
Source: *adapted from Porter* (2004)

2.1 The threat of new entrants (and barriers to entry to keep them out)

A new entrant into an industry will bring extra capacity and more competition. The strength of this threat is likely to vary from industry to industry, depending on:

(a) The strength of the **barriers to entry**. Barriers to entry discourage new entrants.

(b) The likely **response of existing competitors** to the new entrant.

The diagram below outlines the driving forces and critical success factors of competition.

The driving forces

- Customers demand products and services increasingly customised to their needs
- Customer satisfaction standards are increasingly established by global competition
- Reductions in international trade barriers
- Industrialisation of Pacific Rim countries
- Slow growth in the mature economies
- New overseas competitors in mature production and service sectors
- Technology is rapidly changing and easily transferable
- Public sector financial constraints, political pressures for higher value for money and privatisation or market testing
- Communities are becoming more concerned about the effects of economic development on the environment and social well being

How organisations are responding

- Highly differentiated goods and services
- Customer-led organisations; relationships
- 'Step' change and continuous improvement of products, processes and services
- Quicker response times
- Lower costs and sustainable profits
- Flexibility from people and technology
- Investing in and developing the core competences of people

How this is affecting the way people are organised and managed

- Decentralisation and development of decision-making
- Slimmer and flatter management structures
- Total quality and 'lean organisation' initiatives
- Fewer specialists directly employed
- Developing a flexible workforce
- More project based and cross functional initiatives and team working
- Empowered rather than command structures
- Partnership approach to supplier links

What this means for employees

- Customer-orientation to meet the needs of both internal and external customers
- Greater self-management and responsibility for individuals and teams
- Contributing to the continuous improvement of processes, products and services
- Commitment to personal training, development and adaptability

What this means for managers

- Facilitating, co-ordinating roles
- Greater interpersonal, team leadership and motivational skills
- Integrated management and communication systems
- Openness, fairness and a partnership in employment relations
- Managing constructively the interests of groups of employees and their collective and individual representation
- Ensuring part-time and temporary employees and those contracted to supply services are fully integrated

Figure 9.2: Competition – the driving forces and critical success factors

2.2 The threat from substitute products

A **substitute product** is a good/service produced by **another industry** which satisfies the **same customer needs**. Substitutes put a lid on what firms in an industry can charge.

EXAMPLE

Passengers have several ways of getting from London to Paris, and the pricing policies of the various industries transporting them there reflects this.

(a) 'Le Shuttle' carries cars in the Channel Tunnel. Its main competitors are the ferry companies, offering a substitute service. Therefore, you will find that Le Shuttle sets its prices with reference to ferry company prices, and vice versa.

(b) Eurostar is the rail service from London to Paris/Brussels. Its main competitors are not the ferry companies but the airlines. Prices on the London – Paris air routes fell with the commencement of Eurostar services, and some airlines have curtailed the number of flights they offer.

2.3 The bargaining power of customers

Customers want better quality products and services at a lower price. Satisfying this want might force down the profitability of suppliers in the industry. Customer strength depends upon the following.

(a) How much the **customer buys**.

(b) How **critical** the product is to the customer's own business.

(c) **Switching costs (ie the cost of switching supplier).**

(d) Whether the products are **standard items** (hence easily copied) or **specialised**.

(e) The **customer's own profitability:** a customer who makes low profits will be forced to insist on low prices from suppliers.

(f) The customer's **ability to bypass** the supplier or **take over** the supplier.

(g) The **skills** of the customer's **purchasing staff**, or the price-awareness of consumers.

(h) When **product quality** is important to the customer, the customer is less likely to be price-sensitive, and so the industry might be more profitable as a consequence.

EXAMPLE

Although the Ministry of Defence may wish to keep control over defence spending, it is likely as a customer to be more concerned that the products it purchases perform satisfactorily than with getting the lowest price possible for everything it buys.

2.4 The bargaining power of suppliers

Suppliers can exert pressure for higher prices, depending upon the following factors.

(a) Whether there are just **one or two dominant suppliers** to the industry, able to charge monopoly or oligopoly prices.

(b) The threat of **new entrants** or substitute products to the **supplier's industry**.

(c) Whether the suppliers have **other customers** outside the industry, and do not rely on the industry for the majority of their sales.

(d) The **importance of the supplier's product** to the customer's business.

(e) Whether the supplier has a **differentiated product** which buyers need to obtain.

(f) Whether **switching costs** for customers would be high.

EXAMPLE

Food products in the UK are largely sold through supermarket chains, and it can be difficult for a new producer to get supermarket organisations to agree to stock its product. As retailers become more powerful, they are placing more and more demands on food producers: failure to comply can mean exclusion from the channel of distribution. Supplier bargaining power is low. Sophisticated marketing firms try to get round this by using advertising, for example, to stimulate customer demand by implementing 'pull strategies'.

Other suppliers try to restrict distribution outlets to maintain high prices, particularly in the case of perfumes and cosmetics, by banning sales of these items in 'undesirable' outlets.

2.5 The rivalry amongst current competitors in the industry

The **intensity of competitive rivalry** within an industry will affect the profitability of the industry as a whole. Competitive actions might take the form of price competition, advertising battles, sales promotion campaigns, introducing new products for the market, improving after sales service or providing guarantees or warranties.

Activity 1 **(10 minutes)**

Coca-Cola and Pepsi compete on the basis of massive advertising spend on image and packaging to position against each other. They will respond to each other's advertising and promotion with anything except one thing – price. Coca-Cola and Pepsi have experienced price wars and they do not like them. This made the big brands highly vulnerable to attack by cheaper substitutes – Sainsbury own label and Virgin Cola have taken significant market share in the UK market driven mainly by lower prices. Can you think of any other similar examples?

3 MARKET ANALYSIS

Definition

> A **market** is a group of actual and potential customers, who can make purchase decisions.

Businesses also talk about the market 'for' a product (eg the 'confectionery market') as well as other classifications such as 'the youth market'.

Many firms compete in several markets, if they are diversified or if they have a distinctive competence or brand which can be exploited.

EXAMPLE

Conventional financial services providers were wrong-footed by Virgin's entry into the market with simplified products and direct marketing techniques, and seem unable to respond to the entry of diverse firms like supermarkets into financial services.

A **market analysis** will be made up of a range of factors. Here is a checklist.

Statistical data	**2008**	**2009**	**2010 (forecast)**
Company/SBU data			
Market name			
Unit sales			
£ sales			
Profitability			
Market data			
Market size			
Market share			
No. of main customers			
No. of dealers/distributors			
Concentration ratio			
Qualitative data			
Environmental factors			
Critical success factors			
Growing/stable/declining			
Key competitors and their strategies			
Future competitors			
Segmentation opportunities			
Ease of entry			

We can expand upon some elements of the above checklist.

(a) **Market size**. This refers to both actual and potential (forecast) size. A company cannot know whether its market share objectives are feasible unless it knows the market's overall size. Forecasting areas of growth and decline is also important.

(b) **Customers**. The analysis needs to identify who the customers are, what they need, and their buying behaviour (where, when and how they purchase products or services). This will help to point out opportunities.

(c) **Distributors**. The company will need to evaluate its current arrangements for getting goods or services to the customer. Changes in distribution channels can open up new fields of opportunity (eg the Internet).

Often these factors overlap and PEST factors will affect many areas. For example at the present time the UK government is considering how best to free the country's postal systems from monopoly. Parliamentary bills will eventually need to be passed. Here the major driving force could be said to be political, triggered by economic necessity, facilitated by law. The markets will cease to be a monopoly. They might fragment into public and private sectors.

4 COMPETITOR ANALYSIS

Many firms identify key competitors and plan their strategies with competitors in mind.

Definition

> **Competition analysis** is 'a systematic attempt to identify and understand the key elements of a competitor's strategy, in terms of objectives, strategies, resource allocation and implementation through the marketing mix. A sound understanding of these areas enables stronger defences to be built and sustainable competitive advantage to be created and, not least, provides a foundation for outmanoeuvring the competition'. *Brassington & Pettitt (2006)*

4.1 Key questions for competitor analysis

- Who are they?
- What are their goals?
- What strategies are they pursuing?
- What are their strengths and weaknesses?
- How are they likely to respond?

The complexity facing the modern business is that its main competitor, customer and collaborator may be the same company.

EXAMPLE

Kodak and Fuji are intense rivals in the photographic film business, yet they collaborated to bring the Advanced Photographic System (APS) to market while at the same time fighting in the Japanese courts over market protection issues.

Similarly the Efficient Consumer Response programme involves groups of competing manufacturers working together with retailers to streamline supply chains – an alliance of competitors, customers and collaborators. The complexity and ambiguity faced by executives in many modern markets underline yet further the imperative of identifying and understanding competitors.

For many organisations in the voluntary or community sector, collaboration is believed to be one of the key drivers of success and is regadred as essential for survival.

4.2 Who are our competitors?

Identifying current competitors is easy. Identifying **potential** competitors is harder as potential competitors might be:

- Smaller companies attacking the market segment
- Companies operating in other markets wishing to expand
- Companies wishing to diversify

Finally a firm can **define** who its competitors actually are.

EXAMPLE

Coca-Cola competes against:

- Pepsi in the Cola market
- All other soft drinks
- Tea and coffee
- Tap water: Coca-Cola's chief executive has declared that 'the main competitor is tap water: any other share definition is too narrow'

4.3 What are competitors' goals?

Next, you need to discern what competitors' goals and objectives are.

(a) **Relevant goals and objectives**

(i) Goals and objectives of the **parent company,** if the competitor is part of a larger group.

(ii) The competitor's assessment of risk; a higher risk will require a higher return from a market.

(iii) The personal goals of key managers. For example, a new chief executive may be brought in to 'turn the company round' and may have made a **public commitment** and invested a lot of prestige in achieving declared goals.

(iv) A company facing cash-flow problems may do anything to maximise cash inflow.

(v) The competitor's history, position and the underlying assumptions of their management. For example, some firms consider themselves to be 'market leaders'.

(vi) **How dependent** the competitor is on the current business. A competitor with one main business will fight much harder to defend it than a competitor exposed to several sectors.

(b) **Types of goals**

- Profit
- Market share
- Cash-flow
- Technological leadership
- Service leadership

Different competitors put different weights on particular goals, especially with regard to time horizons. Some might sacrifice profit, in the short-term, for market share.

4.4 Current competitor strategies

Assessing current competitor strategies is relatively simple, as competitors send out signals to the same customer base. A company's closest competitor is one competing in the same target market.

4.5 Strategic group analysis: a constraint on competitive choice

Strategic group analysis tries to show how firms are positioned in a particular market or segment. Porter identifies a number of dimensions in which firms can differ.

- **Specialisation.** (Limited number of segments? Narrow product range?)
- **Brand.** Does the firm promote a brand or compete on price?
- **Distribution.** What channels are used? **Push** or **pull** approach?
- **Quality**
- Technological **leader** or follower?
- Degree of vertical **integration**
- **Cost structure**
- **Add-on services**
- **Price policy**
- **Indebtedness**
- Degree of **control** by holding company
- **Government involvement**

Any firm can be defined according to these dimensions. Firms with **low relative prices** are usually **able to control costs,** but **do not have superior product quality**.

Definition

> In any industry, especially with a large number of firms, some will pursue similar strategies in which case they can be considered a **strategic group**.

For any two of the attributes in 4.5 above it should be possible to map how firms relate to each other. The number of dimensions of course is very large, so a strategic group is best identified by taking the two most significant dimensions in the industry.

Mobility barriers constrain organisational endeavours and function as barriers to entry. They make it hard for a firm in one strategic group to develop or migrate to another.

(a) **Market factors**

(i) The brand name may be a mobility barrier, if it is unknown in the particular segment.

(ii) The product line may not be extensive enough.

(iii) Other factors include user technologies and selling systems.

(b) **Industry characteristics.** To move into a mass volume end of the market might require economies of scale and large production facilities. To move to the quality end might require greater investment in research and development.

(c) The organisation may lack the **distinctive skills** and competences in the new market area.

(d) **Legal barriers** might exist.

4.6 Competitors' strengths and weaknesses

SWOT analysis is covered in a later chapter, but it is relatively easy to assess a competitor's **strengths** and **weaknesses.** Here are some examples.

- Brand strengths, customer loyalty
- Market share
- Quality of management team
- Resources, financial and otherwise
- Intellectual property
- Distribution network
- Relative cost structure
- Distinctive competence

Kotler (2008) suggests the following table for consideration for **marketing strengths and weaknesses.**

- Customer awareness
- Product quality
- Product availability
- Technical assistance
- Sales staff
- Market share
- 'Mind' share (% of customers who had heard about the company)
- Share of benefit

4.7 Analysing competitors' costs

Clearly, the strategic response of competitors can depend significantly on the cost profile of the competitor. **Relative costs** are more important than absolute costs.

Where the competitor is not competing on price, despite having a lower cost base, the competitor is:

- Under no pressure to raise prices, thus limiting the firm's ability to raise its own
- More profitable, and hence can invest more

4.8 Competitor reaction and response

Kotler (2008) identifies the following types of competitor response.

Predictable

(i) **Laid-back**: competitor does not respond

(ii) **Selective**: competitor only responds to certain types of attack

(iii) **Tiger**: competitor reacts to any attack

Unpredictable

Unstochastic: **impossible to predict** how **competitor will react**

FOR DISCUSSION

Why might a competitor be 'laid-back'?

Activity 2 **(5 minutes)**

Jot down a list of items of information that might be obtained from an analysis of competitors.

4.9 'Good' competitors

Monopolies are hard to come by, but some competitors are definitely easier to deal with than others. A 'good' competitor:

- Deters new entrants (assuming you are not a new entrant)
- Shares similar assumptions about the industry
- Prefers differentiation and focus to competing on price

	Balance	Strength	Weakness
Competitive maturity	• Understand the rules • Realistic assumptions • Support industry structure	• Credible/viable • Know the industry costs	• Clear weaknesses • Limited strategic concept
Reconcilable goals	• Moderate strategic stake • Accept current profitability • Desire cash generation	• Comparable ROI targets	• Short time horizons • Risk averse

Figure 9.3: Behaviour of 'good' competitors

5 COMPETITORS AND INNOVATION

5.1 Hamel's company types

Gary Hamel (1996) is one of the principal advocates of the view that organisations cannot succeed if they simply imitate what has gone before. In essence, he defines three principal types of company.

Company type	Comment
Rule makers	Dominate their respective marketplaces and who (try to) set the competitive conditions under which they and others will operate. The rule makers in today's environment include Microsoft, Hertz, General Electric and McDonald's.
Rule takers	The companies who, in effect, imitate the rule makers, who accept the competitive framework which has been established by the dominant players, and who try to beat the rule makers at their own game. Rule takers include Avis and Burger King.
Rule breakers	Organisations which refuse to accept the implicit assumptions made by existing competitors, and which therefore seek to establish a new paradigm. Companies in the rule breaker category include Amazon.com. Eventually, if a rule breaker becomes highly successful, it dominates its market place and can fall into the trap of turning into a rule maker.

5.2 Kotler's five dimensions of strategy

A similar framework is offered by Kotler.

Creating Value Through Innovation		
Five dimensions of strategy	**Conventional logic**	**Value innovation logic**
• **Industry assumptions**	Industry's conditions are given.	Industry's conditions can be shaped.
• **Strategic focus**	Competitive advantages to beat the competition.	Competition not the benchmark. A company should pursue a quantum leap in value to dominate the market.
• **Customers**	Further segmentation and customisation, focusing on the differences in what customers value.	A value innovator targets the mass of buyers and willingly lets some existing customers go. It focuses on the key commonalities in what customers value.
• **Assets and capabilities**	A company should leverage its existing capabilities.	A company must not be constrained by what it already has. It must ask, 'What would we do if we were starting a new?'
• **Product and service offerings**	An industry's traditional boundaries determine the products and services a company offers. The goal is to maximise the value of those offerings.	A value innovator thinks in terms of the total solution customers seek, even if that takes the company beyond its industry's traditional offerings.

5.3 Characteristics of innovators

It is of crucial importance to the marketer of an innovation to know who the innovators/early triers are, and how they can be reached and influenced. 'Consumer innovators' is a term for the relatively small group who are the earliest purchasers of a new product or service (whether this is defined as the first 2.5% of adopters of a particular new product, or the people who purchase a number of new products and are therefore inferred to be 'innovative'.)

Characteristics which distinguish innovators from later adopters and non-adopters.

(a) **Interest in the relevant product category**. People who show an interest in fashion or technological inventions, say, are more likely to be the ones who will try out a new 'look' or device. Innovators can be identified and targeted by their tendency to seek information on the areas of their interest from special-interest mass-media sources – publications, conferences and exhibitions. Attitude surveys and lifestyle analysis may also pinpoint people with particular interests.

(b) **Opinion leadership**. We noted earlier that opinion-leaders tend to be innovators, and are therefore gatekeepers of new product information: if the opinion leaders get interested and have positive experience of the innovation, they will tell and influence others. By identifying opinion leaders, marketers can target motivational communication at innovative individuals.

(c) **Personality traits**

(i) Attitude flexibility, or open-mindedness.

(ii) Independence of judgement.

(iii) Variety-seeking, and the ability to deal with complex or ambiguous stimuli.

(iv) High tolerance for risk, low perception of risk, 'venturesomeness'. Innovators tend to be willing to risk a poor choice in order to increase their exposure to new ideas and experience.

Non-innovators seem to possess the opposite characteristics. Separate promotional approaches might therefore be required. Innovators respond to informative messages appealing to their interest, open-mindedness and willingness to make independent evaluations. Non-innovators respond to reference group influence, and the use of trusted/well known spokespersons, to reduce perceived risk and give their evaluation the support of others' opinions.

(d) **Consumption habits**. Innovators are less brand loyal, willing to switch to other brands for variety and respond more to promotional 'deals'. They also consume heavily (in volume) in the product areas in which they are the innovators.

(e) **Media selection**. Innovators expose themselves to more magazines and journals – especially those related to their particular interests. Targeting innovators can thus be efficiently achieved through advertising/editorials in special interest publications.

(f) **Social profile**. Innovators are more socially involved and accepted than non-innovators, meaning that they are more likely to belong to social groups and organisations. They therefore also function well as opinion leaders.

(g) **Demographic factors.** Innovators tend to be younger than non-innovators, although this depends to an extent on the nature of the product. They tend to have higher status in terms of education, occupation (three quarters have professional or technical jobs) and income. Innovators may thus be targeted through the use of geo-demographic techniques.

6 SWOT ANALYSIS

The purpose of **corporate appraisal** (SWOT analysis) is to **combine** the assessment of the environment and the analysis of the organisation's internal resources and capabilities. SWOT analysis relates to a few of the chapters already outlined such as the external environment and organisational capability. It has been put at the end of competitor analysis because it acts as a summary for the entire marketing audit.

It is an important tool to use in order to provide a summary of the external and internal values which should be used to deliver the marketing plan and strategy.

Definition

> **Corporate appraisal:** 'a critical assessment of the strengths and weaknesses, opportunities and threats in relation to the internal and environmental factors affecting the entity in order to establish its condition prior to the preparation of a long-term plan.'

A **strengths and weaknesses** analysis expresses which areas of the business have:

- Strengths that should be exploited
- Weaknesses which should be improved

It therefore covers the results of the position audit.

6.1 Opportunities

- What opportunities exist in the business environment?
- Their inherent profit-making potential
- The organisation's ability to exploit the worthwhile opportunities

6.2 Threats

- What threats might arise?
- How will competitors be affected?
- How will the company be affected?

The opportunities and threats might arise from PEST and competitive factors.

6.3 Bringing the SWOT elements together

The internal and external appraisals will be brought together, and perhaps shown in a cruciform chart.

EXAMPLE

Strengths	Weaknesses
£10 million of capital available	Heavy reliance on a small number of customers
Production expertise and appropriate marketing skills	Limited product range, with no new products and expected market decline. Small marketing organisation.
Threats	**Opportunities**
A major competitor has already entered the new market	Government tax incentives for new investment
	Growing demand in a new market, although customers so far relatively small in number

The company is in imminent danger of losing its existing markets and must diversify its products and/or markets. The new market opportunity exists to be exploited, and since the number of customers is currently small, the relatively small size of the existing marketing force would not be an immediate hindrance. A strategic plan could be developed to buy new equipment and use existing production and marketing to enter the new market, with a view to rapid expansion. Careful planning of manpower, equipment, facilities, research and development would be required and there would be an objective to meet the threat of competition so as to obtain a substantial share of a growing market. The cost of entry at this early stage of market development should not be unacceptably high.

The SWOT technique can also be used for specific areas of strategy such as IT and marketing.

Effective SWOT analysis does not simply require a categorisation of information, it also requires some **evaluation of the relative importance** of the various factors under consideration.

(a) These features are only of relevance if they are **perceived to exist by the customers.** Listing corporate features that internal personnel regard as strengths/weaknesses is of little relevance if customers do not perceive them as such.

(b) In the same vein, threats and opportunities are conditions presented by the external environment and they should be independent of the firm.

The SWOT can now be used to guide strategy formulation. The two major options are **matching** and **conversion**.

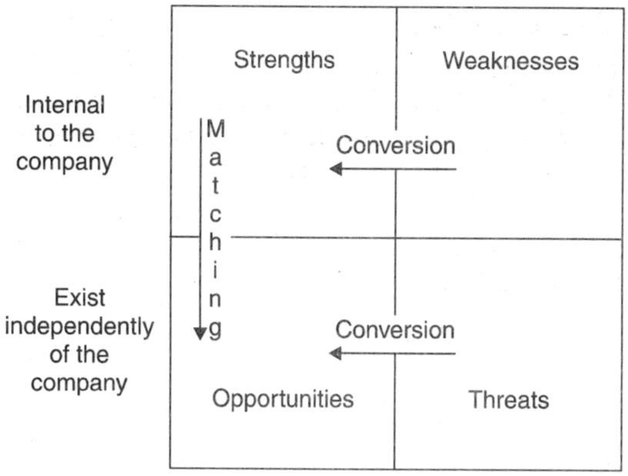

Figure 9.4: SWOT analysis

(a) **Matching**

This entails finding, where possible, a match between the strengths of the organisation and the opportunities presented by the market. Strengths which do not match any available opportunity are of limited use while opportunities which do not have any matching strengths are of little immediate value.

(b) **Conversion**

This requires the development of strategies which will convert weaknesses into strengths in order to take advantage of some particular opportunity, or converting threats into opportunities which can then be matched by existing strengths.

Activity 3 **(20 minutes)**

Hall Faull Downes Ltd has been in business for 25 years, during which time profits have risen by an average of 3% per annum, although there have been peaks and troughs in profitability due to the ups and downs of trade in the customers' industry. The increase in profits until five years ago was the result of increasing sales in a buoyant market, but more recently, the total market has become somewhat smaller and Hall Faull Downes has only increased sales and profits as a result of improving its market share.

The company produces components for manufacturers in the engineering Industry.

In recent years, the company has developed many new products and currently has 40 items in its range compared to 24 only five years ago. Over the same five-year period, the number of customers has fallen from twenty to nine, two of whom together account for 60% of the company's sales.

Give your appraisal of the company's future, and suggest what it is probably doing wrong.

6.4 The marketing SWOT

Having looked at corporate level SWOT analysis we should now turn our attention to the marketing level. It is important to remember that the concept and approach remains the same, it is only the factors which we are considering which vary. Corporate SWOTs are concerned with everything. Marketing SWOTs concentrate more specifically on **markets** and the mix.

6.5 Strengths and weaknesses

The marketing department is probably the most important source of 'bottom-up' information, opinions and views which influence the development of the corporate strategy. But the marketing audit also represents the starting point for developing the **marketing** plan, answering the 'where are we now' question in terms of marketing controllables.

A **marketing audit** as we have seen earlier, should involve a thorough 'taking stock' of the complete marketing activity.

A prime objective as far as the marketing manager is concerned of this internal marketing analysis is to be able to log the company's current market position on a **positioning map**.

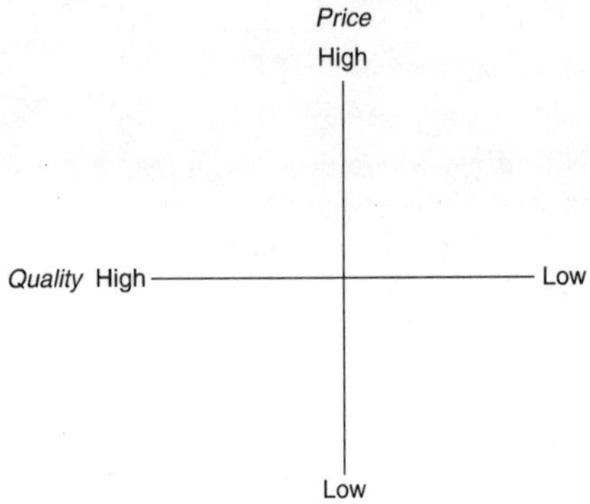

The variables used on this positioning map are dimensions of the marketing mix. You may need several such maps to consider the real position of a complex product, but the variables you should focus on are those recognised as having the greatest influence on purchasing decisions.

Activity 4 **(10 minutes)**

Use the positioning maps above and below to log the positions of your company or college and its key competitors.

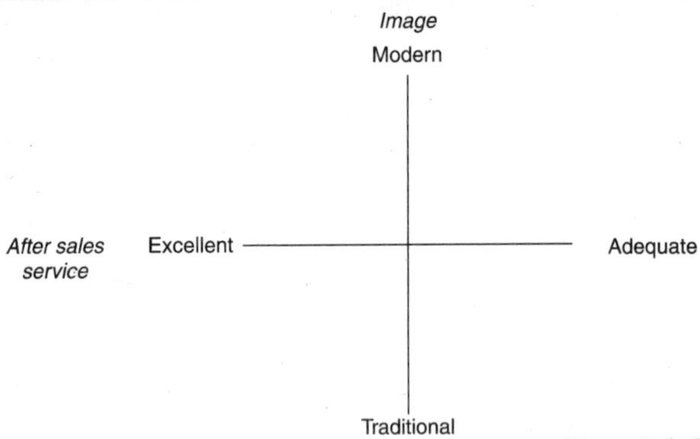

Figure 9.5: Positioning maps

6.6 Opportunities and threats

The external aspects of the marketing SWOT are the product/market opportunities and threats which evolve from changes in the macro environment identified at the corporate level. For example a demographic shift increasing the proportion of older customers for overseas holidays may have been identified in the environmental analysis of a package holiday company. At **marketing** level this translates into a number of possibilities.

(a) An opportunity to sell existing holidays to this new target market.

(b) An opportunity to develop new products specifically developed to meet the needs of this emerging segment.

(c) The possible option of switching resources away from segments which are showing less growth potential.

At marketing level, opportunities can be considered and communicated using the **Ansoff matrix** (see next section) which provides the alternative product/market options available to a company. (*Note.* Although not specifically shown by implication the threats at this level are factors which reduce the viability or potential of any of the product/market possibilities.)

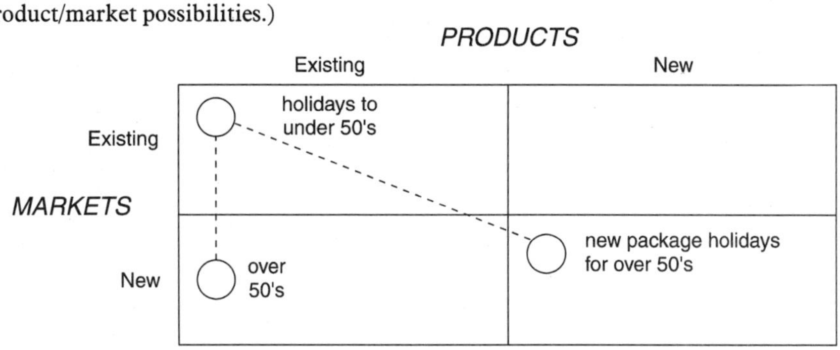

To summarise the marketing SWOT:

Strengths	*Weaknesses*
These are **internal** factors controllable by marketing managers; they are the 7Ps	
Opportunities	*Threats*
These are **external** uncontrollable factors related to an appraisal of changing product/market position	

Chapter roundup

- Companies that have not mastered forecasting are likely to build positions that defend against yesterday's competitors or appeal to yesterday's customers.
- Competition between firms to serve customers is the very essence of modern, market-led economies.
- Systematic analysis of the business environment typically commences at the macro level, highlighting aspects of the broader environment that may impinge on the specific markets the firm operates in.
- Many firms such as Virgin compete in several markets and as such are diversified.
- Without a knowledge of competitors' strengths and their likely actions, it is impossible to formulate the central component of marketing strategy – finding a group of customers for whom one has a competitive advantage over the competition.
- It must also be true that, since competitive advantage is a relative concept, a company that has poor understanding of its competitors can have no real understanding of itself.
- The identification of strategic groups is fundamental to industry analysis since, just as industries can rise or fall despite the state of the overall business environment, so strategic groups with the distinctive competencies of their members can defy the general fluctuations within an industry.
- When a company chooses to enter a market, it also chooses its competitors. Therefore, in the selection of new opportunities, it is important to realise that not all competitors are equally attractive.
- The more a firm innovates, the greater the experience accumulated; the greater the experience gained, the better the firm gets at innovation; the better the firm becomes at this activity, the greater its chances of competitive survival. A cycle of innovation is thus established.
- SWOT analysis is designed to combine an assessment of the organisation's internal resources with the influences of the external environment in order to deliver the marketing plan and strategy.

Quick quiz

1. What is involved in a market forecast?
2. List three factors that govern sales potential.
3. What are Porter's Five Forces?
4. Name three factors which can encourage suppliers to exert pressure for higher prices.
5. What are the five key questions when undertaking a competitive analysis?

6 What types of goals might an organisation establish?

7 What is a strategic group?

8 What are the four main types of competitor response?

9 What three types of company has *Hamel* defined?

10 What are Kotler's five dimensions of strategy?

11 List four factors that distinguish innovators from later or non-adopters.

12 What is 'matching' in the context of SWOT analysis?

Answers to quick quiz

1 An assessment of environmental factors, outside the organisation's control, which will affect the demand for its products and services.

2 The price of the product, sales promotion expenditure, competition.

3 The threat of new entrants and substitute products/services, the bargaining power of suppliers and customers and the rivalry among existing firms.

4 The importance of the supplier's product to the customer's business, whether the supplier has a differentiated product which buyers need to obtain, whether switching costs for customers would be high.

5 Who are they, what are their goals, what strategies are they pursuing, what are their strengths and weaknesses and what are their response patterns?

6 Goals could be concerned with profit, market share, cash flow and technological or service leadership.

7 A strategic group is composed of firms within an industry following similar strategies aimed at similar customers or customer groups.

8 Laid-back, selective, tiger and stochastic.

9 Rule makers, takers and breakers.

10 Industry assumptions, strategic focus, customers, assets and capabilities, product and service offerings.

11 Interest in the relevant product category, they tend to be opinion leaders, their consumption habits and their media selection.

12 Finding a match between the strengths of the organisation and the opportunities presented by the market.

Answers to activities

1 Petrol: supermarkets have entered the market
Financial services/banking
Books and CDs (threat from e-retailers)
Cars. Impact of cheaper imported cars has been to drive down the price
Medicines: some chemists now sell at below the RRP

2
- Their current and future objectives – this will give clues as to the direction it will take and the aggressiveness with which it will pursue that direction.
- Their current strategies – can help to identify threats and opportunities arising from competitor actions.

- Their resources – asset and capability profile will indicate how they will move in the future and how they may react to threats.
- Predict their future strategies – a combination of the above findings should help to indicate what they are most likely to do in the future.

3 A general interpretation of the facts as given might be sketched as follows.

Objectives: the company has no declared objectives. Profits have risen by 3% per annum in the past, which has failed to keep pace with inflation but may have been a satisfactory rate of increase in the current conditions of the industry. Even so, stronger growth is indicated in the future.

Strengths: the growth in company sales in the last five years has been as a result of increasing the market share in a declining market. This success may be the result of the following.

(i) Research and development spending

(ii) Good product development programmes

(iii) Extending the product range to suit changing customer needs

(iv) Marketing skills

(v) Long-term supply contracts with customers

(vi) Cheap pricing policy

(vii) Product quality and reliable service

Weaknesses:

(i) The products may be custom-made for customers so that they provide little or no opportunity for market development.

(ii) Products might have a shorter life cycle than in the past, in view of the declining total market demand.

(iii) Excessive reliance on two major customers leaves the company exposed to the dangers of losing their custom.

Threats: there may be a decline in the end-market for the customers' product so that the customer demands for the company's own products will also fall.

Opportunities: no opportunities have been identified, but in view of the situation as described, new strategies for the longer term would appear to be essential.

Conclusions: the company does not appear to be planning beyond the short-term, or is reacting to the business environment in a piecemeal fashion. A strategic planning programme should be introduced.

Recommendations: the company must look for new opportunities in the longer-term and diversify into new markets or into new products. Diversification opportunities should be sought with a view to exploiting any competitive advantage or synergy that might be achievable.

In the short-term, current strengths (whether in R & D, production skills or marketing expertise) must be exploited to continue to increase market share in existing markets and product development programmes should also continue.

4 The answer to this activity depends on your choice of organisation.

Chapter 10 :
NEW PRODUCTS

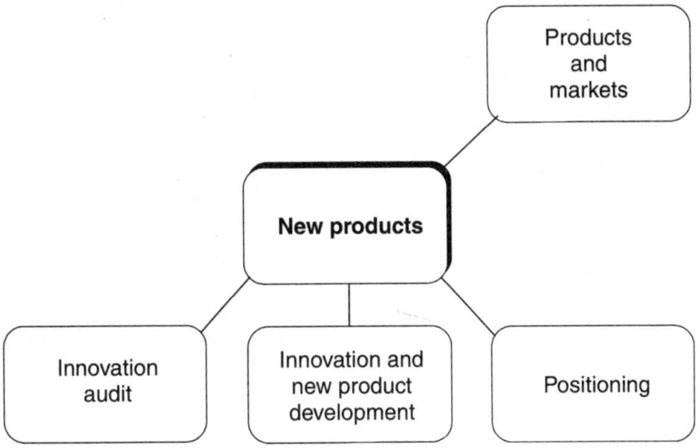

Introduction

This chapter will look at new product development and innovation. First, however, organisations must look at their external and internal environment, their products and markets and associated positioning. This chapter will take the same approach.

Your objectives

In this chapter you will learn about the following.

(a) The importance of product-market analysis

(b) Product-market strategies

(c) The steps involved in a systematic new product development (NPD) process

(d) The importance of innovation to an organisation

1 PRODUCTS AND MARKETS

Ansoff (1987) drew up a **growth vector matrix**, describing a combination of a firm's activities in current and new markets, with existing and new products.

Definition

Product-market mix is a short-hand term for the products/services a firm sells (or a service which a public sector organisation provides) and the markets it sells them to.

Ansoff's product-market growth matrix

	Existing products	*New products*
Existing markets	*Market penetration strategy* 1 More purchasing and usage from existing customers 2 Gain customers from competitors 3 Convert non-users into users (where both are in same market segment)	*Product development strategy* 1 Product modification via new features 2 Different quality levels 3 'New' product
New markets	*Market development strategy* 1 New market segments 2 New distribution channels 3 New geographic areas eg exports	*Diversification strategy* 1 Organic growth 2 Joint ventures 3 Mergers 4 Acquisition/take-over

1.1 Current products and current markets: market penetration

Market penetration. The firm seeks to:

(a) **Maintain or to increase its share** of current markets with current products, eg through competitive pricing, advertising, sales promotion

(b) **Secure dominance** of growth markets

(c) **Restructure a mature market** by driving out competitors

(d) **Increase usage** by existing customers (eg airmiles, loyalty cards)

EXAMPLE

Good examples of strategies for market penetration are air miles and 'frequent flier' services. A decision to fly with an airline gives the customer air miles, which can be redeemed on later flights, and which will encourage the customer to fly again.

1.2 Present products and new markets: market development

Market development is when the firm seeks new markets for its **current** products or services. It is appropriate when its products are strengths which can be matched by opportunities in new markets. Ways of developing markets includes the following.

(a) **New geographical areas** and export markets (eg a radio station building a new transmitter to reach a new audience).

(b) **Different package sizes** for food and other domestic items so that both those who buy in bulk and those who buy in small quantities are catered for.

(c) **New distribution channels** to attract new customers (eg organic food sold in supermarkets not just specialist shops).

(d) **Differential pricing policies** to attract different types of customer and create **new market segments.** For example, travel companies have developed a market for cheap long-stay winter breaks in warmer countries for retired couples.

1.3 New products and present markets: product development

Product development is the launch of new products to existing markets.

(a) **Advantages**

- Product development forces competitors to innovate
- Newcomers to the market might be discouraged

(b) The **drawbacks** include the expense and the risk.

1.4 New products: new markets (diversification)

Diversification occurs when a company decides to make **new products for new markets.** It should have a clear idea about what it expects to gain from diversification. There are two types of diversification, related and unrelated diversification.

(a) **Growth.** New products and new markets should be selected which offer prospects for growth which the existing product-market mix does not.

(b) **Investing surplus** funds not required for other expansion needs: but the funds could be returned to shareholders.

(c) The firm's strengths match the opportunity if:

   (i) Outstanding new products have been developed by the firm's research and development department

   (ii) The profit opportunities from diversification are high.

1.5 Related diversification

Definition

> **Related diversification** is 'development beyond the present product market, but still within the broad confines of the industry ... [it] ... therefore builds on the assets or activities which the firm has developed' (*Johnson and Scholes*). It takes the form of vertical or horizontal integration.

Horizontal integration refers to 'development into activities which are competitive with or directly **complementary** to a company's present activities. Sony, for example, started to compete in computer games. Ferrari launched a range of bicycles.

Vertical integration occurs when a company becomes its own:

(a) **Supplier** of raw materials, components or services (**backward vertical integration**). For example, backward integration would occur where a milk producer acquires its own dairy farms rather than buying raw milk from independent farmers.

(b) **Distributor** or sales agent (**forward vertical integration**), for example where a manufacturer of synthetic yarn begins to produce shirts from the yarn instead of selling it to other shirt manufacturers.

1.6 Advantages of vertical integration

(a) **A secure supply of components** or raw materials with more control. Supplier bargaining power is reduced.

(b) **Strengthen the relationships** and contacts of the manufacturer with the 'final consumer' of the product.

(c) Win a share of the **higher profits**

(d) Pursue a **differentiation strategy** more effectively

(e) Raise **barriers to entry**

1.7 Disadvantages of vertical integration

(a) **Overconcentration.** A company places 'more eggs in the same end-market basket' (*Ansoff*). Such a policy is fairly inflexible, more sensitive to instabilities and increases the firm's dependence on a particular aspect of economic demand.

(b) The firm **fails to benefit from any economies of scale or technical advances** in the industry into which it has diversified. This is why, in the publishing industry, most printing is subcontracted to specialist printing firms, who can work machinery to capacity by doing work for many firms.

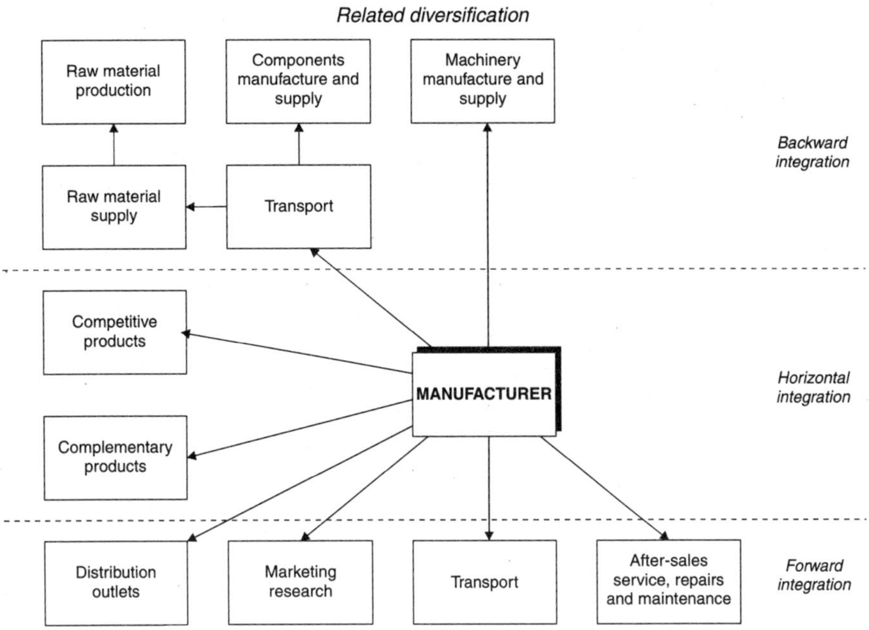

Figure 10.1: *Related diversification*
Source: *Johnson and Scholes*

1.8 Unrelated diversification

Definition

Unrelated or conglomerate diversification 'is development beyond the present industry into products/markets which, at face value, may bear no close relation to the present product/market.'

Conglomerate diversification is now very unfashionable. However, it has been a key strategy for companies in Asia, particularly South Korea. EasyJet and Virgin are key examples of UK organisations adopting this strategy. It is not readily apparent what the relationship is between air travel, cosmetics, bridal fashion, telecommunications and cola – a few of the sectors within which Virgin competes.

1.9 Advantages of conglomerate diversification

(a) **Risk-spreading.** Entering new products into new markets offers protection against the failure of current products and markets.

(b) **High profit opportunities.** An improvement of the **overall profitability and flexibility** of the firm through acquisition in industries which have better economic characteristics than those of the acquiring firms.

(c) **Escape** from the present business. For example, Reed International moved away from paper production and into publishing.

(d) **Better access to capital** markets.

(e) **No other way to grow.** Expansion along existing lines might create a monopoly and lead to government investigations and control. Diversifications offer the chance of growth without creating a monopoly.

(f) **Use surplus cash.**

(g) **Exploit under-utilised resources.**

(h) **Obtain cash,** or other financial advantages (such as accumulated tax losses).

(i) **Use a company's image and reputation** in one market to develop into another where corporate image and reputation could be vital ingredients for success.

1.10 Disadvantages of conglomerate diversification

(a) The **dilution of shareholders' earnings** if diversification is into growth industries with high P/E ratios.

(b) **Lack of a common identity and purpose** in a conglomerate organisation. A conglomerate will only be successful if it has a high quality of management and financial ability at central headquarters, where the diverse operations are brought together.

(c) **Failure in one of the businesses will drag down the rest,** as it will eat up resources.

(d) **Lack of management experience** in the business area. **Japanese steel companies** have diversified into areas completely unrelated to steel such as personal computers, with limited success.

(e) **No good for shareholders.** Shareholders can spread risk quite easily, simply by buying a diverse portfolio of shares. They do not need management to do it for them.

Activity 1 **(20 minutes)**

A large organisation in road transport operates nationwide in general haulage. This field has become very competitive and with the recent down-turn in trade, has become only marginally profitable. It has been suggested that the strategic structure of the company should be widened to include other aspects of physical distribution so that the maximum synergy would be obtained from that type of diversification.

(a) Name three activities which might fit into the suggested new strategic structure, explaining each one briefly.

(b) Explain how each of these activities could be incorporated into the existing structure.

(c) State the advantages and disadvantages of such diversification.

1.11 Withdrawal

It might be the right decision to cease producing a product and/or to pull out of a market completely. This is a hard decision for managers to take if they have invested time and money or if the decision involves redundancies.

Exit barriers make this difficult.

(a) **Cost barriers** include redundancy costs, the difficulty of selling assets.

(b) **Political barriers** include government attitudes. Defence is an example.

(c) **Marketing considerations** may delay withdrawal. A product might be a 'loss-leader' for others, or might contribute to the company's reputation for its breadth of coverage.

(d) **Psychology**. Managers hate to admit failure, and there might be a desire to avoid a 'bloodletting'. Furthermore, people might wrongly assume that carrying on is a low risk strategy, especially if they (wrongly) feel bound to carry on, as they have spent money already.

1.12 Reasons for exit

(a) The **company's business** may be in buying firms, selling their assets and improving their performance, and then selling them at a profit.

(b) **Resource limitations** mean that less profitable businesses have to be abandoned. A business might be sold to a competitor, or occasionally to management (as a buy-out).

(c) A company may be forced to quit, because of **insolvency**.

(d) **Change of competitive strategy**. In the microprocessor industry, many American firms have left high-volume DRAM chips to Asian firms so as to concentrate on high value added niche products.

(e) **Decline in attractiveness of the market.**

(f) **Funds can earn more elsewhere**.

1.13 Section summary

Product-market strategy can be:

- **Penetration**: same products, same markets
- **Product development**: new products, same markets
- **Market development**: same products, new markets
- **Diversification**: new products, new markets
- **Withdrawal**
- Any **combination** of the above, depending on the product portfolio

2 POSITIONING

Definition

> **Positioning** is the act of designing the company's product and image so that it offers a distinct and valued place in the target customer's mind.

Positioning entails using the marketing mix – it is the practical finale of a well-considered and justified marketing plan.

2.1 Problems with positioning

How much do people remember about a product or brand?

(a) Many products are, in fact, very similar, and the key issue is to make them distinct in the customer's mind.

(b) People remember 'number 1', so the product should be positioned as 'number 1' in relation to a valued attribute.

(c) Cosmetic changes can have the effect of repositioning the product in the customer's mind. To be effective, however, this psychological positioning has to be reinforced by 'real' positioning.

Given that positioning is psychological as well as real, we can now identify positioning errors.

Mistake	Consequence
Underpositioning	The brand does not have a clear identity in the eyes of the customer.
Overpositioning	Buyers may have too narrow an image of a brand.
Confused positioning	Too many claims might be made for a brand.
Doubtful positioning	The positioning may not be credible in the eyes of the buyer.

FOR DISCUSSION

Marks and Spencer was criticised for its poor positioning. To what extent was this the cause of this company's difficulties in recent years?

2.2 Positioning strategy checklist

Positioning variable	Comment
• Attributes	Size, for example
• Benefit	What benefits we offer
• Use/application	Ease of use; accessibility
• User	The sort of person the product appeals to
• Product category	Consciously differentiated from competition
• Quality/price	Superior quality/low price

2.3 Perceptual maps

One simple perceptual map that can be used is to plot brands or competing products in terms of two key characteristics such as price and quality.

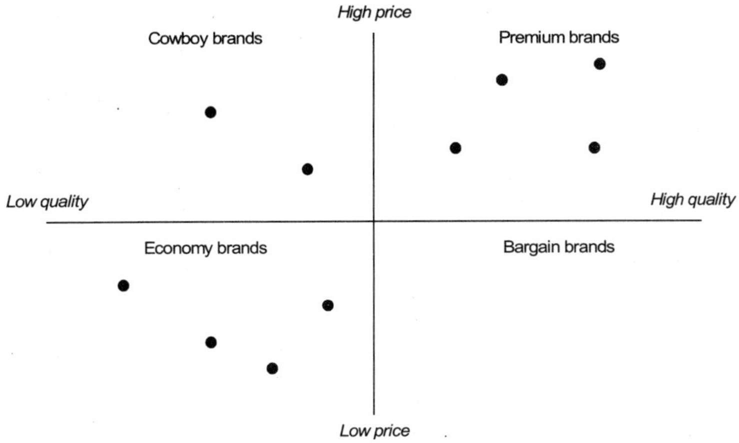

Figure 10.2: Perceptual map

A perceptual map of market positioning can be used to **identify gaps in the market**. This example might suggest that there could be potential in the market for a low-price high-quality 'bargain brand'. A company that carries out such an analysis might decide to conduct further research to find out whether there is scope in the market for a new product which would be targeted at a market position where there are few or no rivals.

2.4 Mapping positions

Kotler (2008) identified a 3×3 matrix of nine different competitive positioning strategies.

Product quality	*Product price*		
	High price	*Medium price*	*Low price*
High	Premium strategy	Penetration Strategy	Superbargain strategy
Medium	Overpricing strategy	Average-quality Strategy	Bargain strategy
Low	Hit-and-run strategy	Shoddy goods Strategy	Cheap goods strategy

Once selected, the needs of the targeted segment can be identified and the marketing mix strategy developed to provide the benefits package needed to satisfy them. Positioning the product offering then becomes a matter of matching and communicating appropriate benefits.

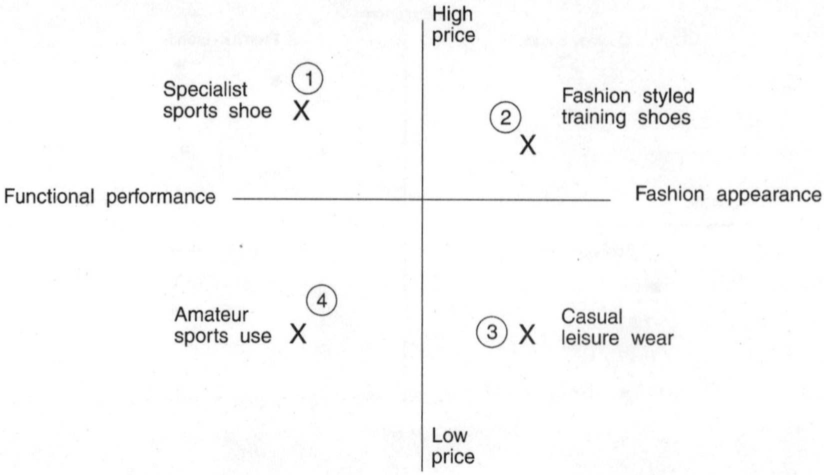

Figure 10.3: Positioning map for hypothetical shoe manufacturer

2.5 Steps in positioning

Step 1 Identify differentiating factors in products or services in relation to competitors

Step 2 Select the most important differences

Step 3 Communicate the position to the target market

The value of positioning is that it enables **tactical marketing mix decisions to be made.**

3 INNOVATION AND NEW PRODUCT DEVELOPMENT

3.1 Where do new ideas come from?

(a) New products may be developed as a result of a **technical breakthrough**, or as a consequence of changes in society, or simply to copy and capitalise on the success of your existing products.

(b) Management, sales people, customers and competitors can all generate new product ideas. One of the tasks of **marketing management** is to '**tap**' these ideas and select some for further development.

(c) Management can adopt a proactive approach to product development by establishing research and development departments to look into ideas for new products.

What is a new product?

(a) One that opens up an entirely new market
(b) One that replaces an existing product
(c) One that broadens significantly the market for an existing product

An old product can be new if:

(a) It is introduced to a new market
(b) It is packaged in a different way
(c) A different marketing approach is used
(d) A mix variable is changed

3.2 New products and strategy

New products feature in a firm's competitive and marketing strategies.

(a) New and innovatory products can **lower entry barriers** to existing industries and markets, if new technology is involved.

(b) The market for any product changes over time and its life. The interests of the company are therefore best met with a **balanced product portfolio.** Managers therefore must plan when to introduce new products, how best to extend the life of mature ones and when to abandon those in decline.

A firm should identify its strategy underlying new product development.

(a) **Leader strategy.** Will the firm gain competitive advantage by operating at the leading edge of new developments? If yes, there are significant implications for the R&D activity and the likely length of product life cycles within the portfolio.

(b) **Follower strategy.** Will the firm be more pro-active, adopt a follower strategy, which involves lower costs and less emphasis on the R&D activity? It sacrifices early rewards of innovation, but avoids its risks. A follower might have to license certain technologies from a leader (as in the case with many consumer electronics companies).

EXAMPLE

Allen and Hamilton Booz (management consultants) identified the following categories, in a survey of 700 firms.

• New to the world: new market	10%
• New product lines to enable a firm to enter a new sector	20%
• Additions to product line	26%
• Repositionings to new segments	7%
• Improvements/revisions	26%
• Cost reductions	11%

FOR DISCUSSION

There are very few truly new products that come into the market.

3.3 Degrees of newness

(a) **The unquestionably new product**, such as such as products for the treatment of AIDS and cancer using nanotechnology and fullerenes (in other words things that have only just been discovered or become possible). Marks of such a new product are: technical innovation – high price – initial performance problems – limited availability.

(b) The **partially new product**, such as the DVD player. The main markof such a product is that it performs better than the equivalent old product.

(c) **Major product change**, such as the digital camera. Marks of such a product: radical technological change altering the accepted concept of the order of things (no need to get your films developed: print them out at home or show them round by e-mail).

(d) **Minor product change**, such as styling changes. Marks of such a product: extras which give a boost to a product. The motor industry does this all the time.

EXAMPLES

Sources for new products

- **Licensing** (eg Formica, Monopoly)
- **Acquisition** (buy the organisation making it)
- **Internal product development** (your own Research and Development team)
- **Customers** (listen to and observe them, analyse and research – eg the Walkman)
- **External inventors** (Trevor Baylis and the wind-up radio)
- **Competition** (Dyson's bag-less vacuum cleaners, now copied by other manufacturers, as are Crocs footwear)
- **Patent agents**
- **Academic institutions** (eg the pharmaceutical industry funds higher education department research)

3.4 The process of NPD in overview

Key factors for NPD success. A systematic NPD process is outlined in Figure 10.3.

Step 1 **Idea generation** requires the maximum number of new ideas to be generated. This necessitates an active search of the environment and for no suggestion to be rejected out of hand. Sources include employees, scientists, competitors, customers.

Step 2 **Screening** sorts the ideas for compatibility with organisational strategy, resources, distribution channels, competitive advantage etc.

Step 3 **Concept development and testing** is focused on customer needs. Can we find a concept that wraps the idea up into a package that will be adopted by enough consumers? Conceptual **positioning maps** are often used.

Step 4 **Marketing strategy**. The next stage is to draft a marketing plan including short and long-term sales, profit and market share objectives and the structure of the marketing mix.

Step 5 **Business analysis** is focused on determining whether the product will meet the plan's objectives. Sales forecasting is used with estimates firstly on the level and speed of first-time sales and secondly the level of replacement sales. Costs and profits are also estimated.

Step 6 **Product development** involves the physical development of the product in the form of a prototype and a substantial increase in commitment and investment. Tests are then conducted (eg food, for taste and shelf life).

Step 7 **Market testing.** Test marketing is often used to arrive at a more reliable sales forecast and to pre-test marketing plans. Store tests are often used in consumer markets with product use tests and trade shows used more in industrial markets.

Step 8 **Commercialisation**. Often, market testing is omitted and full scale product launch occurs. The questions to ask at this stage are: when to launch? Where to launch? Which groups should be targeted? How should the product be launched?

3.5 Responsibility for NPD

At strategic level, NPD is ultimately the responsibility of the **board**. NPD requires, at different stages, the co-operation of R&D, marketing and production departments.

- The **marketing** department should identify the opportunity.
- The **designers** should, ideally, develop the product so that it satisfies customers' need.
- The **products** should be designed also to be produced in the most cost-effective way.

The ideal management structure for the NPD process involves:

- Clear, realistic planning targets
- A project manager to drive the project, perhaps with a sponsor at Board level

A key relationship is that between marketing personnel and R&D. The **danger** is that **NPD will be 'owned' by R&D,** so technically perfect products are produced which do not meet customer needs profitably.

The relationship of the R&D department with marketing personnel is sometimes problematic.

(a) **Cultural**. The R&D department may have an 'academic' or university atmosphere, as opposed to a commercial one.

(b) **Organisational**. If R&D consumes substantial resources, it would seem quite logical to exploit economies of scale by having it centralised.

(c) **Work.** Marketing work and R&D work differ in many important respects. R&D work is likely to be more open ended than marketing work.

3.6 Why R&D should be more closely co-ordinated with marketing

(a) If the firm operates the **marketing concept**, then the 'identification of customer needs' should be a vital input to new product development.

(b) The R&D department might identify possible changes to product specifications so that a **variety of marketing mixes** can be tried out and screened.

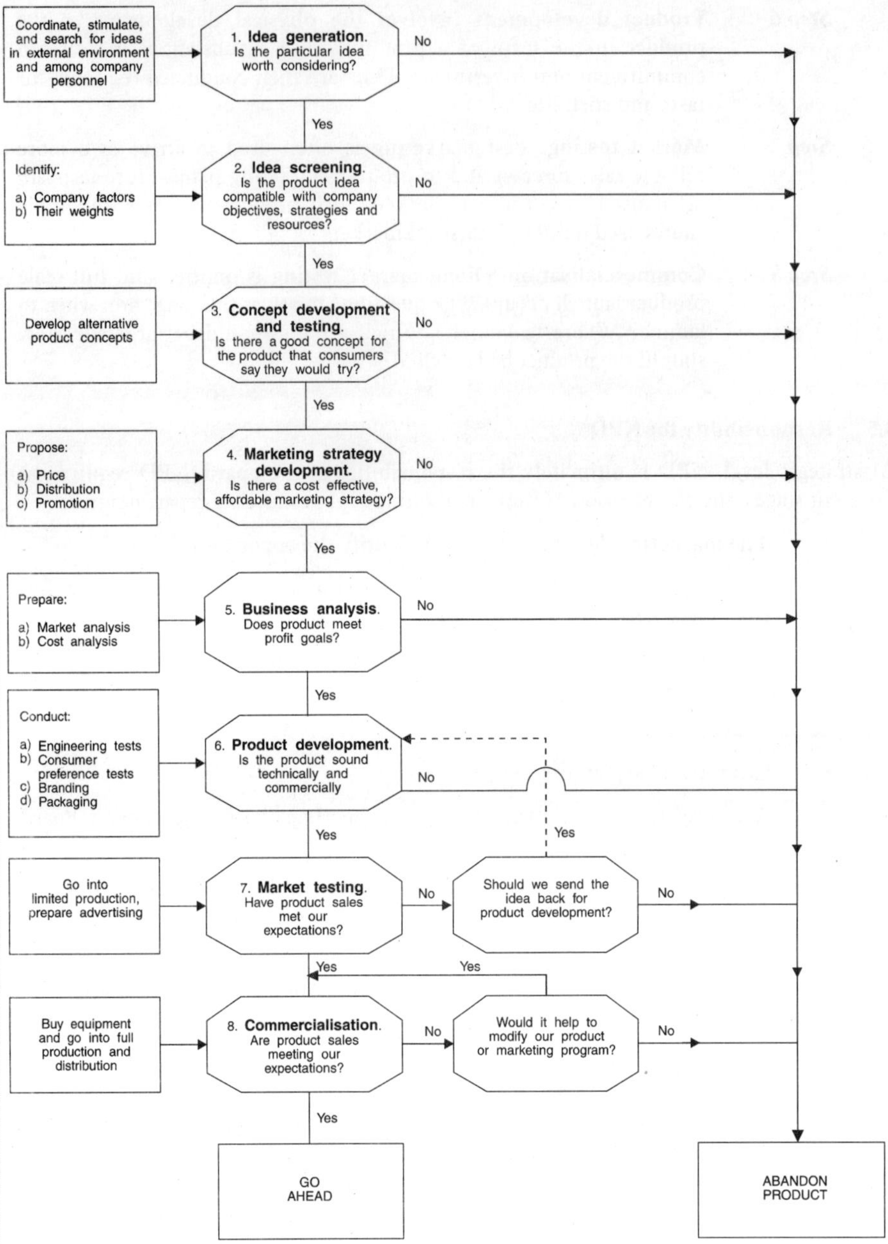

Figure 10.4: NPD process

EXAMPLE

Nestlé once had a central R&D function, with regional development centres. The central R&D function was involved in basic research. 'Much of the lab's work was only tenuously connected with the company's business... When scientists joined the lab, they were told "Just work in this or that area. If you work hard enough, we're sure you'll find something".' The results of this approach were:

- The research laboratory was largely cut off from development centres
- Much research never found commercial application

Nestlé reorganised the business into strategic business units (SBU's). Formal links were established between R&D and the SBUs. This means that research procedures have been changed so that a commercial time horizon was established.

The purpose of **test marketing** is to obtain information about how consumers react to a new product – ie will they buy it, and if so, will they buy it again?

- The total market demand for the product can be made
- The product/service can be amended
- Other aspects of the marketing mix can be changed

A test market involves testing a new consumer product in selected areas which are thought to be '**representative**' of the total market. In the selected areas, the firm will attempt to distribute the product through the same types of sales outlets it plans to use in the full market launch, and also to use the advertising and promotion plans it intends to use in the full market.

3.7 Characteristics of a good test marketing exercise

Size of market	The test market area should be **large enough** to be representative of how the 'full' market might behave, but not so large as to be almost as expensive as a full national market launch. It should also be representative of the target market.
Time	The test period should be sufficiently long to give customers time to become aware of the product, and to monitor not only initial sales demand but also 'repeat buying' habits. This amount of time will therefore vary for different product groups, eg toilet roll may only require a match whereas a product such as shampoo may need at least a couple of matches.
Representative	The test market must be as closely representative of the national market as possible.
Promotional facilities	One of the television regions could be used as a test area.

3.8 Benefits of test marketing

(a) The company **can pre-test a planned marketing mix**. For example, they may be able to identify product faults not identified at the development stage, or they may discover potential distribution problems.

(b) Expensive product failure may be avoided.

(c) **Results** from the test market may enable the company to prepare more accurate **sales forecasts.**

(d) The costs and risks of a full time launch are postponed.

3.9 Disadvantages of test marketing

(a) Unless the test market area is **typical** of the market as a whole, the information obtained about potential demand will be **biased** and misleading.

(b) A lengthy test market will **alert competitors** to what the firm is planning to do, and give them time to prepare their own response to the new product.

(c) Only a **small sample** will be used, which raises statistical problems.

(d) Consumers may be aware of the test and **distort their answers** accordingly.

(e) Estimates for the future cannot reliably be based on results recorded today.

(f) **Competitors** may decide to **sabotage** the test, for example by flooding the area with increased advertising activity.

(g) It is difficult to translate national media plans into local equivalents.

(h) Some goods, for example consumer goods such as household furniture, have lengthy repurchase cycles which would make test marketing far too lengthy to be of any practical forecasting value.

3.10 Other forms of experimentation (different from test marketing).

(a) **Simulated store technique (or laboratory test markets)**. In these tests, a group of shoppers are invited to watch a selection of advertisements for a number of products, including an advertisement for the new product. They are then given some money and invited to spend it in a supermarket or shopping area. Their purchases are recorded and they are asked to explain their purchase decisions (and non-purchase decisions).

(b) **Controlled test marketing.** In these tests, a research firm pays a **panel of stores to carry the new product for a given length of time**. This test helps to provide an assessment of 'in-store' factors.

FOR DISCUSSION

Many product failures could be prevented if adequate market testing was undertaken.

3.11 New product pricing: market penetration and market skimming

There are three elements in the pricing decision for a new product.

- Getting the product accepted
- Maintaining a market share in the face of competition
- Making a profit from the product

When a firm launches a new product on to the market, it must decide on a pricing policy which lies between the two extremes of market penetration and market skimming.

Market penetration pricing is a policy of low prices when the product is first launched in order to gain sufficient penetration into the market. It is therefore a policy of sacrificing short-term profits in the interests of long-term profits.

3.12 In favour of a penetration policy

(a) The firm wishes to **discourage rivals** from entering the market.

(b) The firm wishes **to shorten the initial period of the product's life cycle,** in order to enter the growth and maturity stages as quickly as possible. (This would happen if there is high elasticity of demand for the product.)

(c) A firm might therefore deliberately build excess production capacity and set its prices very low; as demand builds up, the spare capacity will be used up gradually, and unit costs will fall; the firm might even reduce prices further as unit costs fall.

(d) In this way, early year losses will enable the firm to dominate the market and have the lowest costs.

3.13 Market skimming

The aim of market skimming is to gain **high unit profits very early** on in the product's life.

(a) The firm charges **high prices** when a product is **first launched,** eg the Nintendo DSi.

(b) The firm **spends heavily on advertising** and sales promotion to win customers.

(c) As the product moves into the later stages of its **life cycle** (growth, maturity and decline) **progressively lower prices will be charged.** The profitable 'cream' is thus 'skimmed' off in progressive stages until sales can only be sustained at lower prices.

(d) **Conditions suitable for a skimming policy**

  (i) Where the **product is new and different,** so that customers are prepared to pay high prices.

  (ii) **Where demand elasticity is unknown.** It is better to start by charging high prices and then reducing them if the demand for the product turns out to be price elastic than to start by charging low prices and then attempting to raise them substantially when demand turns out to be price inelastic.

  (iii) High initial prices might not be profit-maximising in the long run, but they generate **high initial cash-flows.** A firm with liquidity problems may prefer market-skimming for this reason.

  (iv) Skimming may also enable the firm to identify **different market segments** for the product, each prepared to pay progressively lower prices.

(e) The firm may lower its prices in order to attract more price-elastic segments of the market; however, these price reductions will be gradual. Alternately, the entry of competitors into the market may make price reductions inevitable.

Introductory offers may be used to attract an initial customer interest. Introductory offers are temporary price reductions, after which the price is then raised to its normal 'commercial' rate. Many FMCG products use this approach.

New products can fail in the short-term or in the long-term. The NPD process should improve success rates, but success is never guaranteed.

A successful new product or brand satisfies corporate objectives by:

- Gaining/sustaining market share
- Meeting profit targets
- Generating cash inflows
- Doing (a), (b) and (c) above in the right time.

3.14 Reasons for failure

Reason	Comment
Poor commitment	NPD is a sideline; managers want to do NPD, but are unwilling to risk the resources to develop the competences necessary
Poor thinking	Designers and promoters of NPD within the organisation have their own interests to pursue and downplay potential problems
Poor execution	Many NPD processes involve uncertain outcomes but the product is wanted in an unrealistic timescale
Poor management	The research process for NPD may not be run properly
Poor marketing	The product might fail because of poor marketing research or by poor marketing
Poor analysis	Both the process of NPD and the product can be more time consuming and expensive than anticipated

3.15 Enhancing innovation

The need to speed up innovation is a key issue. Commonly cited spurs to innovation are:

- Shorter product life cycles
- Increasing prosperity
- New technology enabling new services

Many businesses only concentrate on new technology (in other words, option (g) in the list above) rather than the other opportunities ((a) to (f))to innovate. Many businesses feel that their future survival is at stake if they do not innovate. Companies are keen to find out a more **predictable way of emerging with winners**. There is no systematic way to encourage innovation but these steps are an indication.

Step 1 **Imagining**: the initial insight about a market opportunity for a particular technology

Step 2 **Incubating**: nurturing the technology to gauge whether it can be commercialised.

Step 3 **Demonstrating**: building prototypes and getting feedback from potential customers

Step 4 **Promoting**: persuading the market to adopt the invitation

Step 5 **Ensuring** the product or process has as **long a life as possible**

Steps 1, 2 and 3 cannot be managed in a conventional way. Firms could:

- Create a culture in which **innovation and learning exist** throughout the organisation. This is only possible when the barrier of fear of failure is removed or minimised.
- Designate separate teams, or individuals to come up with ideas.

An innovation culture can be considered in the context of a **learning organisation.**

3.16 Creativity and innovation

Creative ideas can come from anywhere and at any time, but if management wish to foster innovation they should try to provide an organisation structure in which innovative ideas are encouraged to emerge.

(a) **Innovation requires creativity**. Creativity may be encouraged in an individual or group by establishing a climate in which free expression of abilities is allowed. Blue skies (or hot water thought) sessions using techniques such as brainstorming etc could be used. These sessions should follow the basis that no idea should be criticised.

(b) Creative ideas must then be **rationally analysed** (in 'cold water thought sessions') to decide whether they provide a viable (commercial etc) proposition. It is paramount that this session is conducted at a later date.

In an article in *Marketing Business* (April 2000), Ty Francis exposed ten myths about innovation. In his view:

(a) Innovation does not depend on doing extensive **marketing research. Creativity** is more important than collecting more data.

(b) Innovation requires **huge creative leaps** into the unknown that change the entire company.

(c) Innovation is the responsibility of the **entire enterprise**. Focusing on existing products and customers will achieve nothing. Functional responsibilities need to be disregarded: 'if you do what you've always done you'll get the results you've always had'.

(d) Innovation is about more than **intellectual** endeavour. **Core creative competences** are needed, and a creative culture needs to be stimulated.

(e) Innovation is not just about **NPD**. Innovation may simply mean a new process or a new component material for an existing product.

(f) Where innovation is concerned, **the future is happening now**. Organisations need to get away from a problem-solving orientation, and become more involved in **creating their future**.

(g) Innovation should not just occur quickly and under duress when a company is **desperate**. Real innovative breakthroughs need proper consideration and thought.

(h) There is no such thing as a foolproof or faddish **toolkit** for innovation. Commercially viable innovations only come from a **proper knowledge** of the company's abilities and its industry.

(i) Innovation is not a **mechanistic business process**, but rather a way of working that should colour everything the company does.

(j) Innovation does not live off **existing brands and products**. Companies must move on. Strong brands can actually stifle innovation, and in any case some competitors are always going to be able to copy what you do.

FOR DISCUSSION

According to Francis: 'Building innovation ... is the only way to achieve significant and sustainable competitive advantage.'

EXAMPLE

The Chartered Institute of Marketing studied the nature of innovation for marketers and discovered that the majority of developments were incremental with minor cosmetic tweaks rather than being breakthrough. The reasons for this were found to be complex but included issues such as marketers reluctance to take risks because they did not feel supported to do so within their organisations, a lack of ownership for innovation, the rapid turnover of brand managers and the pressure for quick profits and fast growth. One problem associated with 'cosmetic' innovation is that consumers become sceptical and tend to wait for future products to enter the market. The car industry is a commonly cited example of consumers taking this approach. Often when it is anticipated that models are changing significantly in the next few years, the latest model of an existing range is discounted because consumers prefer to wait for the next generation range.

EasyJet's easyHotel concept where London hotel rooms are offered at £20 but without a window or cleaner were developed as a result of a good combination of market knowledge and risk taking.

The CIM is firm in that market-shaping innovation is critical for organisations to sustain competitive advantage.

Adapted from CIM Shape the Agenda paper 'The Creative Dilemma' Available from www.shapetheagenda.com [Accessed 3.8.07]

See the follow up to this at:
http://www.adducemarketing.co.uk/Email_Downloads/Innovation_followup.pdf
(accessed 6 December 2009)

---

4 INNOVATION AUDIT

The chief object of being innovative is to ensure organisational success in a changing world. It can also have the following advantages.

(a) Improvements in quality of **products** and **service**

(b) A **leaner structure** – layers of management or administration may be done away with

(c) Prompt and imaginative **solutions to problems**

(d) **Less formality** in structure and style, leading to better communication

(e) **Greater confidence** inside and outside the organisation in its ability to cope with change

Innovation and new product development (NPD) is therefore essential for many firms to survive and prosper. It is an increasingly important area.

Definition

> **Innovation audit:** a critical assessment of the firm's innovation record, the internal obstacles to innovation and how performance can be enhanced.

A firm needs to assess how well it is able to deliver the level and type of innovation necessary to continue to meet customer needs and expectations. Drummond *et al* (2008) identify **four key areas** for the innovation audit.

(a) The current organisational climate

(b) Measures of the organisation's current performance with regard to innovation

(c) Review of policies and practices supporting innovation and facilitating it

(d) The balance of styles of the management team

4.1 Organisational climate

Barriers to innovation include the following.

(a) **Resistance to change**

Any new method of management thinking can experience some resistance from established managers. This resistance may be due to concern to protect the status quo, or because managers are ignorant of the new thinking.

(b) **Old structures/functional specialists**

A lack of a natural 'home' for innovation often causes problems. In some companies marketing has a role while in others R&D departments take control.

(c) **Cost consideration**

Innovation is an expensive process. Contingency plans for finding additional budget it required should be considered at the planning stage otherwise development work can very often be put on the backburner when costs escalate.

Methods of overcoming these barriers include those described below.

(a) **Top management commitment**

The most effective way of overcoming these barriers to change is through the commitment of top management. The chief executive in particular needs to be convinced of the appropriateness of the new thinking and be enthusiastic about its implementation throughout the organisation.

(b) **Marketing reorganisation**

One way in which the chief executive can take advice is through a reorganisation of the marketing function in the organisation. In particular the company should seriously consider the appointment of an individual with overall responsibility for brining about the adoption of an innovation programme throughout the organisation.

(c) **Producing the results**

Nothing succeeds like success. Producing the business results as a consequence of effective launches will boost confidence and gain management converts to the new thinking on an innovative approach.

4.2 Encouraging innovation

To encourage innovation the objective for management should be to create a more outward-looking organisation.

- People should be encouraged to look for new products, markets, processes and designs
- People should seek ways to improve productivity

An innovation strategy calls for a management policy of **giving encouragement** to innovative ideas. This will require the following.

(a) Giving **financial backing** to innovation, by spending on R & D and marketing research and risking capital on new ideas.

(b) Giving employees the **opportunity** to work in an environment where the exchange of ideas for innovation can take place. Management style and organisation structure can help here.

(i) Management can actively encourage employees and customers to put forward new ideas.

(ii) **Development teams** can be set up and an organisation built-up on project team-work.

(iii) **Quality circles** and brainstorming groups can be used to encourage creative thinking about work issues.

(c) Where appropriate, **recruitment policy** should be directed towards appointing employees with the necessary skills for doing innovative work. Employees should be trained and kept up to date.

(d) Certain managers should be **made responsible for obtaining information** from outside the organisation about innovative ideas, and for **communicating** this information throughout the organisation.

(e) **Strategic planning** should result in targets being set for innovation, and successful achievements by employees should if possible be rewarded.

4.3 Measures of performance

This may include measures such as the rate of successful **new product development** and related sales over the past years, or **customer satisfaction ratings.**

Customer satisfaction ratings. An important input to innovation is the degree of customer satisfaction, both from the product itself and service levels.

(a) Customer satisfaction can be measured on a scale (eg from **highly satisfied** to **highly dissatisfied**).

(b) Customers can also be asked to identify which features of a service/product they found most useful.

(c) Firms should **actively measure** customer satisfaction, rather than simply **react to complaints**.

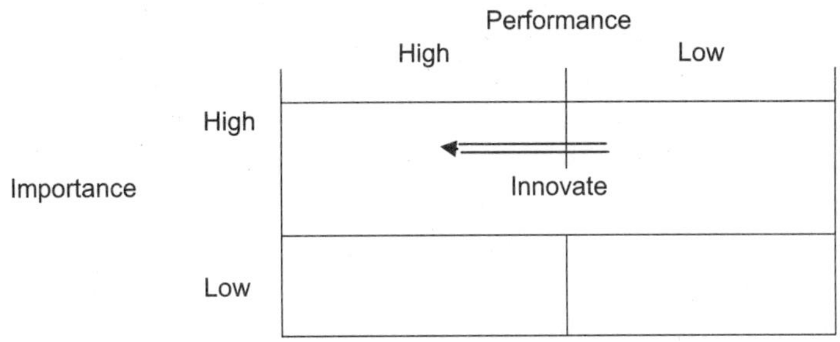

Clearly, a firm should be most concerned about matters of high importance with 'low' performance. Innovation may be necessary to ensure that high performance is achieved on matters of high importance.

4.4 Innovation/value matrix

(a) A similar methodology can apply to innovation and its **value** to the customer. Clearly, the best sort of innovation gives highest customer value for the lowest cost or effort. Businesses can be categorised between those that offer the normal level of innovation and market value, those that offer some improvement on the offerings of competition, and finally those that offer significant innovations and value for the customer.

(b) There is a danger that too many innovations can, in fact, confuse the customer. Recent research has encouraged some companies (such as Procter & Gamble) to reduce the variety of goods on offer.

(c) The innovation process should consider both the **technology** and **customer needs.**

(d) For example, once the limitations of the silicon chip are reached, optical computers might be invented. In some cases, instead of technical developments being used to predict future technologies, future social developments can be predicted, in order to **predict future customer needs.** The likely technologies which will satisfy these needs can then be considered.

4.5 The management team

The management team are key in setting the scene for innovation. The management team is also a critical influence on corporate culture. Belbin (1993) drew up a list of the characteristics of an ideal team.

Member	Role
Co-ordinator	Presides and co-ordinates; balanced, disciplined, good at working through others.
Shaper	Highly strung, dominant, extrovert, passionate about the task itself, a spur to action.
Plant	Introverted, but intellectually dominant and imaginative; source of ideas and proposals but with disadvantages of introversion.
Monitor-evaluator	Analytically (rather than creatively) intelligent; dissects ideas, spots flaws; possibly aloof, tactless – but necessary.
Resource-investigator	Popular, sociable, extrovert, relaxed; source of new contacts, but not an originator; needs to be made use of.

Member	Role
Implementor	Practical organiser, turning ideas into tasks; scheduling, planning and so on; trustworthy and efficient, but not excited; not a leader, but an administrator.
Team worker	Most concerned with team maintenance – supportive, understanding, diplomatic; popular but uncompetitive – contribution noticed only in absence.
Finisher	Chivvies the team to meet deadlines, attend to details; urgency and follow-through important, though not always popular.

The dynamics of the management team affects how it perceives the work environment.

Although the **environment poses strategic questions,** it is **people who make sense of it** and devise strategies. While the recipe provides cultural coherence it can impede strategic renewal. If the corporate strategy is failing, a company will:

(1) Place tighter **controls** over implementation (eg give tougher performance targets to sales staff); but if **this** fails ...

(2) Develop a new strategy (eg sell in a new market); but if this fails as well ...

(3) Only now will the company abandon the recipe (eg realise that the product is obsolete).

This is significant if it impacts on the management team's attitude to innovation. A management team might be unbalanced if it has too many 'ideas' people and not enough implementers able to bring projects to fruition.

To summarise here are some suggested stages for an innovation audit.

Step 1 **Benchmark with leading competitors**. For example, many motor firms regard the rate and speed of NPD as something they must emulate.

Step 2 **Identify performance indicators** for innovation and compare with previous years (Davidson), such as the **rate of NPD.**

- Number of innovations
- Success rate (more important than quantity)
- Percentage of revenue derived from **innovations** (3M has a target)
- **Incremental** sales resulting from innovation
- Average annual sales per new product/service

Note that if a higher percentage of revenue comes from **innovation** then **incremental** products, it looks as if innovatory products are **cannibalising** existing sales.

Step 3 Identify obstacles to innovation which typically reside in the corporate culture of structure.

Step 4 Recommend innovation objectives.

Activity 2 **(1 hour)**

Bowland Carpets Ltd is a major producer of carpets within the UK. The company was taken over by its present parent company, Universal Carpet Inc, in 1993. Universal Carpet is a giant, vertically integrated carpet manufacturing and retailing business, based within the USA but with interests all over the world.

Bowland Carpets operates within the UK in various market segments, including the high value contract and industrial carpeting area – hotels and office blocks etc – and in the domestic (household) market. Within the latter the choice is reasonably wide ranging from luxury carpets down to the cheaper products. Industrial and contract carpets contribute 25% of Bowland Carpets' total annual turnover which is currently £80 million. During the late 1980s the turnover of the company was growing at 8% per annum, but since 1992 sales have dropped by 5% per annum in real terms.

Bowland Carpets has traditionally been known as a producer of high quality carpets, but at competitive prices. It has a powerful brand name, and it has been able to protect this by producing the cheaper, lower quality products under a secondary brand name. It has also maintained a good relationship with the many carpet distributors throughout the UK, particularly the mainstream retail organisations.

The recent decline in carpet sales, partly recession induced, has worried the US parent company. It has recognised that the increasing concentration within the European carpet manufacturing sector has led to aggressive competition within a low growth industry. It does not believe that overseas sales growth by Bowland Carpets is an attractive proposition as this would compete with other Universal Carpet companies. It does, however, consider that vertical integration into retailing (as already practised within the USA) is a serious option. This would give the UK company increased control over its sales and reduce its exposure to competition. The president of the parent company has asked Jeremy Smiles, managing director of Bowland Carpets, to address this issue and provide guidance to the US board of directors. Funding does not appear to be a major issue at this time as the parent company has large cash reserves on its balance sheet.

Required

(a) To what extent do the distinctive competences of Bowland Carpets conform with the key success factors required for the proposed strategy change?

(b) Suggest and discuss what might be the prime entry barriers prevalent in the carpet retailing sector.

(c) In an external environmental analysis concerning the proposed strategy shift, what are likely to be the key external influences which could impact upon the Bowland Carpets' decision?

Chapter roundup

- SWOT analysis is an assessment of a company's strengths and weaknesses (internal to the organisation) and opportunities and threats (external to the organisation).
- A SWOT analysis should also include some evaluation of the relative importance of factors.
- Following a SWOT analysis strategy formulation should try to match company strengths to industry opportunities. Weaknesses should be developed into strengths if at all possible.
- SWOT analysis can be done at corporate or functional levels.
- Ansoff developed a product-market growth matrix and corresponding strategic implications of market penetration, product development, market development and diversification.
- Diversification can be vertical (backwards or forwards) or horizontal, which are complementary or competitively positioned to a company's present activities.
- If there is diversification that has no relation to the company's existing products/markets this is termed as unrelated or conglomerate diversification.
- Positioning is designing a product/service, so it holds a certain image in the consumer's mind.
- The foundation of a positioning strategy is to align what the company can do with what customers want.
- New products can either be new to the market or new to the company.
- There are eight steps to a systematic new product development process.

  1 Idea generation
  2 Screening
  3 Concept development
  4 Marketing strategy
  5 Business analysis
  6 Product development
  7 Market testing
  8 Commercialisation

- The relationship between the research and development department and the marketing department needs to be strong.
- A critical assessment of an organisation's record of innovation can be audited. Innovation strategy should encourage innovative ideas.
- Positioning can be 'psychological' and 'real'. Perceptual maps enable users to identify positioning options.
- An innovation audit identifies a firm's record of innovation and how it can be enhanced. It covers the organisation climate and culture, the value to the customer and the management team.

Quick quiz

1. What does Ansoff's growth vector matrix show?
2. Give two advantages of vertical integration.
3. What is positioning?
4. What does a perceptual map look like?
5. What is a 'new' product?
6. What is the purpose of test marketing?
7. What is market penetration pricing?
8. What are some of the barriers to innovation?
9. What are the main components of the ideal management team?

Answers to quick quiz

1. It describes a combination of a firm's activities in current and new markets, with existing and new products.
2. Secure supply of components

   Strengthening relationships.
3. The act of designing the company's product and image so that it offers a distinct, and valued place in the target customer's mind.
4.

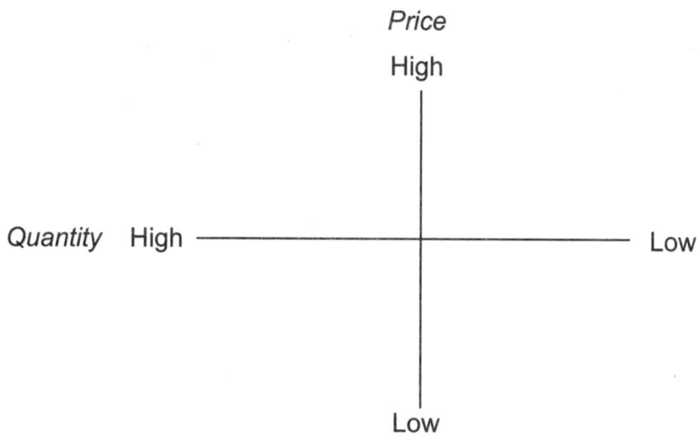

5. One that:

   (a) Opens up an entirely new market
   (b) Replaces an existing product
   (c) Broadens the market for an existing product
6. To obtain information about how consumers react to a new product – will they buy it?
7. A policy of low prices when the product is just launched to gain sufficient penetration in the market. It sacrifices short-term profits in the interests of long-term market development.
8. See paragraph 4.1
9. Co-ordinator
   Shaper
   Plant
   Monitor-evaluator
   Resource-investigator
   Implementor
   Team worker

   Finisher

Answers to activities

1 (a) Your answer might include:

- Acquiring specialist knowledge eg frozen foods
- Developing a nationwide courier service
- Developing a European haulage service

(b) Each one of these could be put into the existing structure by running, as a division or SBU (Strategic Business Unit). It could either be autonomous or closely integrated with the general haulage business.

(c) Advantages would include increased markets, possible increased profits.

Disadvantages would include additional costs in terms of specialist lorries/vans, additional staff, specialist knowledge required.

2 (a) An organisation's **distinctive competences**, highlighted in its internal analysis, are those features, skills or processes that differentiates an organisation and is performance/products attractively from its competitors and enable it to obtain a special sphere of influence or a strong competitive position. Competences derive from experience, staff skills and the quality of co-ordination.

Key or critical success factors. Organisations need to identify the key success factors, assets and skills needed to compete successfully in a market.

(i) **Strategic necessities** do not necessarily provide an **advantage,** because others have them, but their **absence** will cause a substantial weakness.

(ii) **Strategic strengths** (in which the organisation excels), are superior to those of competitors and provide a base of advantage. The market analysis will also be looking at how these will change in the future and how the assets and skills of competitors can be neutralised by strategies.

Key success factors include good distribution networks, advanced office systems and up-to-date marketing intelligence.

Mismatches between competences and success factors

Most organisations doing a SWOT analysis will find a mismatch somewhere. A company may be successful at establishing a strong position during the early stages of market development, only to lose ground later when the key success factors have changed. With consumer products marketing and distribution skills are dominant during the early phases but operations and manufacturing become more crucial as the product moves into the maturity and decline stage.

Bowland's new strategy. The management at the US parent company of Bowland Carpets have come up with a new strategy in an attempt to solve the problem of the declining carpet sales in the UK, mainly in the domestic market. The contract and industrial carpet segment will not be affected radically as the distribution network generally uses direct sales.

Bowland UK's competences are the ability to:

(i) Offer a wide range of high quality products at **competitive prices**.

(ii) Sustain **powerful brand names**, presence in different market segments.

(iii) Sustain **good relationships** with distributors.

Success factors for retailing

The proposed option of vertical integration into retailing will require a set of key success factors which will include some of these competences. However, there are gaps which are a cause for concern.

The key success factors for vertical integration into retail sales which have been developed in the US will not be totally transferable to the UK and the domestic company has no expertise in this field.

(i) **Distribution.** It is not clear whether the intention is to introduce this strategy as an addition to the current distribution network or instead of it. Both of these options would affect the **relationship with distributors** that has built up over a period and could be very **damaging to sales**. To compensate for this loss, Bowland Carpets would need to have a strong **geographical** presence either in High Street positions or in out-of-town developments. This could be **very costly** in both site selection and development.

(ii) **Expertise** in **retailing** and **distribution**. Staffing and servicing the retail outlets and training the staff in the skills required will be time-consuming and expensive. When customers buy carpets they expect a measuring, fitting and laying service as well as after-sales support. It may be that the UK company can learn from the USA but the culture of marketing household durables is different in both countries.

(iii) The **ability to provide a choice of products and services for the customer**. If there is insufficient choice, Bowland Carpets will have to find competitive manufacturers to fill the gap. This action may defeat the strategy to raise the sales in the **domestic** carpet market.

Conclusion. Bowland's distinctive competences are not appropriate to the key success factors required for retailing.

(b) **Entry barriers prevalent in the carpet retailing sector**

- The number of established carpet retailers in an already mature market
- The variety of 'own brands' available in dominant department stores
- The cost, availability and maintenance of suitable retail sites
- Suitable suppliers and reasonable terms
- The retailing skills which will need to be developed
- Marketing investments (research, staffing)
- The ability to offer a broad product line
- The level and nature of the service offered
- Brand loyalty

(c) An external environmental analysis identifies emerging trends, **opportunities** and **threats** created by the forces outside the organisation.

(i) Firms must avoid major surprises by anticipating major changes in their business circumstances.

(ii) Firms must make daily responses to changes among their customers, suppliers and workforce. Those who discover the longer-term patterns can decide whether they pose a threat or an opportunity and can gain a headstart on their competitors.

Contents of the analysis

(i) The **competitive** environment. Knowledge of the reactions of the other players in the market, both manufacturers and retailers, could be crucial to the success or otherwise of a new entrant's plan. Established businesses can adopt **retaliation strategies** to make it difficult for new companies to enter the market.

(ii) **Economic** factors include the **rate of growth** and the associated increase/decrease in **disposable income**, the **rate of inflation**, the state of the domestic housing market (house moves are often associated with new refurbishments), unemployment, interest rates and the availability of credit, taxation levels and incentives.

(iii) **Political** factors include laws on the safety of the product, town planning, selling practices adopted and the way a firm treats its employees.

(iv) The **social, demographic and cultural** environment analysis would highlight issues such as: the growth or decline in population; changes in ages when people leave home and start their own household; trends in house refurbishments; trends towards car-centred shopping in superstores and out-of-town shopping 'cities'.

(v) The **technological** environment. Consumers expect modern carpets to have properties which keep stains and insects away. The manufacturing environment is undergoing rapid changes with the growth of advanced manufacturing technology. Retail outlets are using point of sale equipment which can be used for stock control and to analyse the customer trends. Some DIY stores allow customers access to large cutting machines to avoid expensive cutting and laying services.

Chapter 11 :
THE EXTENDED MARKETING MIX

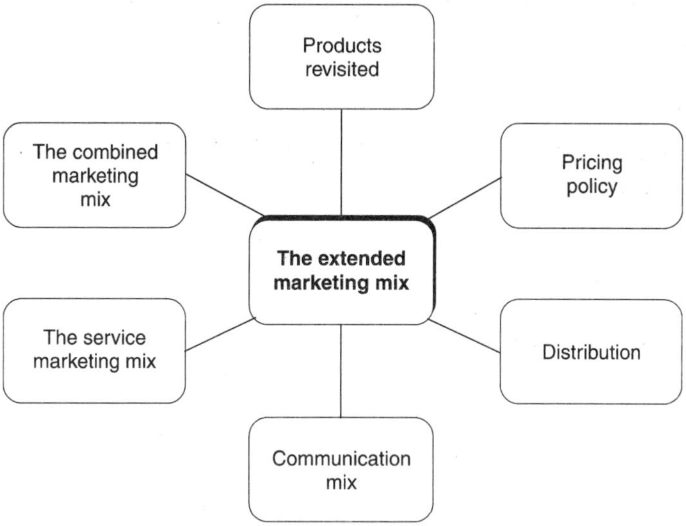

Introduction

The marketing plan is made up of decisions relating to the marketing mix for a product or service. This chapter will cover the integration of the elements of the extended marketing mix.

Your objectives

In this chapter you will learn about the following.

(a) The elements of the marketing mix

(b) Specific characteristics of services

1 THE COMBINED MARKETING MIX

Definition

> Kotler (2008) defines the mix as follows. '**Marketing mix** is the set of controllable variables and their levels that the firm uses to influence the target market.'

Each of the mix elements will be turned into a plan, at a more tactical level within the organisation. Each of these plans is prepared using the same basic framework that we have identified at both corporate and marketing level.

(1) Where are we now? (audit)
(2) Where are we going? (objectives)
(3) What are the alternative ways of getting there?
(4) Choosing the best option
(5) Developing an action plan (tactics)
(6) Implementation and control

The balance is often between a 'push' and a 'pull' strategy.

(a) A **push strategy** is concerned with moving goods out to wholesalers and retailers who then have the task of selling to customers, **ie getting dealers to accept goods.**

(b) A **pull strategy** is one of influencing final consumer attitudes so that a **consumer demand is created which dealers are obliged to satisfy;** a pull policy usually involves heavy expenditure on advertising, but holds the promise of stimulating a much higher demand.

(c) **A proper balance between 'push' and 'pull' is necessary to optimise sales.** Both require consideration within the same marketing plan.

Stages in the formulation of a marketing mix

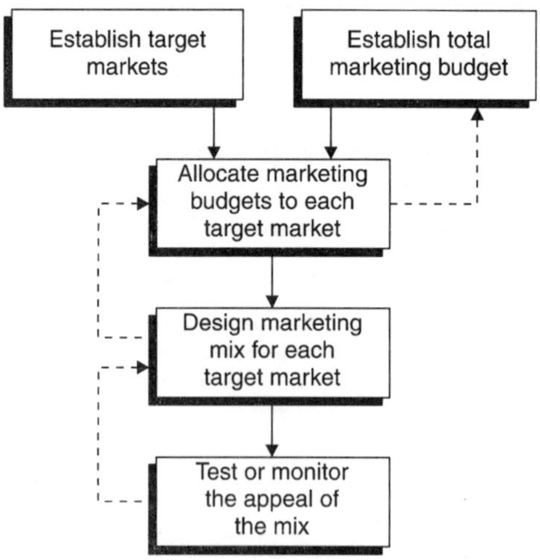

Figure 11.1: Formulation of the marketing mix

1.1 Design issues for the marketing mix

Issue	Comment
Profit/volume	The sales response function shows how different areas of the mix affect volume sales and **profits.** All other things being equal, the mix design should maximise profits.
Brand value	The mix should, where relevant, support the brand value, if a strong brand is important. Not all firms depend on branding.
Customers and distribution, segmentation	The mix should satisfy customer needs, but note in many cases there are two customers to consider: the end-user and the intermediary or reseller.
Life cycle	The appropriate mix changes over the life cycle of the product. For example a firm might adopt **penetration** or **skimming** prices at launch.
Marketing environment	This affects the optimal mix, but should be taken into account earlier in the planning process.
Seasonality	Clothes retailers are seasonally based, hence 'sales' after Christmas.
Integration	The elements of the marketing mix must support each other. There is no point promising the earth (promotion) if this cannot be delivered.
Push/pull	The mix can pull demand through the distribution chain or push it down.
Competitive strategy	The mix will support the competitive strategy.

EXAMPLES

You might like to contrast the marketing mix of these **holiday firms**. Each has been designed to appeal to a particular market segment.

(a) *Explore Worldwide*. This firm offers escorted holidays to small groups, in a variety of locations, which may involve some trekking and camping. Locations might include isolated villages in northern Thailand. The firm advertises itself on the basis of 'You'll see more'. The firm advertises in newspapers, but also likes to generate repeat business and word of mouth recommendation. Poster or TV advertising is not used. (www.explore.co.uk)

(b) *Club 18 to 30*. Targeted at a specific age group, these promise 'fun' or 'activity' holidays in or round beach resorts. Holidays are fairly cheap. "This is the time of your life. Love every single minute".
(www.club18-30.co.uk)

1.2 Combining the marketing mix in practice

For high-selling products some firms prepare a demand function showing the relationship between price and quantity of demand. This is not always possible.

(a) It may not be possible to establish, scientifically, how the different elements of the mix might interact.

(b) Many smaller businesses do not have the resources to prepare complicated models in this way.

(c) Another problem, especially true of business-to-business markets, is that there might be relatively **few customers**, who might be able to dictate, quite precisely, product specifications and other arrangements. The price may be negotiated after the sort of hard bargaining rarely encountered in consumer markets.

We will now briefly identify some issues regarding each element of the mix. This section is partly revision and partly to get you thinking about key issues of each element of the mix, including the marketing mix for services. In the **UK and most of the developed world, services account for greater economic output than manufacturing,** so we will take a 7P rather than a 4P approach to this issue.

- Product
- Place
- Price
- Promotion
- People
- Processes
- Physical evidence

2 PRODUCTS REVISITED

What is a product?

Definition

> A **product** is a 'package of benefits' meeting particular needs. It is anything that can be offered to a market, for attention, acquisition, use or consumption that might satisfy a want or need.

Product decisions were dealt with in the previous chapter in detail.

Aspect	Example
Physical aspect: what the product is	Bank account
Functional aspect: what the product does	Keeps your money safe
Symbolic aspect: what the product means	If you bank with Coutts, you are a member of an exclusive set of people

Levels of a product (Kotler)

Level	Comment
Core benefit	A hotel offers rest and sleep away from home
Generic product	Any hotel is a building with rooms to rent
Expected product	Most expect cleanliness and quiet
Augmented product	Additional benefits (eg taxi service)
Potential product	Possible augmentations in the future (for example, Internet connections in the room)

The expected product in one country may be the augmented product in a poor country. Most **competition** in the developed world is based around the **augmented product**.

Activity 1 **(10 minutes)**

Compare the levels of a product such as a car to a service such as home insurance.

Strategic issues for product

(a) **Defining the product.** Product/service is key in differentiation strategy, as the product can be manipulated to satisfy the needs of different market segments.

(b) **Selecting the product range**, in terms of **width** (how many segments) and **depth** (variety of options in each segment).

(c) Building a **brand**.

(d) Managing the **product portfolio** with new launches and deletions.

(e) **Quality**: this is 'fitness for use' and can be analysed as quality of design, and quality of conformance (the product has been manufactured without defects).

3 PRICING POLICY

3.1 The dimensions of price

Definition

Price can be defined as a measure of the value exchanged by the buyer for the value offered by the seller. It might be expected, therefore, that the price would reflect the costs to the seller of producing the product and the benefit to the buyer of consuming it.

Pricing is the only element of the mix which generates revenue rather than creating costs. It also has an important role as a competitive tool to differentiate a product and an organisation and thereby exploit market opportunities. Pricing must also be consistent with other elements of the marketing mix since it contributes to the overall image created for the product.

No organisation can hope to offer an exclusive high quality product to the market with a low price – **the price must be consistent with the overall product** offer.

Activity 2 **(15 minutes)**

In what circumstances would you expect price to be the main factor influencing a consumer's choice?

Although pricing can be thought of as fulfilling a number of roles, in overall terms a price aims to produce the **desired level of sales** in order to **meet the objectives** of the business strategy.

Pricing must be systematic and at the same time take into account the internal needs and the external constraints of the organisation.

Two broad categories of objectives may be specified for pricing decisions; not mutually exclusive, but different nonetheless.

(a) **Maximising profits** is concerned with maximising the returns on assets or investments. This may be realised even with a comparatively small market share depending on the patterns of cost and demand.

(b) **Maintaining or increasing market share** involves increasing or maintaining the customer base which may require a different, more competitive approach to pricing, while the company with the largest market share may not necessarily earn the best profits.

Either approach may be used in specifying pricing objectives, and they may appear in some combination, based on a specified rate of return and a specified market share. It is important that stated objectives are consistent with overall corporate objectives and corporate strategies.

3.2 Factors to consider when making pricing decisions

The selling price of a product should exceed its average unit cost in order to make a profit, but cost is only one of the factors to bear in mind when setting a price.

(a) **The organisation's objectives**. Although we generally assume that an organisation's objective is to maximise profit, have we already seen that increased market share could be an objective. Maximisation of sales revenue, being known as a supplier of luxury goods or providing a service to the community may also feature.

(b) **The market in which the organisation operates**. If the organisation is operating under conditions of **perfect competition** (many buyers and many sellers all dealing in an identical product), neither producer nor user has any market power and both must accept the **prevailing market price**. If the organisation is in the position of a **monopolist** (one seller who dominates many buyers), it can use its market power to set a profit-maximising price. Most of British industry can be described as an **oligopoly** (relatively few competitive companies dominate the market). While each large firm has the ability to influence market prices, the **unpredictable reaction** from the other giants makes the price difficult to determine.

(c) **Demand**. Economic theory suggests that the volume of demand for a good in the market is influenced by variables such as the price of the good, price of other goods, size and distribution of household income, tastes and fashion, expectations and obsolescence. The volume of demand for one organisation's goods rather than another's is influenced by three principal factors: **product life cycle, quality** and **marketing.**

(i) **Product life cycle.** Most products pass through the phases of introduction, growth, maturity and decline. Different versions of the same product may have different life cycles, and consumers are often aware of this. For example, the prospective buyer of a new car is more likely to purchase a recently introduced Ford than a Vauxhall that has been on the market for several years, even if there is nothing to choose in terms of quality and price.

(ii) **Quality.** One firm's product may be perceived to be better quality than another's. Other things being equal, the better quality good will be more in demand than other versions.

(iii) **Marketing.** The 7Ps of the extended marketing mix (or 7Ps for services) all influence demand for a firm's goods or services.

(d) **Price elasticity of demand.** The price an organisation charges will be affected by whether demand for an item is **elastic** (a small change in the price produces a large change in the quantity demanded) or **inelastic** (a small change in the price produces only a small change in the quantity demanded).

(e) **Costs.** An organisation has to decide whether a price should be based on fully absorbed cost or marginal cost.

EXAMPLE

Pricing is a key decision as it can very easily affect margins and profits.

	A	*B*
	£	£
Price	10	9.50
Cost	8	8.00
Profit	2	1.50

B is priced at 5% cheaper than A, but is 25% less profitable. In other words, a 5% cut in price leads to a 25% cut in profits. Clearly more of the unit will have to be sold to make up the shortfall.

The problem is that the **cost of producing something is not determined by the price** charged. As firms aim to make profits for shareholders, prices are often set with costs in mind, as a floor. The marketer thus does not have complete freedom to determine prices.

(f) **Competition.** When competitors sell exactly the same product in the same market, price differences are likely to have a significant effect on demand. For example, the price of petrol at filling stations in a local area will be much the same. When organisations sell similar products which are not exactly identical, or where the **geographical location** of the sales point is of some significance, there is more scope for charging different prices.

EXAMPLE

Developing drugs to combat AIDS has been expensive. The prices charged put the treatment way out of reach of sufferers in poorer countries where AIDS is prevalent. Some say that this pricing strategy is unethical. Others say that the money spent researching into drugs for AIDS could be spent on dealing with other life-threatening illnesses in poorer countries. Price does have 'ethical' connotations.

(g) **Inflation**. An organisation should recognise the effects of inflation on its pricing decisions. When its costs are rising, it must try to ensure that its prices are increased to make an adequate profit or to cover its costs (in the case of non-profit-making organisations).

(h) **Legislation**. Certain organisations have their prices controlled by legislation or regulatory bodies.

(i) **Availability of substitutes**. When an organisation is making a pricing decision it must take into account products/services that customers could switch to if they were not happy with the price set.

3.3 Approaches to pricing

Full cost plus pricing

A traditional approach to pricing products is **full cost plus** pricing.

Definition

Full cost plus pricing is a method of determining the sales price by calculating the full cost of the product and adding a percentage mark-up for profit.

A business might have an idea of the **percentage profit margin** it would like to earn and so might decide on an average profit mark-up as a general guideline for pricing decisions. The percentage profit mark-up does not have to be fixed, but can be varied to suit the circumstances. In particular, it can be varied to suit demand conditions in the market.

This approach to pricing fails to recognise that since demand may be determined by price, there will be a **profit-maximising combination** of price and demand.

The **advantage** of full cost plus pricing is that since the size of the profit margin can be varied at management's discretion, a decision based on a price in excess of full cost should ensure that a company working at normal capacity will cover all its fixed costs and make a profit. It is also a simple and quick method.

Marginal cost plus or mark-up pricing

Instead of pricing products or services by adding a profit margin on to **full cost**, a business might add a profit margin on to **marginal cost**. This is sometimes called **mark-up pricing**.

Definition

> **Marginal cost plus pricing/mark up pricing** is a method of determining the sales price by adding a profit margin on to marginal cost.

The **advantages** of a marginal cost plus approach to pricing are as follows.

(a) It can be adjusted to reflect demand conditions.

(b) It draws management attention to **contribution** and the effects of higher or lower sales volumes on profit.

(c) Mark-up pricing is convenient where there is a **readily identifiable basic variable cost**. Retail industries are the most obvious example, and it is quite common for the prices of goods in shops to be fixed by adding a mark-up (20% or 33⅓%, say) to the purchase cost. The price must of course be high enough to ensure that a profit is made after covering fixed costs.

Minimum pricing

A **minimum price** is the price that would have to be charged so that the **incremental costs** of producing and selling the item, and the **opportunity costs** of the resources consumed in making and selling the item, are just covered. A minimum price would leave the business no better or worse off than if it did not sell the item.

Two essential points about a minimum price are as follows.

(a) It is based on **relevant costs.**

(b) It is unlikely that a minimum price would be charged because it would not provide the business with any profit. However, the minimum price for an item shows the **absolute minimum below which the price should not be set** and the incremental profit that would be obtained from any price that is charged in excess of the minimum.

Limiting factor pricing

Another approach to pricing might be taken when a business is working at full capacity, and is restricted by a shortage of resources from expanding its output further. By deciding what target profit it would like to earn, it could establish a **mark-up per unit of limiting factor**.

The demand-based approach to pricing

We have now looked at a variety of cost-based approaches to pricing. **Demand-based approaches** are less common and more difficult to set.

(a) Price theory or demand theory is based on the idea that a connection can be made between price, **quantity** demanded and sold, and total **revenue**. The theory of demand cannot be applied in practice, however, unless **realistic estimates of demand at different price** levels can be made.

(b) In practice, businesses might not make estimates of demand at different price levels, but they might still make pricing decisions on the basis of **demand conditions** and **competition** in the market. When competitors sell exactly the same product in the same market, price differences are likely to have a significant effect on demand.

When companies sell similar products which are not exactly identical, or where the geographical location of the sales point is of some significance, there is more scope for charging different prices. Even so, the prices charges by competitors cannot be ignored altogether. Price differences can be achieved in a number of ways.

- Through product quality
- Through design differences (motor cars are an obvious example)
- Through geographical location
- Through **brand loyalty**

EXAMPLE

The prices of crossing the English Channel by ferry vary between different ports of departure. Holiday flights from different regional airports may attract varying regional supplements.

Competitor-influenced pricing and price leadership

The problem of pricing under **oligopoly** has been mentioned and it is observable that oligopolists tend not to compete on price, for fear of provoking increased competition and a **price war**.

There may be small differences in the prices charged by the various suppliers, but these tend to be fairly constant and seem to be based on market status, with the well-known brands able to charge a small premium. Generally, oligopolists prices tend to fall or rise together. The establishment of a formal cartel to decide industry price is illegal in all developed economies, so why do oligopoly prices display this behaviour?

Usually, there is a market leader, which may be the firm with the largest market share, and other firms in the same industry generally follow the price movements initiated by the leader in an informal way. Their defence against charges of establishing an illegal price-fixing cartel is that they are merely charging the **going rate**. This is an **average price** strategy.

EXAMPLE

This is the case with oil companies and the price of petrol at filling stations: different companies sell the same product and so, within a local area, the prices charged at each station will be much the same. If they were not, customers would go to the cheapest place.

Sometimes a price war will, in fact, break out in an oligopoly market. This used to be quite common among UK national newspapers. The aim is to increase market share. The problem is to keep the extra share when competitors follow the price cut. In the case of identical products such as bulk commodities, the strategy is self-defeating. Where there is an element of product differentiation, a price cut can encourage customers to at least try out the price-cutter's product and may lead to an increase in market share, though at considerable cost in lost turnover.

3.4 Pricing and market share

Generally speaking, price cuts to increase market share will be matched by competitors in some way. If a rival firm cuts its prices in the expectation of increasing its market share, a firm has the following options.

(a) **Maintain its existing prices.** This would be done if the expectation is that only a small market share would be lost, so that it is more profitable to keep prices at their existing level.

(b) **Maintain prices but responding with a non-price counter-attach.** This is a more positive response, because the firm will be securing or justifying its current prices with a product change, advertising, or better back-up services, etc.

(c) **Reduce prices.** This should protect the firm's market share so that the main beneficiary from the price reduction will be the consumer.

(d) **Raise prices and respond with a non-price counter-attack.** A price increase would be based on a campaign to emphasise the quality difference between the rival products.

3.5 Pricing strategies

New product pricing strategies

A **new product pricing strategy** will depend on whether the product is the first of its kind on the market, in which case the company will be able to set a price at which it thinks its profits will be maximised, or if it is following a competitor's product onto the market, in which case the pricing strategy will be constrained by what the competitor is doing. There are two alternative strategies.

(a) **Market penetration pricing** is a policy of **low prices** when the product is **first launched** in order to obtain sufficient penetration into the market. A penetration policy may be appropriate in the following circumstances.

  (i) If the firm wishes to **discourage new entrants** into the market

  (ii) If the firm wishes to **shorten the initial period of the product's life cycle** in order to enter the growth and maturity stages as quickly as possible

  (iii) If there are significant **economies of scale** to be achieved from a high volume of output, so that quick penetration into the market is desirable in order to gain unit cost reductions

  (iv) If demand is **highly elastic** and so would respond well to low prices

(b) In contrast, **market skimming** involves charging **high prices** when a product is first launched and spending heavily on **advertising and sales promotion** to obtain sales. As the product moves into the later stages of its life, progressively lower prices will be charged. The aim of market skimming is to **gain high unit profits early in the product's life**.

Product mix pricing strategies

The strategy for setting a price often has to be changed when the product is part of a **product mix**. The organisation looks for a set of prices that maximise the profit on the total mix. Various pricing strategies exist.

(a) **Product line pricing** involves developing a product line in which each successive item in the line offers more features/higher quality for a higher price. If the price difference between two successive products is small, buyers will usually buy the more advanced/better quality product. If the cost difference is smaller than the price difference, profits are increased, and the profitability of the line as a whole is maximised.

(b) **Optional product pricing** involves selling optional or accessory products along with the main product. For example a car buyer can order electric windows and a sunroof. Airlines have adopted this approach with the choice of buying an in-flight meal or not.

(c) **Captive product pricing** involves selling products that must be used along with a main product. The main products (such as razors) are priced low and the related products (such as blades) are priced high. In the case of services this strategy is called **two-part pricing**. The price of the service is broken down into a fixed fee (entry into an amusement park) plus a variable usage rate (fees for food and rides).

(d) **By-product pricing** involves accepting any price for a low value by-product that covers more than the cost of storing and delivering it. The price of the main product can then be reduced to make it more competitive.

(e) **Product bundle pricing** involves combining several products and offering the whole bundle at a reduced price. Mobile phone providers tend to use this approach with their bundle options with additional services such as internet access minutes, additional texts and inclusive call minutes.

EXAMPLE

Hotels sell specially-priced packages which include room, meals and entertainment. Entire holidays, especially in the Caribbean, are now sold on this all-inclusive basis, covering everything from flights to jet ski hire.

3.6 Price adjustment strategies

Basic prices may need to be **adjusted** to account for customer differences and changing situations. There are a number of relevant strategies.

(a) **Discount pricing and allowances**

(i) **Cash discount** is a price reduction for buyers who pay their bills promptly.

(ii) **Quantity discount** is a price reduction for buyers who buy large volumes.

(iii) **Trade discount** (also called a **functional discount**) is a price reduction given to an intermediary for performing certain functions such as storage.

(iv) **Seasonal discount** is a price reduction for buyers who buy products or services out of season, such as cheaper hotel prices in the winter.

(v) **Allowances** include **trade in allowances and promotional allowances**.

Activity 3 **(5 minutes)**

What are the disadvantages of offering price discounts to cash customers in an attempt to increase customer numbers?

(b) **Discriminatory pricing.** Where a company can sell to two or more separate markets, it might be able to charge a different price in each market to maximise its profits. There are several ways in practice by which price discrimination can be exercised.

(i) **Negotiation with individual customers.** For example, customer A might buy a video cassette recorder from Firm X for £600 cash, whereas customer B might buy the same item and negotiate a discount for cash of, say, 10%.

(ii) **On the basis of quantities purchased.** Bulk purchase discounts are a well-established form of price discrimination, offering favourable prices to large customers.

(iii) **By product type.** This involves some form of product differentiation so that customers in one market segment will buy a product basically similar to (but differentiated from) a product sold to another market segment, but at a different price. Examples of price discrimination through product differentiation are to be found in the sale of clothing and cars (customers may pay disproportionately higher amounts for a car with a larger engine capacity or a more comfortable interior).

(iv) **By time.** Examples are services with peak time and off-peak tariffs, such as hotel accommodation in holiday resorts and charges for telephone calls.

(v) **By location.** Higher prices may be charged in some locations than in others so that a firm with several branches in various towns may set different prices in each branch. Branches in remote locations might set higher prices and in poorer areas they might set lower prices.

For successful price discrimination, certain **market conditions** must exist.

(i) The producer must enjoy a **dominant position** in the market, perhaps as a monopolist or as the provider of a branded product or quality product which commands a high degree of **customer loyalty**.

(ii) Where price discrimination is exercised on the basis of individual negotiation or by geographical area, there must be no opportunity for rivals to buy the product at the cheaper price and sell it at a competitive higher price to the higher priced market.

EXAMPLE

Many supermarkets and multiple retail stores sell their 'own label' products, often at a lower price than established branded products. The supermarkets or multiple retailers do this by entering into arrangements with manufacturers, to supply their goods under the 'own brand' label. This is a form of price discrimination. More recently, this strategy has changed with regard to retailers' premium own brands. These superior quality products are often sold at a higher price than branded alternatives.

(c) **Psychological pricing** considers the psychology of prices and not simply the economics. The price is used to say something about the product.

(d) **Promotional pricing** involves temporarily pricing products below list price, and sometimes below cost, to increase short-run sales.

   (i) **Loss leaders** are used to attract customers in the hope that they will buy other goods at normal mark-up.

   (ii) **Special event pricing** might be used in certain seasons.

   (iii) **Cash rebates** are offered to consumers who buy the product from dealers within a specified time.

   (iv) **Discounts** may be offered.

(e) **Geographical pricing strategies** cover different freight charging strategies (which depend on the location of customers).

EXAMPLE

'Everyday low pricing strategies – the policy of scrapping promotions in favour of sharp, permanent price cuts – were pioneered by Procter & Gamble in the US where they helped the company reclaim market share from competing brands and "own label" products.

The latest company to adopt this strategy is Esso which launched its "Pricewatch" initiative offering "normally unbeatable" prices within a distance of three miles. The policy was introduced after research showed that customers valued lower prices above collections and promotions. Asda in the UK tries to differentiate itself from rivals by emphasising its "permanently low prices", while Tesco uses the term "Every little helps" as a slogan.

The logic of getting away from promotions is supported by research which shows that promotions are only taken up by people who were already customers.'

3.7 Discount policy and competitive bidding

The purpose of discounts is to encourage **more sales (or earlier payment)**. The cost of discounts should not exceed the benefits from extra sales or earlier payment, and the size of discounts offered should not be excessive. After all, why offer a 15% discount for a sale if the customer would still buy if he obtained a 10% discount?

Discounts help to make a firm's products more price-competitive, but the size of discount that can be offered must depend on the **variable cost/sales price ratio**. For example, a firm whose variable costs are 25% of the gross sales price will have more flexibility with discount policy than a firm whose variable costs are 80% of the gross sales price, because it has a bigger contribution margin to play with. Stepped discounts, ie bigger discounts rising in steps for bigger sales orders, must also be planned carefully, and the size of the price breaks should be sensible.

Competitive bidding calls for the preparation of cost data for the purpose of submitting a bid to a potential customer, in the hope of securing his order. There will be three factors in the customer's choice of supplier from among the tenders submitted.

(a) The **price** itself

(b) **Performance**, especially if the product is new and largely untested in the open market, reliability, service etc

(c) **Financial matters,** such as inflation (and cost escalation clauses) and foreign exchange rates (for overseas contracts), export credit insurance

Co-operation is needed between the accounting and marketing departments of a bidding company because a balance has to be drawn between putting in a bid which is too low to make an adequate profit, but keeping the bid low enough to stand a good chance of winning the contract. Consideration must be given to the following.

(a) The **contribution to profit** that would be obtained from the contract

(b) The **consequences** for the company if it failed to win the order

(c) The **probability** of winning the order, which might be assessed on the basis of past experience

(d) **Possible non-price product differentiation** in favour of the supplier eg quality of service, reliable delivery times, finance facilities offered

3.8 Other pricing decisions

Promotional prices are short-term price reductions or price offers which are intended to attract an increase in sales volume. (The increase is usually short-term for the duration of the offer, which does not appear to create any substantial new customer loyalty.) Loss leaders and 'money off' coupons are a form of promotional pricing.

A **temporary price cut** may be preferable to a permanent reduction because it can be ended without unduly offending customers and can be reinstated later to give a repeated boost to sales. They may be used as sales promotions to establish new brands.

Short-term pricing. Marketing management should have the responsibility for estimating the relationship between price and demand for their organisation's products.

(a) The sales-revenue maximising price for a product and the profit-maximising price might not be the same.

(b) Simple **CVP analysis** can be used to estimate the breakeven point of sales, and the sales volume needed to achieve a target profit figure. We cover this in the next chapter.

(c) As we have seen in this chapter, many organisations use a **cost-plus approach** to pricing. Accounting figures are needed for cost in order to establish a floor for making a cost-plus pricing decision. The size of the profit margin will be decided by marketing management.

The marketing department's contribution to **short-run pricing decisions** is not only to assess a basic demand curve relationship between price and sales volume, and an assessment of the elasticity of demand for the firm's products, but also to consider how prices might be adjusted to allow for particular product, market or customer characteristics.

(a) **Product analysis pricing** combines the effects of cost-plus pricing and what the market will bear. An attempt is made to add up all the attributes of the product to ascertain the price that the customer will pay. The characteristics will include finish, strength, durability etc, and the pricing model will be built up using a sample of products with known selling prices and values for each of the characteristics. A price for other products can then be decided accordingly. It works well if the decision is fairly routine.

(b) **Quality adjusted pricing** brings in the aspect of product quality into the assessment of price.

3.9 Data for pricing decisions

Organisations need a multitude of data to make pricing decisions.

(a) **Cost data**

This can be obtained from internal cost and management accounting records and other internal secondary data sources.

(b) **Demand data**

To be able to estimate demand for products or services at different price levels an organisation may well have to commission pricing research. We will be looking at pricing research in detail in Part D of the Course Book. Such research will need to consider, for example, elasticities of demand and customer perceptions of price and quality.

(c) **Competitor data**

Information about competitors is vital for pricing decisions. The sources of competitor information are summarised below.

(i) Published data sources (eg published financial statements, press releases)

(ii) Salesforce data

(iii) Trade databases

(iv) Industry experts

(v) Trade press

(vi) Distributors

(vii) Suppliers

(viii) Customers

4 DISTRIBUTION

Distribution or ('place') comprises all the activities that make a physical product available to the customer.

It involves two main areas:

(a) **Logistics**, which are the activities undertaken within the firm for movement and storage of products.

(b) The **distribution channel**, which is made up of other firms involved in moving, storing and selling the products. These firms include wholesalers, retailers and agents.

The distribution between these two elements is not clear cut since, for example, a firm may buy in some of its logistic services from contractors, while distribution channel partners may have their own logistic activities.

4.1 Intermediaries

How intermediaries add value

Companies may distribute direct to customers, or choose from a wide range of intermediaries: retailers, wholesalers, dealers, agents, franchisees and multiple stores. Intermediaries provide an important service and add value in several ways.

(a) They provide **finance** for logistic and selling effort.

(b) They **break bulk**, enabling customers to buy in much smaller quantities than suppliers may be prepared to offer.

(c) They make goods available at **convenient times** and in **convenient places.**

(d) They provide **transport** and **storage.**

(e) They undertake the procedures required for **import** and **export** of goods.

(f) They hold stock from more than one manufacturer, providing customers with **choice.**

The **distribution channel** dilemma facing management is that of the trade-off between cost and control. The shorter the distribution channel the more control managers have over the marketing of the products, but the higher their distribution costs. Long distribution channels cut the costs but also reduce the firm's control. The various channels are outlined in the diagram below.

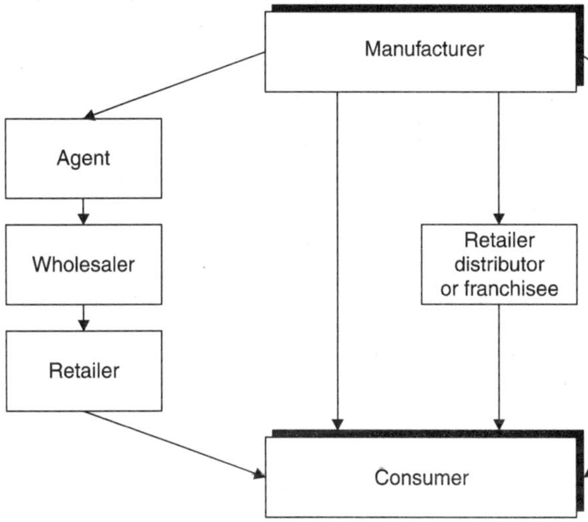

Figure 11.2: Distribution channels

Functions of the distribution channel

In order for a product to be distributed a number of basic functions usually need to be fulfilled.

(a) **Transport**

This function may be provided by the supplier, the distributor or may be sub-contracted to a specialist. For some products, such as perishable goods, transport planning is vital.

(b) **Stock holding and storage**

For production planning purposes, an uninterrupted flow of production is often essential, so stocks of finished goods accumulate and need to be stored, incurring significant costs and risks.

For consumer goods, holding stock at the point of sale is very costly; the overheads for city centre retail locations are prohibitive. A good stock control system is essential, designed to avoid stockouts whilst keeping stockholding costs low.

(c) **Local knowledge**

As production has tended to become centralised in pursuit of economies of scale, the need to understand local markets has grown, particularly when international marketing takes place. The intricacies and idiosyncrasies of local markets are key marketing information.

(d) **Promotion**

While major promotional campaigns for national products are likely to be carried out by the supplier, the translation of the campaign to local level is usually the responsibility of the local distributor, often as a joint venture.

(e) **Display**

Presentation of the product at the local level is often a function of the local distributor. Specialist help from merchandisers can be bought in but decisions on layout and display need to be taken by local distributors, often following patterns produced centrally.

Activity 4 **(5 minutes)**

For many goods, producers use retailers as middlemen in getting the product to the customer. Try to think of some of the disadvantages of doing this from the producer's point of view.

4.2 Types of distribution channel

Choosing distribution channels is important for any organisation, because once a set of channels has been established, subsequent changes are likely to be costly and slow to implement.

Distribution channels fall into one of two categories: direct and indirect channels.

(a) **Direct distribution** means the product going directly from producer to consumer without the use of a specific intermediary. These methods are often described as active since they typically involve the supplier making the first approach to a potential customer. Direct distribution methods generally fall into two categories: those using media such as the press, leaflets and telephones to invite response and purchase by the consumer and those using a sales force to contact consumers face to face.

(b) **Indirect distribution** is a system of distribution, common among manufactured goods, which makes use of intermediaries; wholesalers, retailers or perhaps both. In contrast to direct distribution, these methods are often thought of as being passive in the sense that they rely on consumers to make the first approach by entering the relevant retail outlet.

In building up efficient channels of distribution, a manufacturer must consider several factors.

(a) How many **intermediate stages** should be used and how many dealers at each stage?

(b) What **support** should the manufacturer give to the dealers? It may be necessary to provide an after-sales and repair service, and regular visits to retailers' stores. The manufacturer might need to consider advertising or sales promotion support, including merchandising.

(c) To what extent does the manufacturer wish to **dominate a channel of distribution**? A market leader might wish to ensure that its market share is maintained, so that it could, for example, offer exclusive distribution contracts to major retailers.

(d) To what extent does the manufacturer wish to **integrate its marketing effort** up to the point of sale with the consumer? Combined promotions with retailers, for example, would only be possible if the manufacturer dealt directly with the retailer (rather than through a wholesaler).

4.3 Channel design decisions

In designing a channel of distribution, the supplier must consider five things.

(a) Customers
(b) Product characteristics
(c) Distributor characteristics
(d) The channel chosen by competitors
(e) The supplier's own characteristics

Customers

The number of potential customers, their buying habits and their geographical locations are key influences. The use of mail order for those with limited mobility (rural location, illness) is an example of the influence of customers on channel design. Marketing industrial components to the car industry needs to take account of the geographic distribution of the car industry in the UK.

The growth of Internet trading, both in consumer and business-to-business markets, has been built on the rapid spread of fast Internet access.

Product characteristics

Some product characteristics have an important effect on the design of the channel of distribution.

(a) **Perishability**

Fresh fruit and newspapers must be distributed very quickly or they become worthless. Speed of delivery is therefore a key factor.

(b) **Customisation**

Customised products tend to be distributed direct. When a wide range of options is available, sales may be made using demonstration units, with customised delivery to follow.

(c) **After-sales service/technical advice**

Extent and cost must be carefully considered, staff training given and quality control systems set up. Training programmes are often provided for distributors by suppliers.

Distributor characteristics

The capability of the distributor to take on the distributive functions already discussed above is obviously an important influence on the supplier's choice.

Competitors' channel choice

For many consumer goods, a supplier's brand will sit alongside its competitors' products and there is little the supplier can do about it. For other products, distributors may stock one name brand only (for example, in car distribution) and in return be given an exclusive area. In this case, new suppliers may face difficulties in breaking into a market if all the best distribution outlets have been taken up.

Supplier characteristics

A strong financial base gives the supplier the option of buying and operating their own distribution channel. The market position of the supplier is also important: distributors are keen to be associated with the market leader but the third, fourth or fifth brand in a market is likely to find more distribution problems.

Why do firms use intermediaries?

(a) **Geography**: customers may live too far away to be reached directly, or may be too dispersed

(b) **Consolidation** of small orders into large ones

(c) Better use of **resources** elsewhere

(d) **Lack** of **retailing know-how**

(e) **Segmentation**, with different segments for each market being reached by different distribution channels

---

EXAMPLE: MAKING THE CHANNEL DECISION

So, producers (and their marketing planners!) have a number of decisions to make.

(a) **What types of distributor are to be used?**

ie wholesalers, retailers, agents?

(b) **How many of each type will be used? The answer to this depends on what degree of market exposure will be sought.**

(i) *Intensive* – blanket coverage
(ii) *Exclusive* – appointed agents for exclusive areas
(iii) *Selective* – some but not all in each area

(c) **Who will carry out specific marketing tasks?**

(i) Credit provision
(ii) Delivery
(iii) After-sales service
(iv) Sales and product training
(v) Display

(d) **How will the performance of distributors be evaluated?**

(i) In terms of cost?
(ii) In terms of sales levels?

(iii) According to the degree of control achieved?
(iv) By the amount of conflict that arises?

4.4 Current strategic developments in distribution

(a) **Physical distribution costs** are increasing **relative** to other costs (ie as production costs fall). Sometimes these amount to 50% of the price the end-consumer pays.

(b) **Changing consumer lifestyles**: people work longer hours. They have more money, but less time. Home delivery is a popular option.

(c) Established **distribution channels are beginning to 'leak'** (eg beer-buyers can go to France and stock up with lower-taxed drinks).

(d) Offering EDI (**electronic data interchange**) enables a firm to cut lead times for orders. This can be a source of differentiation.

(e) **Distribution has a 'branding effect'**. Distribution can be a central and, explicit part of a brand's identity, such as First Direct (HSBC's telephone banking subsidiary). Many internet-based organisations rely on the power of their 'online' brand.

(f) **Distribution channels' generation of customer information opens the door to marketing insight and power.** Retailers (through using EPOS) probably know more about customers than manufacturers.

(g) There has been a move towards a **concentration of retailer power** with large **retailers** tending to gain **power over the manufacturers in the distribution channel**. This shift in the balance of power has two consequences. **Large multiples** are able to **dictate product specifications,** and drive much harder bargains on matters of price and delivery. The large multiples' **own-label brands** are increasingly the major competition against branded goods.

(h) **Just-in-time** is a philosophy which applies to the whole production chain, but it is increasingly relevant to distribution, in satisfying the needs of demanding customers, particularly in business-to-business markets.

    (i) Manufacturers are seeking to reduce their stocks of components and raw materials, to eliminate stock holding costs and wasteful activities.

    (ii) Consequently they expect their suppliers to deliver in very small batches as and when demanded.

Mail order, in which goods are sold by catalogue or over the Internet and delivered by post or directly, is common in some markets. Reasons why include:

(a) **Retailers are eliminated and therefore do not have to be offered a mark-up**. This is why **book clubs** are able to offer discounts on recommended retail prices.

(b) **Customers can be reached** who might not normally be able to purchase the product **from a shop.**

(c) This makes it easier to sell to customers who **cannot do their shopping in normal shopping hours**.

(d) **No large and expensive display area** in a shop.

(e) Mail-order facilities can be **combined with an Internet website.**

However, not all mail order and internet distributors are themselves manufacturers. Many traditional store-based retailers have turned themselves into **multi-channel** distributors. They continue to attract customers into their stores, especially for major purchases where brand comparison and technical information are important, but they also offer catalogue and internet sales.

Activity 5 **(10 minutes)**

What social trends do you think might increase home delivery?

4.5 Evaluating current distribution channels

Criteria which may be used to evaluate distribution channels and logistics include:

(a) **Effectiveness** in getting products to customers (ie sales) and in performing each of the distributive functions that leads to sales;

(b) **Efficiency and economy** in terms of the costs of distribution;

(c) **Level of service** offered to customers, supporting loyalty and repeat sales;

(d) **Degree of control** achieved over the distribution channel, where desired for competitive advantage or integration of marketing effort up to the point of sale;

(e) **Degree of co-operation or conflict** with the distributor (channel dynamics).

4.6 Effectiveness

The measure of effectiveness will depend on specific objectives and criteria appropriate to the processes and channels used. **Sales** made through the distribution channels(s), however, are a key indicator and can be either compared month-on-month or year-on-year to show growth or decline trends or compared for different channels, to show which are more effective than others.

Sales results are, however, only the reflection of underlying factors, relating to the distributor's capabilities for undertaking and fulfilling the objectives of distribution tasks.

(a) A retail outlet may or may not give attention to point-of-sale display of the product, since it has a wide product portfolio and limited space.

(b) A retail outlet may or may not distinguish between competing products, or favour the competing brand in its shelf space or promotions.

(c) Intermediary's profit margins may affect the sale price to the consumer, with a depressing effect on sales.

(d) A distributor or transporter may or may not be able to service a widely-dispensed market swiftly and effectively. There may be regional gaps or delays which waste sales potential.

(e) Customers' buying habits and geographical location may favour one type of distribution channel over another. In remote areas, for example, retailers may not be as effective as mail order.

(f) The product may be better suited to one type of distribution channel than another. 'Perishable' products (such as fresh food and newspapers) need to be distributed quickly, or they become worthless.

(g) The supplying/marketing organisation itself may be responsible for insufficient 'pull' promotion motivating consumers to approach the point of sale.

4.7 Efficiency

Cost of distribution is one of the key factors in selecting distribution channels. Intermediaries may reduce the costs of selling for the manufacturer by bearing or sharing the costs of stockholding, transportation and display. In addition, manufacturers may receive payment more quickly from intermediaries than by selling direct to the consumer.

Distribution costs should be monitored to ensure that:

(a) Cost savings are being obtained, compared to estimated costs of other channels

(b) Costs are in line with negotiated and budgeted expenditure

(c) The channel is cost-efficient: that is, that no re-organisation of the network or logistics could reduce costs while maintaining the present level of service to the customer

---

EXAMPLE: ONLINE GROCERIES

The online grocery war continues. Tesco.com's pick-from-store business model took an early lead and was quickly profitable. Competitor Sainsbury's to You took longer to make a profit.

Waitrose, John Lewis and European investment bank UBS invested more than £60m in Ocado, a pick-from-warehouse online grocer that opened a 111,484 square metre warehouse in Hatfield, north of London.

Picking in-store is fine in the short-term, but warehouse fulfilment makes sense as online grocery orders increase, because warehouse space is cheaper than retail space, and offers more reliability and efficiency.

Successful online ventures require a lot of scaleable storage space, but walk-in supermarkets are geared to keeping smaller stocks of a wide variety of items. The warehouse fulfilment model will get more cost-effective as order volumes grow, but the pick-from-store model will not.

One of the main gripes of online shoppers is substitution. If an item in their order is not available, something similar (which they may or may not like) is put in to replace it. An online venture needs enough stock to keep substitutions to a minimum, and warehouse fulfilment can do this more reliably because the website is kept updated about exactly what it has to offer.

Picking in-store is not ideal for online selling because it is unpredictable. Operators can't promise to deliver a certain item because an in-store shopper may have just taken the last one.

Picking items for online order delivery is more efficient in warehouses, which are designed purely for picking speed, and not for luring customers or helping them navigate a store. And warehouse pickers aren't hampered by store customers, who could slow down in-store pickers.

Thus advantages for warehouse fulfilment increase as order volumes grow.

The cost of retail space in city centres is high, so expanding home-delivery capacity using picking in-store will be much more expensive than using out-of-town warehouses. Similarly, efficiency will increase greatly in pick-from-warehouse systems specially designed for high throughput, as opposed to stores that have been adapted for home delivery.

But capital cost and distance can hamper warehouse fulfilment. It is much cheaper to base online operations on existing infrastructure, such as premises and stock. This has given Tesco a head start, allowing it to bolt on an Internet arm at a much lower capital cost than the dedicated new facilities of rivals.

4.8 Level of service

Customer service is a key source of competitive advantage, and therefore a key objective of distribution systems. It may include:

(a) The availability of, and charges for, installation, repair and after-sales service

(b) Readiness to take back and quickly re-supply defective goods

(c) The preparation of orders delivered with correct contents and in good condition

(d) Lead time from placement of an order to delivery

(e) Choice and flexibility in product specifications, size of order accepted and ordering convenience

(f) The availability of product information and/or demonstration (particularly for technical products)

(g) A customer service orientation in front line staff

Such factors are part of the offer to the customer, and responsibility for them should be clearly apportioned by negotiation between manufacturers and intermediaries and monitored. If the manufacturer has a service policy of re-supplying faulty goods, the willingness of a retailer (for example) to mediate the return and exchange should be ascertained.

4.9 Degree of control

Manufacturers may wish to control or dominate a distribution channel.

(a) Ensuring that its policies with regard to pricing, promotion and sales service are carried out, and its marketing message is integrated all the way to the point of sale

(b) Maintain closer contact with consumers and sources of marketing information.

(c) Gain competitive advantage by having exclusive distribution through major retailers or distributors (like car dealers)

EXAMPLE

Champneys, the spa brand, launched a range of toiletries exlcusively through Sainsburys in order to generate significant visibility, while retaining a sense of exclusiveness.

4.10 Degree of co-operation or conflict

As business relationships, channels are subject to conflicts of interest, culture, priorities and personalities. Attention will need to be given to channel management where negotiations and problem-solving take up an unacceptable amount of managerial time, or result in lost sales (for example, though lack of co-operation on promotions or point-of-sale display).

5 COMMUNICATION MIX

This is covered in detail in Unit 18 in the context of advertising and promotion.

5.1 Categories

Marketing communications convey information about the product and the company.

Kotler (1999) identifies four **categories of promotional activity**.

Promotional	Comment
Advertising	Any **paid** form of non-personal presentation and promotion of ideas, goods or services by an identified sponsor.
Sales promotion	Encourage through incentives, over a short-term period, the purchase of the good or service.
Personal selling	The oral presentation of the goods or services, either to make a sale, or to create goodwill to improve the prospects of sales in the future.
Public relations	Unlike advertising, publicity cannot be bought and it might be thought of as unpaid advertising. Although organisations will spend large sums of money on publicity, they do not formally buy 'PR' space in a newspaper or time on television or radio. Nor do they usually control the content of the publicity message, and so some publicity can be bad. However, they often try to manage publicity through the use of public relations.

Recently, the trend is towards **integrated marketing communications**. In other words, the marketing communications should be integrated with the business strategy, the other elements of the marketing mix, and with each other. Few organisations practise an integrated communications approach in any systematic way. The various tools of marketing communications have traditionally been the exclusive preserve of different groups within the organisation.

Promotion is the element of the mix most under control of the marketing department. Piercy (2008) suggests that, as far as managers are concerned, there are a number of issues which must be considered strategically for each form of promotional communication.

5.2 Piercy's issues

Issue	Comment
Role	**Each form of communication has a different target.** Media advertising is direct to the end user, whereas personal selling may be preferred for distributors.

Issue	Comment
Objectives	Each form of communication needs specific objectives: • Advertising: raising awareness, repositioning • Public relations: favourable press exposure • Personal selling: sales targets, client relationships • Sales promotion: sample rates
Process management	This covers relationships with external suppliers, budgeting, recruiting and personnel
Integration	The elements of the mix should be integrated so that all customers get the appropriate message, and the different elements of the mix do not conflict with each other.

5.3 Key strategic developments in promotional communications

Development	Consequence
Database marketing and data mining	This enables targeting of promotional messages.
Digital TV, many channels	It will be harder to reach a single audience: rather like the trade magazine sector, fragmentation may cut advertising rates.
Internet	Internet advertisements are generally **sought** out by 'surfers', possibility of interactive marketing, concerns about junk e-mail, concerns about low profitability of Internet firms.
Call centres	Telephone call centres are mushrooming over the country. They provide sales and customer support activity. They tend to be rigid and bureaucratic in style.
Sponsorship	Sports and cultural organisations are seeking sponsors. Like all forms of activity, the sponsor has objectives to fulfil. This can be a difficult relationship.
Personal advice and loyalty	As service industries develop, there will be greater scope for personal service such as financial services.
Lobbying	Some decisions regarding product standardisation and safety will be taken at EU level. Expertise in this area is necessary.

6 THE SERVICE MARKETING MIX

6.1 The importance of services

(a) The service sector accounts for most economic activity in the UK accounting for more employment than manufacturing, although many services cannot be exported.

(b) Competition has been introduced to service industries.

(c) Many 'products' contain a service element.

(d) Service can be a differentiating factor in a firm's offer to the market.

(e) Bad service is costly.

A study by the Henley Centre indicated that 17% of a typical company's customers were affected by a range of service problems, such as poor information or inefficiency. 15% of people who switched bank account cited poor service as the reason. An unhappy customer tells up to nine others about bad service received.

6.2 Elements of services

Services differ from physical goods.

Intangibility	A service cannot be seen, touched or displayed until after purchase sometimes not even then (eg life assurance). The service is often difficult for the consumer to understand.
Inseparability	For many services, it is impossible to separate the production and consumption of a service. (For example, a theatrical event is consumed when it is produced.)
Perishability	Services are perishable. They cannot be stored, they must be produced on demand and often can only be produced in the presence of the customer. Transport is a sort of service industry. A bus journey cannot be 'stored'.
Variability	The quality of the service product is typically highly dependent on the quality of the personnel conducting the transaction.

FOR DISCUSSION 

Services that are intangible are difficult to 'sell' to customers.

6.3 Products and services combined

Many offers to the market have **both a product and a service element** to them.

- Teaching is almost entirely a service
- A restaurant meal is part product and part service
- A 'house' is almost entirely a product, but it is acquired with the help of service firms

6.4 Dimensions of service quality

(a) **Technical quality** of the service encounter (what is received by the customer). For example, a customer is going to a bank about a pension. The quality of financial advice received can sometimes be evaluated by a customer. The dimension is based on the technical product training of the staff and their knowledge of the bank's services. It can be backed up by a range of sales aids, such as brochures and even computer-based product illustrations which feed the customer's specific requirements into an interactive programme when then produces a customised quotation.

(b) **The functional quality** of the service encounter is how the service is provided. The dimension relates to the psychological interaction between the buyer and seller and is typically perceived in a very subjective way. It includes elements such as the following: the attitudes and behaviour of the employees, how they appear, how accessible the service is, the interrelationships between employees and customers.

(c) The **corporate image** dimension of service quality is a result of how consumers perceive the firm. This dimension can be affected by many factors including advertising and past experience with the firm.

6.5 Determinants of service quality

Determinant	Quality
Tangibles	The physical evidence, such as the quality of fixtures and fittings of the company's service area, must be consistent with the desired image.
Reliability	Getting it right first time is very important, not only to ensure repeat business, but, in financial services, as a matter of ethics, if the customer is buying a future benefit.
Responsiveness	The staff's willingness to deal with the customer's queries must be apparent.
Communication	Staff should talk to customers in non-technical language which they can understand.
Credibility	The organisation should be perceived as honest, trustworthy and as acting in the best interests of customers.
Security	This is specially relevant to medical and financial services organisations. The customer needs to feel that the conversations with bank service staff are private and confidential. This factor should influence the design of the service area.
Competence	All the service staff need to appear competent in understanding the product range and interpreting the needs of the customers. In part, this can be achieved through training programmes.
Courtesy	Customers (even rude ones) should perceive service staff as polite, respectful and friendly. This basic requirement is often difficult to achieve in practice, although training programmes can help.
Understanding customers' needs	The use of computer-based customer databases can be very impressive in this context. The service personnel can then call up the customer's records and use these data in the service process, thus personalising the process. Service staff need to meet customer needs rather than try to sell products. This is a subtle but important difference.
Access	Minimising queues, having a fair queuing system and speedy but accurate service are all factors which can avoid customers' irritation building up. A pleasant relaxing environment is a useful design factor in this context.

6.6 Deploying the marketing mix in services

As services differ from manufactured products, this causes potential **marketing problems**.

(a) The degree of **complexity** which characterises, for example, many financial products.

(b) **Inseparability**: the difficulty for consumers to distinguish between the service itself and its delivery system. The delivery system will be inextricably linked with the service itself and will often be considered as a component of that product. In this sense, there will be some aspects of the delivery system which must be seen as components of the core or tangible product while others may usefully be characterised as part of the augmented product.

6.7 Marketing services

(a) Poor service quality in one case (eg lack of punctuality of trains, staff rudeness, a bank's incompetence) is likely to lead to widespread distrust of everything the organisation does.

(b) If the service is intangible and offers a complicated future benefit, or is consumed 'on the spot', then attracting customers means promoting an attractive image and ensuring that the service lives up to its reputation, consistently.

(c) The pricing of services is often complicated, especially if large numbers of people are involved in providing the service.

(d) Human resources management, not just customer care, is a key ingredient in the services marketing mix, as so many services are produced and consumed in a specific social context. The human element cannot always be designed out of a service.

Service marketing involves three additional 'P's: people, processes and physical evidence.

6.8 People

That **employees** are relevant as an element in the marketing mix is particularly evident in service industries. After all, if you have had poor service in a shop or restaurant, you may not be willing to go there again. An American retailing firm estimated that there was an identifiable relationship between low staff turnover and repeat purchases. Managing front-line workers (eg cabin-crew on aircraft), who are the lowest in the organisational hierarchy but whose behaviour has most effect on customers, is an important task for senior management.

It involves corporate culture, job design and motivational issues.

- Appearance
- Attitude
- Commitment
- Behaviour
- Professionalism
- Skills
- Numbers
- Discretion

The term 'front-line marketers' refers to the point that service staff who come into contact with customers need to have their needs at the forefront of their minds and actions.

6.9 Processes

Processes involve the ways in which the marketer's task is achieved. Efficient processes can become a **marketing advantage** in their own right. For example, if an airline develops a sophisticated **ticketing system**, it can encourage customers to take connecting flights offered by allied airlines. Efficient processing of purchase orders received from customers can decrease the time it takes to satisfy them. Efficient procedures in the long-term save money.

- Procedures
- Policies
- Mechanisation
- Queuing
- Information
- Capacity levels
- Speed/timing
- Accessibility

6.10 Physical evidence

Physical evidence. Again, this is particularly important in service industries, for example where the ambience of a restaurant is important. Logos and uniforms help create a sense of corporate identity.

Environment	Facilities	Tangible evidence
• Furnishings	• Vans/vehicles/ aeroplanes	• Labels
• Colours	• Equipment/tools	• Tickets
• Layout	• Uniforms	• Logos
• Noise levels	• Paperwork	• Packaging
• Smells		
• Ambience		

EXAMPLE

Telecommunications is a service, and an important aspect of physical evidence in telecommunications is the public phone box. BT replaced its old, expensive-to-maintain red phone boxes and introduced nondescript metallic kiosks.

Chapter roundup

- The marketing mix is the operational aspect of the marketing planning process.
- The 7Ps include product, price, place, promotion, people, processes and physical evidence.
- Product analysis can be at various levels: core, generic, expected, augmented, potential.
- A price aims to produce the desired level of sales in order to meet the objectives of the business strategy.
- Two broad objectives for pricing are maximising profits and maintaining or increasing market share.
- When organisations set prices they should take into account
  - Organisation's objectives
  - The market characteristics
  - Demand and price elasticity
  - Inflation
  - Legislation
  - Availability of substitutes
- Approaches to pricing include full cost plus pricing, marginal cost plus pricing, minimum pricing, limiting factor pricing and demand based.
- In some sectors, especially business to business discounting, bidding and tendering are common.
- Distribution is often referred to as 'place' in the marketing mix. It involves the logistics of getting products from A to B and the distribution channels such as retailers.
- Basic functions of the distribution channel include:
  - Transport
  - Stock holding
  - Local knowledge
  - Promotion
  - Display
- Internet developments are having a major impact on distribution strategies.
- Promotional activities include advertising, sales promotions, personal selling and public relations. Again the Internet is very significant in this area.
- The traditional marketing mix has been extended to the 7Ps for services. Characteristics of services include intangibility, inseparability, perishability and variability.

Quick quiz

1. What are the 7Ps?
2. Why must price be consistent with other elements of the marketing mix?
3. Why do a company's objectives affect pricing decisions?
4. What is the difference between market skimming and market penetration pricing policies?
5. What are the two main categories of distribution channel?
6. Why do firms use intermediaries?
7. What are the four main promotional activities?
8. What is meant by service variability?

Answers to quick quiz

1. Product, price, place, promotion, process, physical evidence, people.
2. It contributes to the overall perception of the product – it must not contradict messages given out by other mix elements (eg quality).
3. Objectives may include maximising profits, improving image and increasing market share, all of which will have different implications to price setting.
4. Market penetration – low prices when launched
Market skimming – high prices when launched
5. Direct and indirect.
6. Geographic factors, consolidation of orders, lack of retailing knowledge, segmentation.
7. Advertising, sales promotion, personal selling, public relations.
8. It is dependent on the person delivering the service.

Answers to activities

1. The answer will depend on the products you have chosen.

2. You might have identified a number of different factors here. Perhaps the most important general point to make is that price is particularly important if the other elements in the marketing mix are relatively similar across a range of competing products. For example, there is a very wide variety of toothpastes on the market, most of them may not be much different from the others. So the price of a particular toothpaste may be a crucial factor in its sales success.

3. Lower revenues
   Customers will expect the discount in future
   Customers will believe all rates are negotiable
   Customers will henceforth only buy for cash

4. Your answer might include some of the following points.

   (a) The middleman's margin reduces the revenue available to the producer

   (b) The producer needs an infrastructure for looking after the retailers – keeping them informed, keeping them well stocked – which might not be necessary in a mail order business

   (c) The producer loses some control over the marketing of the product. The power of some retailers is so great that they are able to dictate marketing policy to their suppliers.

5. People's working hours: evenings, weekends, when shopping is traditionally done

   Greater leisure time: desire to spend it on leisure pursuits

   Higher disposable incomes

   Homeworking: people will not shop on the way home from work, and will have the necessary technology available.

Chapter 12 :

IMPLEMENTATION AND ETHICAL ISSUES

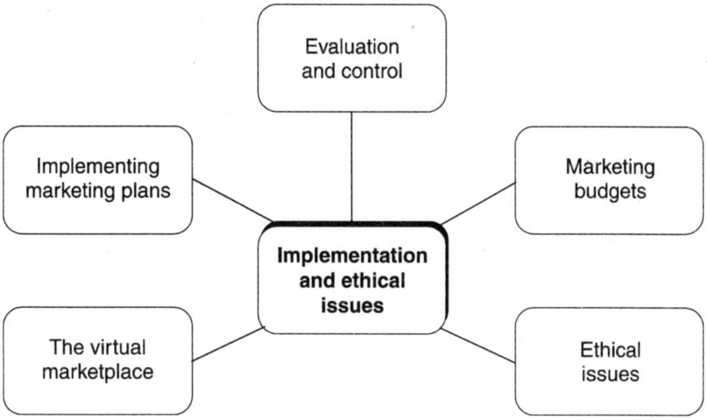

Introduction

This chapter considers those factors affecting the effective implementation and control of marketing plans. Ethical considerations are also coming to the fore, and these will be discussed along with the future of marketing – the Internet 'marketplace'.

Your objectives

In this chapter you will learn about the following.

(a) The issues surrounding the implementation, evaluation and control of marketing plans

(b) Methods of setting marketing budgets

(c) Ethical considerations associated with the elements of the marketing mix

(d) Technology and marketing, in particular the Internet

1 IMPLEMENTING MARKETING PLANS

Having determined objectives, appraised strategy and formulated plans, it is time to put the corporate plan into action. Everyone involved should know what is required and when, and should be committed to the successful accomplishment of the plan.

Senior management cannot just leave it to their middle managers to finish off the work by putting the plans into effect.

(a) Senior managers have the **ultimate responsibility** for ensuring that the organisation achieves its objectives. Monitoring actual results is thus an essential ingredient of the control cycle.

(b) Senior management need to remain committed to the wider picture. Middle management almost invariably, when left to themselves, spend their time on short term or pressing issues, rather than dealing with the less immediate problems of the corporate plan.

(c) The performance appraisal of middle and junior management is based on achieving short-term or budgeted tasks and targets.

1.1 Implementation of the marketing plan

(a) Converting strategic plans into action plans, ie operations plans and budgets.

(b) Allocating responsibilities and giving authority to individual managers to use resources, for example spend sufficient money to allow them to achieve their individual targets.

(c) Establishing checkpoints to monitor activities, such as:

 (i) Have deadlines been met and are future deadlines going to be met?

 (ii) Are any targets in danger of being missed?

 (iii) Will the required resources be available to make the products/services?

 (iv) Will the products be available in sufficient numbers to achieve the aims of the marketing plan?

(d) **Exerting pressure for control action** where necessary, to ensure that things get done according to the aims of the plan.

(e) **Modifying the plan** in the light of changing circumstances.

There are always **unforeseen** events to deal with, some of them controllable and others uncontrollable and unavoidable.

1.2 External factors

By now you should have a thoroughly realistic idea of external environmental factors which affect marketing, both in PEST/SLEPT terms, and in the actions of competitors, suppliers and customers.

1.3 Internal factors

As problematic are the internal factors. The marketing department is only one of many, and competes with others for resources. Moreover, the marketing department **depends** on other business functions to deliver the marketing mix.

1.4 Frequently encountered implementation problems

Problem	Comment
Weak support from the chief executive and top management	Without this support it is unlikely that other functional managers will take the marketing manager's initiatives very seriously.
Lack of a plan for planning	It is naïve to assume that once a marketing planning system has been designed that it will operate smoothly from day one. The evidence indicates that a period of around three years is required in a large company to overcome resistance to the change that planning inevitably brings. Internal marketing is required.
Lack of line management support	Operational managers are often unwilling to participate fully because of hostility, lack of skills, lack of information, lack of resources and an inadequate organisational structure without a fully integrated marketing function.
Confusion over planning terms	The initiators of the system often use academic planning terminology which line managers see as meaningless jargon.
Numbers *in lieu* of written objectives and strategies	Prior to a planning system, often all that is used is sales forecasts and financial projections. Making explicit the route to achieving these objectives is a new and difficult skill. It requires managers to express the logic of their objective and in this sense is a creative process requiring qualitative rather than quantitative information.
Too much detail, too far ahead	Overplanning is often associated with too much information and ends with piles of paperwork which confuses and demotivates rather than promoting positive participation. Marketing auditing can result in far too many issues demanding management attention. Key issues need to be identified – the wood needs to be drawn from the trees.
Once a year ritual	This is a common barrier to effective implementation, when the task is seen as just another job to do which gets in the way of the really pressing day-to-day activities. Plans which are written and then filed away until next year do not work. Planning needs to be an integral part of the manger's job with progress towards objectives being reviewed and discussed on a regular basis.
Separation of operational planning from strategic planning	Strategic plans need to be built up from sound analysis at grass-roots level, and all managers need to consider not just continuing in the same direction but what longer term changes may be required.
Failure to integrate marketing planning into a total corporate planning system	Unless marketing plans are considered in relation to the plans of finance, production and personnel it becomes impossible to resource accurately the plan's product/market requirements.

Problem	Comment
Delegation of planning to a planner	When planning is divorced from the reality of operations, and the people who are expected to put the ideas into action are not involved, it is not surprising that resistance and lack of commitment can exist.

2 EVALUATION AND CONTROL

2.1 The marketing control process

The **marketing control process** is vital to the achievement of marketing objectives and the successful completion of marketing plans. Control is every bit as important a feature of the role of the marketing manager as new product development or promotional creativity.

Definition

To **control** is to measure results against targets and take any action necessary to adjust performance.

Because marketing is essentially concerned with people, who can be both unpredictable and awkward, controlling marketing activities is particularly problematic. Difficulties arise with information, timing and the cost aspects of marketing plans.

The marketing control process can be broken down into four stages.

(a) Development of **objectives and strategies** (covered in more detail in Chapter 6)

(b) Establishment of **standards**

(c) **Evaluation** of performance

(d) **Corrective action**

Part of the corrective action stage may well be to adjust objectives and strategies in the light of experience.

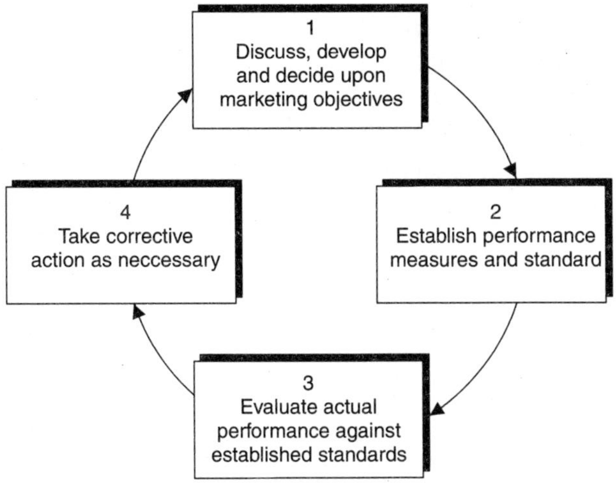

Figure 12.1: Marketing control process

2.2 Establishment of performance measures

In many organisations, the establishment of **performance measures** and standards revolves around a system of **budgeting.** This involves the setting in advance of detailed, quantified targets and the allocation of resources, normally for a year at a time. A large company's budget is an extensive document, stating in great detail what is to be done by the responsible executives and defining the criteria by which their success or failure will be measured. It incorporates a process of hierarchical summarisation leading to a forecast profit and loss account and balance sheet for the entire enterprise.

The process of setting a budget involves much forecasting and estimation. It is therefore to some extent likely that actual results will diverge from those planned. Control measures are then needed to adjust actual performance back towards what is required.

The first input into the budget is normally the **sales forecast.** A careful estimate must be made of the likely extent of sales during the coming year, and this must be broken down by product, month and, if appropriate, region. From the sales budget it is possible to draw up the production plan and from this estimates of the resources needed for the year, such as raw materials purchases, labour costs and distribution facilities, may be prepared.

Within the marketing function it will be necessary to establish budgets for marketing and sales **staff costs, promotional expenditure** of all types, **marketing research** and departmental **administration.**

EXAMPLE

Promotional expenditure is often a major expense, especially in consumer goods marketing. To some extent, sales volumes depend on the extent and quality of advertising and sales promotion campaigns. It is usual, therefore, to undertake some research into the effectiveness of promotional effort, and the cost of this must also be included in the budget.

Budgetary control

Budgetary control is the management technique that allocates resources and responsibility in accordance with a forecast budget and exercises control by reference to reports that compare actual achievement with budget requirements.

We look at budgets in more detail in Section 3 of this chapter.

Quantitative and qualitative targets

Performance can be measured in quantitative or qualitative terms.

(a) **Quantitative measurements** are expressed in figures, such as cost levels, units produced per week, delay in delivery time and market penetration per product.

(b) **Qualitative targets,** although not directly measurable in quantitative terms, may still be verified by judgement and observation.

Where possible, performance should be measured in quantitative terms because these are less subjective. Qualitative factors such as employee welfare and motivation, protection of the environment against pollution, and product quality might still all be gauged by quantitative measures (such as employee pay levels, labour turnover rates, the level of toxicity in industrial waste, reject and scrap rates).

2.3 Marketing performance standards

Performance standards are set for two reasons

(a) To tell managers what they are **required to accomplish,** given the authority to make appropriate decisions

(b) To indicate to managers how well their **actual results measure against their targets,** so that control action can be taken where it is needed

In setting standards for performance, it is important to distinguish between controllable items and uncontrollable ones. Any matters which cannot be controlled by an individual manager should be excluded from his or her standards for performance.

The most common measures by which marketing performance is judged are **sales levels, costs** and **market shares**. However, responsible companies will also have ethical and social responsibility standards. The most marketing-orientated organisations will be likely to pursue relationship marketing which entails a high degree of customer care. Thus, in addition to sales measures, many companies will seek to measure customer satisfaction.

EXAMPLE

Performance standards could thus be set at sales of £X for the period, Y% market share and Z% profit, all set against a maximum number of customer complaints.

Evaluation of performance

The organisation monitors performance at given time intervals **by comparing actual results with the standards set** to determine whether it is on, above or below these targets.

Corrective action

Where performance against standard is below a tolerable level then **remedial action** needs to be taken. This may mean invoking **contingency plans** previously drawn up for this purpose, or taking *ad hoc* action.

3 MARKETING BUDGETS

3.1 What to spend?

There is no one uniform method of deciding what to spend on marketing. The following are some of the considerations that can affect the amount of expenditure.

(a) What **marketing mix** is to be employed?
(b) What **tasks** are to be undertaken?
(c) How **competitive** is the market place?
(d) How **well known** is the organisation?
(e) Are there any **special requirements**?

EXAMPLE

Typical marketing costs to be budgeted include:

- Air time and broadcast media
- Space and printed media
- Production costs
- Staff salaries
- Overheads and expenses
- Agency fees
- Promotional spend
- Research
- NPD

3.2 Approaches to budgeting

Theoretical approaches to setting budgets, for example by marginal costing approaches, have not found favour in industry because the effects of **any marginal increase in expenditure are likely to be hidden**, by many other marketing variables. The effects of any expenditure will have both long-term and short-term effects. It is worthwhile emphasising the view here that **marketing should be treated as an essential long-term investment**.

EXAMPLE: MARKETING METRICS

On the one hand, marketing is vital to business and accounts for truly staggering sums of money; on the other, much of it is ill-defined and unaccountable. There is little understanding, outside the discipline, of how marketing budgets are arrived at, even though they are sometimes the largest single company expenditure.

There is no standard vocabulary and no agreement on how to measure the effectiveness of these vast budgets. There isn't even an agreed definition of what constitutes 'spending on marketing'. It probably includes advertising, direct marketing, promotions and public relations. But what about price maintenance and a host of other activities?

Although no company will admit that the setting of marketing budgets amounts to little more than guess work, there is consensus among commentators that the process leaves much to be desired.

Methods of deciding budgets have been developed over a period of time and, in the absence of clearer guidance, are useful in approaching a budget decision for the first time. After several years' operations it is possible to use experience to make decisions. One or a combination of the following methods can be used to approach the problem.

- Completely arbitrarily
- All you can afford
- Historical basis
- Matching the competition
- Percentage of sales
- Experiment and testing
- Modeling and simulation
- Objective and task method

Recent research has indicated a growing trend towards database methods and especially favours the **objective and task** method.

We now cover each of these in turn.

Completely arbitrarily

There are many examples of budgets being set in an apparently **arbitrary way by senior management**. There may be a link between the **personality** of the **decision-maker and the level of expenditure**. Subsequent arbitrary cuts in expenditure if trading becomes difficult and the profit margins begin to suffer are more worrying.

All you can afford

This often applies to a new company starting up or to an existing company advertising for the first time. The conscious decision has to be taken to forego immediate profits (or to forego an investment in another area) in favour of an **investment in marketing**. This often means **investing at a minimum level**. This will necessarily limit the scope of the work, however, and limit the results to be achieved.

Historical basis

We have already indicated that with experience managers are able to form their own judgment of the effectiveness or otherwise of particular expenditure levels and different promotional methods. **Year-on-year figures** provide the basis for **following trends** and making decisions accordingly. Some factors to consider are these below.

(a) The **danger of inertia**: a temptation just to keep it the same, in which case all the elements of the environment and the costs associated with the task facing the organisation are ignored.

(b) A slight improvement is to use a **media multiplier**, which at least recognises that **media rate card costs** may have increased.

Matching the competition

In many cases an organisation is trying to reach **exactly the same customers** through **exactly the same channels**. In order to obtain a certain market share it is then necessary to match the competition and particularly the market leader.

Percentage of sales method

The percentage of sales is a commonly used method of determining a marketing budget because:

- It is easy to calculate
- It is precise
- It can be quickly monitored
- It can be varied in progressive steps
- It appears logical
- It is financially safe

Activity 1 **(10 minutes)**

What do you think is the logical flaw associated with the percentage of sales method as an effective technique for budget allocation?

Once a sales forecast has been made, then the approximate budget level can be obtained. It can then be moderated for special circumstances such as the degree of competition experienced in the previous year, or expected in the next year.

Experiment and testing method

This method involves **selecting a set of matched markets**. Different final budgets can be set for each of these markets and the results carefully monitored. The resulting levels of awareness and sales delivered can be compared. This method can be used to evaluate alternative media schedules. Problems associated with this method include:

- The cost of conducting the experiment
- The time it takes to get results
- The premature informing of competitors
- The fact that markets can never be completely matched

Modelling and simulation method

With advancing use of **computer databases** and more precise promotional media, it is possible to build models to **forecast the likely performance** of different media schedules. There are likely to be an increasing number of PC-based modelling programs available which will allow a number of business variables to be examined including:

- Sales levels
- Purchase frequency
- Awareness levels
- Profits achievable

Both the experimental and modelling methods lend themselves to a cost-benefit analysis approach to evaluating the results. The costs of adopting a particular option should be fairly easy to establish, while the likely benefits are forecast by the experiment or simulation undertaken. This can form the basis for rational assessment of possible courses of action.

The objective and task method

The objective and task method is probably the one which is most **logical and appropriate** to the complex situation found in planning marketing programmes. The **logic of the method is as follows.**

(a) Determine the **marketing objectives**

(b) Determine **tasks** necessary to achieve these objectives

(c) Determine the **cost** of each element

It is necessary to be realistic about the objectives and accurate in the costing of the tasks. A systematic approach to applying the objective and task method will lead to disciplined thinking, and provide an excellent communication and decision device.

Ten steps in applying the objective and task method

Step 1 Define marketing and promotion objectives
Step 2 Determine the tasks to be undertaken
Step 3 Build up expenditure by costing the tasks
Step 4 Compare the results against industry averages
Step 5 Compare the results as a percentage of sales
Step 6 Reconcile differences between steps 3, 4 and 5
Step 7 Modify estimates to meet company policies
Step 8 Specify when expenditures are to be made
Step 9 Maintain an element of flexibility
Step 10 Monitor actual results against these forecasts

Activity 2 **(30 minutes)**

Compare the advantages and disadvantages of the various methods that can be used to determine the appropriate level for a marketing budget.

As you study, consider how who is involved in setting the budget might impact upon incentivising and motivation.

4 ETHICAL ISSUES

4.1 The nature of ethics

In simple terms, ethics is concerned with right and wrong and how conduct should be judged to be good or bad. Ethics is about how we should live our lives and, in particular, how we should behave towards other people. It is therefore relevant to all forms of human activity. Business ethics is not really separate or different from ideas that apply in the general context of human life.

FOR DISCUSSION

Professionals of all specialisations should be aware of the general principles of ethics and be capable of applying them in their everyday work.

4.2 Perspectives on ethics

Critics of marketing argue that it is dedicated to selling products which are potentially damaging to the health and well-being of the individual or the society in which consumers live. Examples include tobacco, alcohol, automobiles, detergents and even electronic goods such as computers and video recorders.

Kotler (2008) suggested that a **societal marketing concept** should replace the marketing concept as a philosophy for the future.

Definition

> The **societal marketing concept** is a management orientation that holds that the key task of the organisation is to determine the needs and wants of target markets and to adapt the organisation to delivering the desired satisfactions more effectively and efficiently than its competitors in a way that preserves or enhances the consumers' and society's well being'.

FOR DISCUSSION

It has been argued that even seemingly beneficial, or at least harmless, products, such as soft drinks, sunglasses or agricultural fertiliser, can damage individuals and societies.

EXAMPLE

The alcohol industry, often accused of encouraging binge drinking and using inappropriate sexual and sporting imagery in its advertising campaigns, is taking steps to clean up its act as it tries to fend off legislation aimed at curbing its marketing activities.

Many in the industry fear that it could be next in line – after tobacco – to face an advertising ban. These fears have already promoted major players to take radical steps towards promoting 'responsible drinking'.

"Diageo targeting students during the 2009 university freshers' week with a responsible drinking campaign to encourage young drinkers to think about and moderate how much alcohol they drink.

As part of its 'One Too Many' campaign, Diageo has partnered with 10 UK universities to carry out on campus activity to promote a more responsible freshers' week. The owner of drinks brands Smirnoff, Guinness and Baileys seeks to remind students that drinking too much can potentially see them ending up in negative situations.

Students' Union bathrooms are being adorned with floor vinyls depicting someone passed out on the floor, to remind student drinkers of the dangers of excessive drinking.

Curved mirrors are also being installed to reflect a distorted image and ask the question whether they have had one too many drinks.

As part of its commitment to promoting responsible drinking Diageo is currently trialling a lower alcohol strength Guinness variant in Scotland. Guinness Mid-Strength, which has an alcohol level of 2.8% compared to regular Guinness which is 4.1%."

www.mad.co.uk (2009)

How should the marketer react to these problems? There appears to be a clear conflict; **what is profitable for a business organisation may well not be in the interest of the customer**, or the society within which the transaction is taking place.

EXAMPLE

Different cultures view marketing practices differently. While the idea of intellectual property is widely accepted in Europe and the USA, in other parts of the world, standards are quite different. Unauthorised use of copyrights, trademarks and patents is widespread in countries such as Taiwan, Mexico and Korea. According to a US trade official, the Korean view is that ' ... the thoughts of one man should benefit all', and this general value means that, in spite of legal formalities, few infringements of copyright are punished.

A number of companies have moved to adopt more ecologically-friendly policies. HSBC was one organisation to offer a paperless banking option. AOL added 'Green' content to their homepage and energy and water companies became more active in their promotion of green initiatives.

4.3 Ethics in marketing

Product issues

Ethical issues relating to products usually revolve around **safety, quality**, and **value** and frequently arise from failure to provide adequate information to the customer. This may range from omission of uncomfortable facts in product literature, to deliberate deception.

A typical problem arises when a product specification is changed to reduce cost. Clearly, it is essential to ensure that product function is not compromised in any important way, but a decision must be taken as to just what emphasis, if any, it is necessary to place on the changes in product literature. Another, more serious, problem occurs when product safety is compromised. **Product recall** is the issue here.

EXAMPLE

When the French company Perrier discovered that its mineral water was in danger of contamination, they immediately withdrew all supplies, suffering huge losses. By acting ethically, the company's reputation was enhanced. When Coca Cola suffered a similar problem in Europe it dithered, played down the issue, denied liability and suffered a huge blow to its image.

In the summer of 2007, Mattel recalled products from their Polly Pocket, Disney Cars and Barbie ranges due to high lead content in the products' paint. Discoveries were made regarding the use of the paint in different product ranges gradually. The effect on consumer trust could therefore become a major issue for the toy manufacturer.

Counterfeiting and imitation

Intellectual property in the form of trademarks, registered designs and patents is generally protected within individual countries, but foreign suppliers may infringe upon it. Counterfeits of well-differentiated branded consumer products, such as Rolex watches, are common, as are 'pirate' or 'bootleg' CDs and DVDs. Even where the products concerned are not direct copies, unauthorised use of brand names is common.

The Internet brings further threats to brand value such as the legal but unscrupulous registration of brand and company names as domain names.

(a) Registration of 'Brand X.com' before the owners of Brand X register it deprives them of the use of their brand name on the Web. They may have to register a second-best name or pay the prior registrant to release the domain name.

(b) If the owners of Brand X have succeeded in registering 'Brand X.com', they may find themselves faced with a rash of websites with slightly different names such as 'Brandx.com' and 'Brand X.org'. These may be set up in an attempt to extract further fees or may actually be used by competitors.

A related threat is the theft of intellectual property in the form of software, music, video and printed material by means of unauthorised downloads through peer-to-peer file sharing sites.

Promotion issues

Ethical considerations are particularly relevant to **promotional practices**. Advertising and personal selling are areas in which the temptation to select, exaggerate, slant, conceal, distort and falsify information is potentially very great indeed. Questionable practices here are likely to create cynicism in the customer and ultimately to preclude any degree of trust or respect for the supplier. It was because so many companies were acting unethically with regard to marketing communications that the **Trade Descriptions Act 1968** came into being.

FOR DISCUSSION

Persuading people to buy something they don't need is intrinsically unethical, especially if hard sell tactics are used.

Also relevant to this area is the problem of corrupt selling practices. It is widely accepted that a small gift such as a mouse mat or a diary is a useful way of keeping a supplier's name in front of an industrial purchaser. On the other hand, most business people would condemn the payment of substantial bribes to purchasing officers to induce them to favour a particular supplier. But where does the dividing line lie between these two extremes?

(a) **Extortion**. Government officials in some countries have been known to threaten companies with the complete closure of their local operations unless suitable payments are made.

(b) **Bribery**. Payments may be made to obtain services to which a company is not legally entitled. If they are used to acquire public works contracts political contributions are bribery.

EXAMPLE

In the UK political contributions are supposed to be made at arm's length, and not to benefit the contributor with specific political favours. The Blair Labour Government suffered a number of political contribution scandals, the most noteworthy being the Ecclestone/Formula 1 case in which the business interest of a major donor appeared to be protected from restrictive EU regulations.

(c) **Grease money**. Multinational companies are sometimes unable to obtain services to which they are legally entitled because of deliberate stalling by local officials. Cash payments to the right people may then be enough to oil the machinery of bureaucracy.

(d) **Gifts**. In some cultures (such as Japan) gifts are regarded as an essential part of civilised negotiation, even in circumstances where to Western eyes they might appear ethically dubious. Managers operating in such a culture may feel at liberty to adopt the local custom.

Pricing issues

There are several pricing practices that have attracted criticism.

(a) **Active collusion** (price fixing) among suppliers to fix prices is **illegal** in most countries, though the existence of a more or less fixed market price does not necessarily imply that collusion is taking place. A tendency to compete in areas other than price is a natural feature of oligopoly markets.

(b) **Predatory pricing** is an issue when newcomers attempt to break into a market. Established suppliers utilise their cash reserves and economies of scale to sell at prices the newcomer cannot match and still make a profit. Withdrawal from the market follows.

(c) **Failure to disclose the full price** associated with a purchase has been rightly criticised as unethical. However, it must be recognised that there are occasions when it is impossible to compute the eventual full price, as when cost escalation is accepted by both parties to a contract. The measure of propriety is whether there is any **intention to deceive.**

(d) The UK popular press have attempted to create a climate of opinion in which very large suppliers of consumer products are condemned if they ever raise prices or, indeed, if they make profits that are large in absolute terms.

FOR DISCUSSION

Just as consumers may sometimes need protecting from profiteering companies, so might companies need protecting from dishonest consumers.

Place issues

Where long and complex distribution channels are used, there is potential for **disputes and conflicts of interest.**

There will often be inequality of power between suppliers and distribution partners.

(a) Large suppliers will have power over small distributors, especially where a distributor is dependent on a single supplier for a large percentage of purchases. The relationship between UK breweries and their pub tenants is an extreme case of this kind of relationship.

(b) Large distributors may have power over smaller suppliers, as is the case with the large UK supermarket chains. Even large suppliers such as Procter and Gamble are unable to dominate distributors such as Tesco and may have to accept the conditions they are offered.

Where there is significant difference in power, there is always the possibility of abuse.

Even where relationships of trust have been built up over long periods of time, business pressures can lead to hard decisions and a perception by distributors that they have been treated unfairly. Here are some examples of conduct by manufacturers that distributors could reasonably complain of.

- Requiring high levels of **stock holding**
- Manipulating **price structures** to the detriment of distributors
- **Ending distribution agreements** at short notice
- **Dealing direct** with end users

Cause-related marketing

Increasing prosperity in the western world has led to the emergence of well-funded and active advocacy groups promoting corporate social responsibility. Great success has attended this development and many consumers are now ready to give or withhold loyalty according to their perception of a brand's efforts to promote improvements in such fields as animal welfare, labour conditions and the natural environment. Firms have therefore sought to enhance their reputations and understanding of their values through partnership with charities and other good causes. A cynical approach is unlikely to work, but, used with integrity, cause-related marketing can have undoubted beneficial effects on corporate reputation and success. Careful choice of partner is important. Ideally, the 'good cause' partner's priorities will reflect the best aspirations of the commercial partner. Thus, Tesco's 'Computer's for Schools' coupon related donations reflect an aspiration to support families. Constellation, a global alcohol products corporation supports programs to educate consumers on responsible alcohol consumption.

Fair trade

Fair trade is an important aspect of cause-related marketing. Perceptions of transnational companies as exploitative of poor agricultural producers have led to great support for the fair trade concept of above-market price payments for the products of such producers. A very good example of the success of the idea has been the growth of 'Fairtrade' (The Fairtrade Foundation, UK) as, effectively, a brand in its own right in the retail market for coffee, both as a grocery staple and in chain cafes such as Starbucks. Fairtrade also illustrates the importance of careful selection of cause-related marketing partner. The activities of the UK Fairtrade Foundation and the Fairtrade labelling organisations have both been heavily criticised by Phillip Booth, Editorial and Programme Director of the Institute of Economic Affairs and Professor of Insurance and Risk Management at Cass Business School, City University, London:

> I am now concerned about many aspects of the Fairtrade network, including the high fees it charges its growers; the huge proportion of the premium charged to wholesalers that is spent purely on promotion of the brand – it is no wonder we only hear good things about it!; aspects of the policing of the brand of which there have now been numerous verified reports; the potentially damaging insider/outsider markets it creates; and the damaging line it takes on trade policy issues. (http://www.iea.org.uk/record.jsp?type=news&ID=417)

A full discussion by Philip Booth and Linda Whetstone of the problems with Fairtrade can be found at http://www.iea.org.uk/files/upld-book408pdf?.pdf

EXAMPLE: AMA CODE OF ETHICS

The American Marketing Association has produced a Code of Ethics to which it expects its members to adhere. This includes the following principles relating to the implementation of individual elements of the marketing mix.

In the area of product development and management

- Disclosure of all substantial risks associated with product or service usage.
- Identification of any product component substitution that might materially change the product or impact on the buyer's purchase decision.
- Identification of extra-cost added features.

In the area of promotions

- Avoidance of false and misleading advertising.
- Rejection of high pressure manipulation, or misleading sales tactics.
- Avoidance of sales promotions that use deception or manipulation.

In the area of distribution

- Not manipulating the availability of a product for purpose of exploitation.
- Not using coercion in the marketing channel.
- Not exerting undue influence over the resellers' choice to handle the product.

In the area of pricing

- Not engaging in price fixing.
- Not practicing predatory pricing.
- Disclosing the full price associated with any purchase.

In the area of marketing research

- Prohibiting selling or fund raising under the guise of conducting research.
- Maintaining research integrity by avoiding misrepresentation and omission of pertinent research data.
- Treating outside clients and suppliers fairly.

Activity 3 **(20 minutes)**

A UK chemical products company turning over £10 million a year makes extensive sales to a company in China, and has good relations with its executives. The CEO of the Chinese company contacts the MD of the UK company and asks for help with a problem. In this industry a great deal of business is done at the annual trade fair in Hanover: a company that fails to send a strong sales team to this event will find itself being rapidly overtaken by competitors. The Chinese company finds it very difficult to do this since the Chinese currency is non-convertible and it cannot obtain sufficient foreign currency from the state banking system to pay its team's expenses.

The Chinese CEO proposes that the UK company should over-invoice its deliveries (invoicing is in US dollars). There will be no difficulty in obtaining the dollars from the bank to pay the inflated invoices since they will appear to represent purchases of essential materials. The UK company will then deposit its excess receipts in a bank account in the West. The Chinese company will then draw on the account to pay its trade fair expenses.

What should the UK CEO do?

5 THE VIRTUAL MARKETPLACE

5.1 The impact of technology

Relationships with other members of the marketing channel are increasingly being influenced and developed by the Internet. In recent years new technologies have emerged that have changed, and are continuing to change, the way business is conducted. Among the most significant changes are those relating to the following.

- Mobile communications
- Electronic communications and commerce (eg Electronic Data Interchange (EDI))
- Satellite and cable digital television
- The Internet

The full impact of new technology has only just begun, but already significant changes have occurred in some distribution channels.

5.2 Internet distribution

Display

Information gathering is still the most common Internet activity, whether it be information about a historical fact, a medical problem or, hopefully, **about your product**. At present the five most common online **purchase** categories are books, CDs, clothing, toys and games, and computer software. The range of products and services bought online is increasing rapidly as is the opportunity to read and write reviews of products and services prior to purchase.

FOR DISCUSSION

Why do many buyers do their initial 'window shopping' online and then go to a more conventional distribution outlet to actually make their purchase?

A website offers an effortless and impersonal way for customers to find out the details of the products and services that a company provides, and **spend as long as they like** doing so: much longer than they might feel comfortable with if they had a sales person hanging over them.

EXAMPLE

For businesses the advantage of a website is that it is much cheaper to provide the information in electronic form than it would be to employ staff to man the phones on an enquiry desk or walk the shop floor, and much more effective than sending out mailshots that people would either throw away or forget about.

In September 2007, the Conservative Party launched the first entirely online political campaign. The practice had been common in the US for a few years previously, with politicians such as Hilary Clinton using the web as their key practical tool.

In January 2009, UK ministers shelved plans to exempt MPs' expenses details from the Freedom of Information Act, after the Tories and Lib Dems said they would fight it. Campaigners said that it was a victory for "people power" after a web protest. An Internet campaign by MySociety, urging MPs to vote against the change, attracted more than 6,000 supporters on the Facebook website.

Transport

The Internet can be used to get certain products **directly** into people's homes. Anything that can be converted into **digital form** can simply be uploaded onto the seller's site and then downloaded onto the customer's PC. The Internet offers huge opportunities to producers of text, graphics/video, and sound-based products. Much computer software is now distributed in this way.

5.3 Strategic and operational impact of the Internet

Strategic ('board level')

- Improve corporate image
- Increase visibility in the market
- Create market growth opportunities
- Lower costs
- Appeal to customers
- Access to the full competitive arena

Operational ('day-to-day' on the factory floor)

- Speed of transactions increased
- Management of information improved
- Increased service levels
- Removal of time and distance constraints
- Complete transactions electronically
- Opportunity for new revenues
- Cost effectiveness
- Closer relationships with business partners
- Improved understanding of customer requirements

5.4 Information technology and marketing planning

Information technology (IT) is becoming increasingly useful in many aspects of marketing. These include not only applications such as **market research** and **relationship marketing**, both of which utilise large quantities of structured data, but also creative, **communications** aspects that can make use of computer-aided design and desktop publishing programmes.

The increasing use of IT is partly a result of developments in IT systems themselves, which have made them more productive and easier to use.

(a) Hardware and software have both **fallen in price** and become **more powerful.**

(b) The explosive growth of the Internet has created a powerful new **research** and **communication tool**. Corporate **intranets** use Internet technology for publishing information internally.

(c) Devices such as **EPOS scanners** and **barcode readers** allow rapid acquisition and manipulation of data.

(d) **Hand held devices** such as mobile phones, laptop computers and personal digital assistants allow sales force people to send reports and receive information and instructions without a personal visit to the office.

Applying IT to the marketing planning process

The Marketing Information System database contains live and ever-changing information of importance to the marketing process. Modern **relational database management systems** allow rapid access to chosen aspects of this information without wading through reams of paper. Such information would include both internally generated and externally generated items.

Internal information examples

- Sales records
- Customer records
- Marketing communications records
- Market research information
- Cost records
- Stock records

External information examples

- Trade association information
- Published market information
- Competitor information
- Government information

IT and implementing the marketing plan

IT can be useful in four aspects of plan implementation.

(a) **Segmentation**. Datamining is a technique that reveals hidden connections between items of data. For example, one supermarket chain found that there was a link between purchases of disposable nappies and purchases of beer. Simpler techniques can be used to organise data by potential segmentation variables.

(b) **Targeting**. Analytical techniques such as sales forecasting can be used for the evaluation of promising segments.

(c) **Positioning**. Marketing communications intended to create a position can be enhanced by the use of e-mail, websites and Internet broadcasts.

(d) **Monitoring and control**. Large volumes of feedback data can be handled by IT systems. Examples include analysis of EPOS information and its correlation with such events as sales promotions.

Chapter roundup

- Implementing the marketing plan includes:
  - Converting strategy into action
  - Allocating responsibilities and resources
  - Establishing checkpoints and deadlines
  - Taking control action
  - Modifying the plan where necessary
- Frequently encountered implementation problems include:
  - Weak support from top management
  - Lack of a 'plan' to bring the planning into action
  - Lack of line management support
  - Confusion over terms/jargon
  - Numbers replacing strategies on how to achieve them
  - Too much detail
  - Ritual, done once a year
  - Operational planning not related to strategic planning
  - Failure to integrate the marketing plan into the overall corporate plan
  - Planning department in its own 'ivory tower', divorced from operations
- Controls need to be in place for implementing marketing plans where critical analysis of the effectiveness of the plan should be made.
- The marketing control process can be broken down into four stages,
  - Development of objectives and strategies
  - Establishment of standards
  - Evaluation of performance
  - Corrective action
- A system of budgeting is usually established as a central method of measurement and control. The first input is usually the sales forecast.
- Performance can be measured in quantitative or qualitative terms.
- The most common measures by which marketing performance is judged are:
  - Sales levels
  - Costs
  - Market share
- Corrective action may be taken where the actual performance is below standard.
- Approaches to the budgeting include:
  - Arbitrary
  - 'All you can afford'
  - Historical basis
  - Matching the competition
  - Percentage of sales
  - Experiment and testing
  - Modelling and simulation
  - Objective and task
- Ethical concerns of marketing are becoming more important to companies and customers.
- Societal marketing strives to preserve or enhance customers' and/or society's well being.

Chapter roundup (con't)

- Ethical issues are important in all aspects of the marketing mix.
- New technology having a significant impact upon marketing includes:
  - Mobile communications
  - Electronic commerce
  - Satellite and digital TV
  - The Internet
- The Internet has both a strategic and operational impact. It is a powerful research and communication tool.
- Information technology can be useful in plan implementation:
  - Segmentation
  - Targeting
  - Positioning
  - Monitoring

Quick quiz

1 Who has the ultimate responsibility for ensuring that an organisation achieves its objectives?

2 What is 'control' in the context of achieving marketing objectives?

3 What is budgetary control?

4 Why should performance ideally be measured in quantitative terms?

5 What are some examples of marketing costs to be budgeted?

6 What is predatory pricing?

7 What is the strategic impact of the Internet?

8 Give some examples of internal and external information for planning purposes.

Answers to quick quiz

1 Senior management

2 Measuring results against targets and taking any action necessary to adjust performance.

3 The allocation of resources and responsibility in accordance with a forecast budget; comparing actual achievement with budget.

4 Quantitative measures are less subjective.

5 Media costs (air time, space, print etc)
Production costs
Staff salaries
Overheads and expenses

6 Predatory pricing occurs when established suppliers utilise their power (economies of sale, cash reserves) to undercut a newcomer.

7 See paragraph 5.3.

8 See paragraph 5.4.

Answers to activities

1 The main deficiency of the percentage of sales method is that it turns the traditional cause and effect relationship on its head. Promotion causes sales. Hence, the amount of sales is a function of the amount spent on promotion. The strict implementation of the percentage of sales method means that the promotional spend becomes a function of the level of sales. Therefore, if sales decrease, then the amount spent on promotion is also decreased, whereas it might be wiser to keep the promotional spend constant in the face of declining sales.

The problem in forecasting future sales is the uncertainty of knowing what resources will be available to achieve the sales targets. Hence, this method should only be used to determine how much needs to be spent if conditions remain static. Beyond that, the budget needs adjusting in view of the new objectives.

2 Check back to the points made in paragraph 3.2.

3 Here are some considerations.

The UK company is not large and would probably be hard hit if it lost its Chinese customer to a competitor.

The proposed deal is probably illegal under Chinese law since it evades Chinese monetary controls – but China does not have the rule of law as it is understood in the West, and custom is very important.

A refusal to co-operate would probably cause the Chinese CEO to lose face.

The trade fair problem could be a cover story – the Chinese CEO could be setting up the scheme for his own self-enrichment.

Chinese exchange controls tend to protect what is left of the command economy in China and with it, the position of the Chinese Communist party. Is this a good thing?

Should the Chinese be encouraged to integrate as closely as possible with the global economy in the interests of peaceful development and normal international relations?

Will anybody lose as a result of this arrangement?

Bibliography

Allen, C. (2002) 'Presentation to Lehman Brothers media conference, London, 17 September'

Ansoff, I. (1987), *Corporate Strategy* revised ed, London: Penguin

Arnold, M. (2001), Can Railtrack Ever Win Back The Public's Trust?, *Marketing*, 28 June, p.1

Beard, M. (2002) Sainsbury Signs Jamie Oliver in £2M Deal, *The Independent*, 17 January, p.11

Belbin, M. (1993) *Team Roles at Work*, Oxford: Butterworth: Heinemann

Bickerton, P. Bickerton, M. and Simpson-Holley, K. (1998) *Cyberstrategy*, Butterworth-Heinemann

Bowen, D. (2002), Handling the Bad News, *Financial Times*, 25 January, p.11

Brassington, F. and Pettitt, S. (2006), *Principles of Marketing* (4th edition), FT Prentice Hall

Burt, T. (2002) He's Bond, James Bond, the man who's licensed to sell, *Financial Times*, 5 October, p.22

Carter, H. C. (1986) *Effective Advertising*, The Daily Telegraph Guide for Small Businesses, Kogan Page

Chaffey, D. (2002) *E-business and E-commerce Management; Strategy; Implementation and Practice*, FT – Prentice Hall, Pearson Education

Chisnall, O.M. (1997), *Marketing Research*, McGraw-Hill

Colley, R. (1961) Defining Advertising Goals for Measured Advertising Results, *Association of National Advertisers*

Cowell, D. (1995), *The Marketing of Services*, Heinemann

Cowlett, M. (2001), Research Can Be Child's Play, *Marketing*, 10 May p. 35

Crosby, P.B. (1978), *Quality is free*, McGraw-Hill Education

CyberAtlas, (2002), *B2B E-Commerce Headed for Trillions*, http:/cyberatlas.internet.com

Daffy, C. (2000) *Once a Customer, Always a Customer*, Oak Tree Press

Dow, B. (2001), Tanks a Lot, Boss, *Daily Record*, 3 December, p.7

Drummond, J. , Ensor, G. & Ashford, R. (2008), *Strategic Marketing: Planning and Control*, 3rd edition,Butterworth-Heinemann

Ehrenberg, A. S. C. (1992), Comments on How Advertising Works, *Marketing and Research Today*, August, pp.167–9

Engel, J. F., Warshaw, M.R. and Kinnear, T. C. (1994), *Promotional Strategy*, Irwin

Engel, J. F., Blackwell, R. D. and Miniard, P. W. (1990), *Consumer Behaviour*, Dryden

Festinger, L. (1957), *A Theory of Cognitive Dissonance*, Stanford University Press

Fill, C. (2002), *Marketing Communications: Contexts, Strategies and Applications*, (3rd edition), FT Prentice Hall

Flack, J. (1999), Child Minding, *Marketing Week*, 8 July, pp 41–4

Folkard, C. (eds), (2003) *Guinness World Records*, Gullane Education

Francis, R. (2000), Leaders of the Pack, *Brandweek*, 26 June, pp.28–38

Grunig, J. E. and Hunt, T. (1984), *Managing Public Relations*, Thompson Learning

Gummesson, E. (1987), *The New Marketing: Developing Long-Term Interactive Relationships*, Long Range Planning, 20: pp.10–20

Hall, M. (1992) Using Advertising Frameworks: Different Research Models for Different Campaigns, *Admap*, March, pp.17–21

Hamel, G. (1996) Strategy as Revolution. *Harvard Business Review* July/August

Hamel, G. and Prahalad, C. K. (1996), *Competing for the Future*, Harvard Business School Press

Heider, F. (1958), *The Psychology of Interpersonal Relations*, Wiley

Herzberg, F. (1968) *Work and the Nature of Man*, Cleveland: World

Hill, L. and O'Sullivan, T. (1999), *Marketing*, (2nd edition), Longman, Essex

Hill, L. and O'Sullivan, T. (2004), *Foundation Marketing* (3rd edition), FT Prentice Hall, London

Hooley, G. Saunders, J. and Piercy, N. (2003), *Marketing Strategy and Competitive Positioning*, FT Prentice Hall

Jobber, D. 2007) *Principles and Practice of Marketing* (5th edition), McGraw Hill, Maidenhead

Johns, T. (2003), *Perfect Customer Care*, Random House Business Books

Johnson, G., Scholes, K. & Whittington, R. (2007), *Exploring Corporate Strategy* (8th edition), Harlow: FT Prentice Hall

Keating, M. (2001) Milk in a Bag Knocks Old-time Bottles off the Doorstep, *The Guardian*, 14 August, p.15

Kent, R. (1993), *Marketing Research in Action*, Routledge, London

Kotler, P. 2008), *Marketing Management*, 13th edition, Prentice Hall

Kotler, P & Lee, N. (2008), *Social Marketing: Influencing Behaviors for Good*, 3rd edition, Sage Publications

Kotler, P., Armstrong, G., Saunders, J. and Wong, V. (2008) *Principles of Marketing*, 5th edition, FT Prentice Hall

Lannon, J. (1991), Developing Brand Strategies Across Borders, *Marketing and Research Today*, August, pp.160–7

Marketing, (2001) 'Outstanding Marketing Achievement' The Marketing Society Awards 2001 supplement to *Marketing*, 14 June pp. 6–7

Maslow, A. (1954) *Motivation and Personality* New York: Harper and Row

McDaniel, C. and Gates, R. (1996), *Contemporary Marketing Research* (3rd edition), West Group

McDonald, M. and Christopher, M. (2003), *Marketing: A Complete Guide*, Palgrave Macmillan, Hampshire

McDonald, M. 2007), *Marketing Plans: How to Prepare Them, How to Use Them*, Butterworth-Heinemann

McLuhan, R. (2002), Brands Put Service Under the Spotlight, *Marketing*, 21 February, p 33

Morgan, R. M. and Hunt, S. D. (1994), The Commitment – Trust Theory Of Relationship Marketing, *Journal of Marketing*, pp.58 : 20–38

Museums Journal, (2002), *Free Entry means traditional audience keep coming back*, October, p.13

Oakland, J. S. (2003), *Total Quality Management Text with Cases*, Butterworth-Heinemann

Ohmae, K. (1983), *The Mind of the Strategist*, Penguin

Osgood, C. E. Suci, G. J. and Tannenbaum, P. H. (1957), *The Measurement of Meaning*, University of Illinois Press

Pastore, M. (2001) *Global Companies Lead B2B Charge*, 14 August, http:/cyberatlas.internet.com

Peattie, K. and Peattie, S. (1993), Sales Promotion: Playing to Win?, *Journal of Marketing Management.* 9, pp 255–69

Phillips, K. (2001), *Marketing Quality*, Research, June, pp.30–1

Piercy, N. and Evans , M. (1983) *Managing Marketing Information*, CroomHelm

Piercy, N. 2008), *Market-Led Strategic Change – Transforming the Process of Going to Market*, 4th edition, Butterworth Heinemann

Piercy, N. (1987), The Marketing Budgeting Process: Marketing Management Implications, *Journal of Marketing*, pp.51 (4), 45–59

Porter, M. (2004), *Competitive Advantage*, New edition, Free Press

Rogers, E. M. (1962) *Diffusion of Innovation*, The Free Press

Saunders, M. Lewis, P. and Thornhill, A. (2003), *Research Methods for Business Students (2nd edition)*, Financial Times Pitman Publishing

Schiffman, L.G. and Kanuk, L.L. (2004) *Consumer Behaviour* (8th edition), Pearson Prentice Hall

Schultz, D. , Tannenbaum, S. & Lauterborn, R. (2000) *Integrated Marketing Communications: Putting It Together & Making It Work*, illustrated edition, McGraw-Hill Contemporary

Sclater, I. (2002) Wish you were here, *Marketing Business*, July/August, pp 26–27

Simms, J. (2001), The Value of Disclosure, *Marketing*, 2 August, pp 26–7

Smith P.R. and Taylor, J. (2004) *Marketing Communications: An Integrated Approach* (4th edition), Kogan Page

Snodly, J. (2001), Fallen for an old flame? Just Log on for Counselling, *The Independent*, 9 September, p 8

Solomon, M. Bamossya, G. and Askegaard, S. (1999), *Consumer Behaviour*, Prentice Hall

Sunderland, P. (2002), Wish you were here, *Marketing Business*, July/August, pp 26–27.

Vroom, V. (1964) *Some Personality Determinants of the Effects of Participation*, Englewood Cliffs, New Jersey: Prentice Hall

Williams, K. C. (1981), *Behavioural Aspects of Marketing*, Heinemann Professional Publishing

Woods, R. (2002) Pop Idol or Puppet, *Sunday Times*, 10 February, p 12

www.marketingpower.com (American Marketing Association)

Zikmund, W. G. (1997), *Exploring Marketing Research* (Sixth edition), Dryden

Index

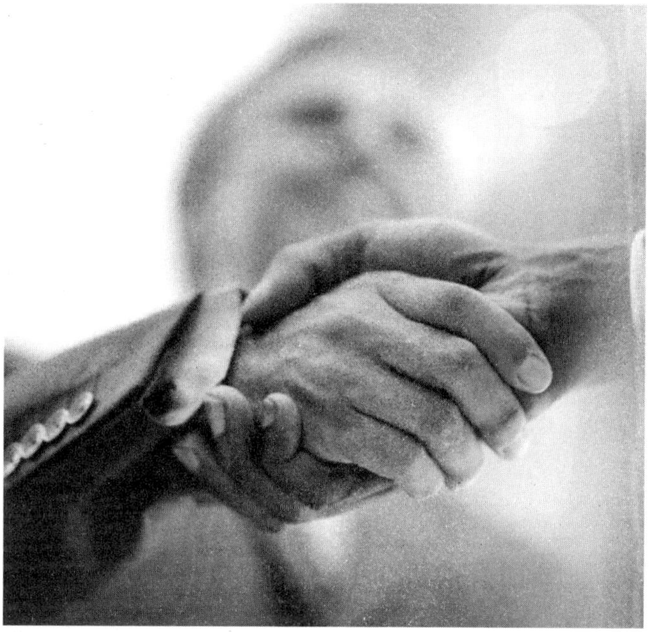